T0354321

A Collection of Plays
By Mark Frank
Volume III

*The Land of Never, I Swear By The Eyes
of Oedipus!, The Rainy Trails, Hurricane
Iphigenia-Category 5-Tragedy in Darfur,
Iphigenia Rising, Humpty Dumpty, The
Musical?, Troubles Revenge, Mahmudiyah
Incident, The Rock Of Troy, A Christmas Play*

Mark Frank

iUniverse, Inc.
New York   Bloomington

iUniverse books may be ordered through booksellers or by contacting:

iUniverse
1663 Liberty Drive
Bloomington, IN 47403
www.iuniverse.com
1-800-Authors (1-800-288-4677)

ISBN: 978-1-4401-3997-0 (sc)
ISBN: 978-1-4401-3998-7 (ebook)

Printed in the United States of America

iUniverse rev. date: 12/09/2009

Contents

Contents

The Land Of Never

Cast of Characters:

Smee

James

Peter

Bell

SPECIAL NOTE ON SONGS AND RECORDINGS

For all performance songs, arrangements and recordings mentioned in this play that are protected by copyright, the permission of the copyright owners must be obtained; or other songs, arrangements and recordings in the public domain substituted.

Time: Present

Place: A nursing home in New York.

AT RISE:

An elderly man enters pushing another elderly man in a wheel chair due to not having any arms or legs. "Disneyland" by Five for Fighting plays in the background until the dialogue starts.

JAMES: It's good to see you old friend. I thought you abandoned me long ago.

SMEE: I would never abandon you Captain.

JAMES: Don't call me that. That was long ago and I'm no longer your captain. Call me James.

SMEE: This is her room.

JAMES: Why don't you come back for me in ten minutes?

SMEE: Are you sure you want to do this?

JAMES: It's been long enough. Time heals old wounds.

SMEE: I'll be outside the door if you need me.

(James enters the room and an old lady lies in a bed as an old man sits at her bedside holding her hand. He looks up. There is a long pause.)

JAMES: Do you recognize me old friend? Do you know who I am?

PETER: Yes

JAMES: Not a very warm welcome.

PETER: Bell is dying.

JAMES: I know, that's why I came.

PETER: They said anytime now.

JAMES: Then it's good the ones she loved are close to her when she goes no matter what our differences were in the past. *(Long pause. They both stare at Bell)*

PETER: What happened to us?

JAMES: We got old Peter, very, very old.

PETER: We should have never left the island; you know the three of us.

JAMES: And Smee?

PETER: Him too.

JAMES: Yes. We all left for the world of the unknown, the world of opportunity.

PETER: We became selfish, greedy, and then later... bored with life.

JAMES: Never grow old.

PETER: Never grow old

JAMES: We sure discovered a lot when we left didn't we?

PETER: What, that we weren't real?

JAMES: Created by J.M. Barrie in a storybook and then the stage musical.

PETER: Cartoons, Disney, movies, adaptations, video games...

JAMES: ...marketing, clothes, and of course... copyrights.

PETER: I don't dare use my name or say my name for anything for fear I will be sued for copyright infringement. Disney owns my name, likeness, story...

JAMES: I hear you; I'm in the same boat, no pun intended. I hate Disney!

PETER: Disney owns us all, they own everything these days.

JAMES: Careful Peter, I'm sure they're listening.

PETER: To find out we weren't real, just fictional characters, it doesn't seem fair.

JAMES: It does suck to know your whole existence in life was for the amusement of others.

PETER: Why did we grow old?

JAMES: We left the island. It's our punishment.

PETER: Wendy, Michael, John.....all dead.....later Jane even died.

JAMES: We will die soon too Peter.

PETER: After Jane died I swore I'd never fall in love with another mortal.

JAMES: So you and Bell left the island to be normal.

PETER: I loved her. I just was blind to it all these years. She loved me for so long and I...

JAMES: You married her Peter. She was patient. She waited for you.

PETER: My little Tink...

JAMES: Careful Peter, lawyers are everywhere... listening, shhhh.

PETER: Bell.

JAMES: Bell.

PETER: You knew how she felt about me all those years?

JAMES: Everyone knew.

PETER: Why didn't you tell me?

JAMES: Peter, we were enemies. I lost both arms and legs because of you, I wasn't about to do you any favors.

PETER: *(Pause)* You hate me for that.

JAMES: No, you didn't write what happened to me, you just played the part you were given. We all do in life.

PETER: Bell gave up the life of a fairy and all of her powers to be a grown woman, my wife, and left the island to be with me and now look at her. Look what I've done.

JAMES: She loved you Peter.

PETER: I'd never thought we would grow old so fast. I never thought she would get lung cancer.

JAMES: Never leave a land that has no diseases. A land of make believe is harmless.

PETER: I'm surprised you survived all of our famous battles. I thought you were dead.

JAMES: After I lost my arms and legs to that crocodile I left the island with Smee and moved to New York. It got too boring after you and Bell left. He brought me to this nursing home to be cared for. I've been here ever since.

PETER: You were the greatest villain of all time. We had some classic battles.

(Bell coughs)

JAMES: Classis, classic battles.

PETER: You remember that one time we had that sword fight and my shadow and Bell surprised you from behind and cut the draw of your pants and they fell to your ankles?

(They both laugh.)

JAMES: Or how about when I captured you and your lost boys with the help of Lilly.

PETER: You never captured me.

JAMES: You're out of your mind. I did so.

PETER: The hell you did.

(They continue to argue until Bell coughs again. Long pause)

PETER: It doesn't matter anymore, those days are gone.

JAMES: No more battles Peter, those days are gone, time flies. No wonder I hated clocks so much. They measure our existence how long we have left to live.

PETER: What going to happen to us when we die James? Where do we go?

JAMES: Well, we'll never die since we're in print so we will live in spirit but our soul will no longer exist.

PETER: Will they remember us?

JAMES: On DVD and in books and musicals, live performances, and all that other merchandising crap.

PETER: God love Cathy Rigby.

JAMES: She's too old now, she can no longer fly. She's retired.

PETER: Wow, flying...I forgot how. It's been so long. I couldn't if I wanted to, too much arthritis. I lost all my magic abilities when I left the island.

JAMES: At least you have limbs to have arthritis. (*They share another laugh.*)

PETER: *(Looking at Bell)* What happens to our soul when we die James? Where do we go?

JAMES: Nowhere.

PETER: Surely characters have a heaven.

JAMES: The ink bleeds to black and then runs dry Peter. Then there's nothing.

PETER: But what was our purpose then?

JAMES: Everyone asks that question Peter. Our purpose is what we create in this world.

PETER: And what we leave behind?

JAMES: Correct and what we left was a classic for the ages!

PETER: I don't want Bell to die.

JAMES: She died a long time ago Peter just like the rest of us when we left the Land of Never.

PETER: She was the best wasn't she?

JAMES: She was something else. They got to her too, made her talk and rebranded her with tons of merchandise, she hated it all. She was their best money maker after we got stale and they turned to her to rejuvenate the product. Re-create the magic in a new direction.

PETER: She was the best, a little rambunctious, but the best.

JAMES: *(Looking at Bell)* I do believe in fairies.

PETER: I do believe in fairies. I've tried that a million times, it no longer works. She's no longer a fairy, just a normal woman... dying.

JAMES: I do believe in fairies.

PETER: I want to tell you something James.

JAMES: Yes.

PETER: As much as you were my enemy I was really glad you were in my life. You brought out the best in me just like Bell did.

JAMES: What about Wendy? Jane?

PETER: I miss both of them every day but treasure my memories with you always for as long as I live.

JAMES: Well you've always been like a rebellious son to me.

(Bell coughs again.)

PETER: She's losing.

(Bell breathes one last breath and dies. Long pause. "Never Land" plays softly in the background.)

PETER: Bell's gone

JAMES: She'll always be with us. She'll never be too far behind. She's in flight now. *(Long pause)*

PETER: Thanks for coming.

JAMES: I'm up the hall if you ever want to play cards, talk of old times…

PETER: I'm not sure I'll see you again after today James.

JAMES: I understand. I sort of already knew that.

PETER: Bell would have been happy to see you.

JAMES: Are you sure? I did poison her once.

PETER: Life is too short to hold grudges. Some people take them to the grave, Bell was never like that. Look how forgiving you were with me.

JAMES: You aren't to blame for my misfortunes. It was written to be so.

PETER: Thank you James. I'm going to do something I've never done to you before. *(Stands up and salutes him.)*

JAMES: Dismissed.

PETER: Be good.

JAMES: I can't or the children might start liking me. Are you going to be okay Peter?

PETER: By hook or by crook. Goodbye James. *(They stare at each other. Long pause)*

PETER: James, I ….

JAMES: I know Peter-let's not get emotional and say it; we both know how we feel.

PETER: I just wanted you to know.

JAMES: I know, goodbye Peter.

PETER: Oh, I have something for you, a present if you will. *(He gives James a pocket watch)*

JAMES: Is there a crock behind me?

PETER: (*Laughing*) No.

JAMES: Time.

PETER: It's been chasing you for years, now it chases all of us.

JAMES: Goes so fast doesn't it.

PETER: That it does old friend. That it does.

(Smee enters and rolls James out in his wheel chair as they exit. Peter sits next to Bell in an empty room and sings "Never Land" as a lullaby to Bell. The lights dim except a spot that continue to light Bell. The spot dims slowly to black as the play ends.)

I SWEAR BY THE EYES OF OEDIPUS!

I Swear by the Eyes of Oedipus! was originally produced by Coffeyville Community College on May 3-4-5, 2005 in the Spencer/Rounds Performing Arts Theatre. It was directed by Mark Frank. The production stage manager was Emily Wilson. The cast was as follows:

Prologue Girl #1/Chorus member	Michelle Hucke
Prologue Girl # 2/Chorus member	Kerri Davis
Eddie Pius/Chorus member	Zac Freisberg
Uncle Leon/Chorus member	Tyrell Blue/Devon Wesley
China Baby/Chorus member	Miwa Ishii
Tiresias/Chorus member	Jason Inman
Josie/Chorus member	Laura Michael
Lionel/Chorus member #5	Stuart Wolf
Dr. Gender/Chorus member/Ninja	Patrick O Neil
Melba/Chorus member/ Ninja	Emily Wilson
Creon/Chorus member/ Ninja	Nick Bishop

Oedipus/Chorus member/Ninja	Dustin Morby
Iphigenia/Chorus Messenger/#1/Sam/Ninja	Milena Barone
Jimmy/Chorus member #2/ Paramedic/Ninja	Brian Fank
Johnny/Chorus Leader/ Chorus #3/Ninja	Derrick Brewer
Jamie/Chorus member #4/ Paramedic/Ninja	Shannon Moran
Zeus	Zoel Lopez

Cast of Characters

Prologue Girl #1/Chorus member
Prologue Girl # 2/Chorus member
Eddie Pius/Chorus member
Uncle Leon/Chorus member
China Baby/Chorus member
Tiresias/Chorus member
Josie/Chorus member
Lionel/Chorus member
Dr. Gender/Chorus member/Ninja
Melba/Chorus member/Ninja
Creon/Chorus member/Ninja
Oedipus/Chorus member/Ninja
Iphigenia/Chorus Messenger/#1/Sam/Ninja
Jimmy/Chorus member #2/ Paramedic/Ninja
Johnny/Chorus Leader/Chorus #3/Ninja
Jamie/Chorus member #4/ Paramedic/Ninja
Zeus

SPECIAL NOTE ON SONGS AND RECORDINGS

For all performance songs, arrangements and recordings mentioned in this play that are protected by copyright, the permission of the copyright owners must be obtained; or other songs, arrangements and recordings in the public domain substituted.

Time: Present (New York City) and Past (500 B.C. Greece)

Mark Frank

AT RISE:

The Prologue Girls appear and walk directly into two spots of lights downstage center. They are both dressed in elaborate dresses. They each are holding large signs. Prologue Girl # 1 holds her poster board up first and it says, "The play, Oedipus Rex,... in progress" The other Prologue Girl hold up her sign and it says "Thebes, Greece 432 B.C." The lights fade to a black. As the lights come back up fifteen chorus members with long black cloaks and Greek masks act out the last ten minutes of the play Oedipus Rex. They are all standing staggered on a series of steps that lead up to a platform sitting center stage. They speak in a classical Greek vocal pattern as dramatic music plays in the background. A messenger runs on and enters the palace. He is dressed like the chorus.

Scene 1

MESSENGER: Citizens of Thebes, you who are most honored in this city! What dreadful things you will see and hear! What a cry of sorrow you will raise, if, as true Thebans, you have any feeling for the royal house. Not even the great rivers of Ister and Phasis could wash this house clean of the horrors it hides within. And it will soon expose them to the light of day-horrors deliberately willed, not voluntary. Those calamities we inflict on ourselves are those which cause the most pain.

20

CHORUS LEADER: The horrors we knew about before were burden enough. What other dreadful news do you bring?

MESSENGER: Here is the thing quickest for me to say and you to hear. Jocasta, our queen, is dead. *(Chorus leans sharply to listen.)*

CHORUS LEADER: Poor lady, from what cause?

MESSENGER: By her own hand. You are spared the worst of what happened-you were not there to see it. But as far as my memory serves, you shall hear the full story of that unhappy woman's sufferings. *(Quickens delivery, the chorus gathers around quickly)* She came in through the door in a fury of passion and rushed straight towards her marriage bed, tearing at her hair with both hands. Into her bedroom she went, and slammed the doors behind her. She was calling the name of Laius, so long dead, remembering the child she bore to him, so long dead, remembering the child by whose hand Laius was to die, and leave her, its mother, to bear monstrous children to her own son. She wailed in mourning for her marriage in which she had borne double offspring, a husband from her husband and children from her child. And after that, but I do not know exactly how she died. For Oedipus came bursting in, shouting, and so we could not watch Jocasta's suffering to the end; all of us looked at him as he ran to and fro. He rushed from one of us to the other, asking us to give him a sword, to tell him where he could find his wife, no, not his wife, but his mother, his mother and the mother of his children. It must have been some supernatural being that showed the raving man where she was, it was not one of us. As if led by a guide he threw himself against the doors of her room with a terrible cry, he bent bolts out of their sockets, and so forced his way into the room. And there we saw Jocasta, hanging, her neck caught in a swinging noose of rope. When Oedipus saw her he gave a deep dreadful cry of sorrow and loosened the rope around her neck. The poor woman was lying on the ground, and then we saw the most dreadful sight of all. He ripped out the golden pins with which her clothes were fastened, raised them high above his head, and speared the pupils of his eyes. "You will not see," he said, "the horrors I have suffered and done. Be dark forever now, eyes that saw those you should never have seen, and failed to recognize those you longed to see." Murmuring words like these he raised his hands and struck his eyes again, and again. And each time that wounded eye sent a stream of blood down his chin, no oozing flow but a dark shower of it, thick as a hailstorm. There are the sorrows which have burst out and overwhelmed them both, man and wife alike. The wealth and happiness they once had was real while it lasted, but now, weeping, destruction, death, shame, name any shape of evil you will, they have them all.

CHORUS: *(Spoken together)* And Oedipus, poor wretched Oedipus, has he now some rest from pain?

MESSENGER: He is shouting, "Open the doors, someone, show me to all the people of Thebes, my father's killer, my mother's…" I cannot repeat his unholy words. He speaks of banishing himself from Thebes, says he will not remain in his house under the curse which he himself pronounced. But he has no strength; he needs someone to guide his steps. The pain is more than he can bear. But he will show you himself. The bolts of the doors are opening. Now you will see a spectacle that even enemies would pity.

(Enter Oedipus, blind and bleeding from his eye sockets. He is holding his bloody eyes in his hands.)

CHORUS: O suffering dreadful for mankind to see, most dreadful of all I ever saw. What madness came over you? What unearthly spirit, leaping farther than the mind can conceive, swooped down on your destiny? I pity you. I have many questions to ask you, much I wish to know, my eyes are drawn towards you, but I cannot bear to look. You fill me with horror.

OEDIPUS: Where am I going? Pity me! Where does my voice range to through the air? O spirit, what a leap you made!

CHORUS: To a point of dread, too far from men's ears and eyes.

OEDIPUS: Darkness, dark cloud all around me, enclosing me, unspeakable darkness, irresistible, you came to me on a wind that seemed favorable. Ah, I feel the stab of these sharp pains, and with its memory of my sorrow.

CHORUS: In such torment it is no wonder that your pain and mourning should be double.

OEDIPUS: My friend! You are by my side still, you alone. You still stay by me, looking after the blind man. I know you are there. I am in the dark, but I can distinguish your voice clearly.

CHORUS: You have done a dreadful thing. How could you bring yourself to put out the light of your eyes? What superhuman power urged you on?

OEDIPUS: It was Zeus, friends, Zeus, who brought to fulfillment all my sufferings. But the hand that struck my eyes was mine and mine alone. What use had I for eyes? Nothing I could see would bring me joy. (*Holding his eyes*)

CHORUS: It was just as you say. I am moved to pity your misfortunes and your understandings of them, too. I wish I had never known you!

OEDIPUS: I would never have become my father's killer, never have been known to all men as my own mother's husband. Now I am godforsaken, the son of an accursed marriage, my own father's successor in the marriage bed. If there is any evil worse than the worst that a man can suffer-Oedipus has drawn for his lot and cursed his generation after him to the end of time.

CHORUS: Creon, Jocasta's brother and new ruler of Thebes have spoken of banishment. You would have been better dead than blind and banished. *(All bow to Creon as he enters and laughs.)*

OEDIPUS: Take me away, out of this country, quickly, take me away. I welcome banishment. I am lost, accursed, and hated by the gods beyond all other men. Cursed by these eyes I was born with! *(He opens his hands to reveal his bloody eyes in his hands. They fall out of his hand and gently bounce down the steps. They are rubber super balls with eyes painted on them. A chorus member (Creon) snickers and then quickly covers his mouth, the rest of the chorus turns to that chorus member and gasps. Creon cannot hold his laughter in anymore and burst out laughing. "Swing Swing Swing" by Tommy Dorsey starts to play. As the drums in the song start to play Creon takes a cane out of his cloak and starts to dance as the rest of the chorus follows suite except one chorus member (Tiresias) who goes to retrieve Oedipus eyes and puts them into a small box. They all dance down the stairs moving their canes back and forth. As the chorus continues to dance down stage together, the Prologue Girls enter from both sides of the steps and Prologue Girl #1 hold up a sign that say, "I Swear by the Eyes of Oedipus!" Prologue Girl #2 holds up a sign that says, "Written by Mark Frank". Prologue Girl #1 next sign says, "Starring..." The chorus dances some more together as the Prologue Girl hold up a sign for each chorus member who comes downstage and does a solo dance while the Prologue Girls take turns holding up cards that say the actors name as one of the character in the play. They do this for every character including themselves. When this is done the chorus comes back together and dances together some more. It should resemble a musical from the 1920's with top hats and canes. While they continue to dance the stairs and platform center stage split left and right as the chorus continues to dance. There is now a space between the two separated parts of the steps. The Prologue Girls walk down the open space. A chorus member, Tiresias, is running with the box that contains the eyes of Oedipus in them. As he runs in place down stage center the Prologue Girls are on each side of him. An image appears on the back wall that indicates time travel. Prologue Girl #1 holds up a sign that says "A chorus member escapes to the future." Prologue Girl #2 holds up a sign that says, "With the Eyes of Oedipus" As Tiresias continues to run, the chorus continues their dance in big Broadway fashion. During the saxophone part in the song a chorus member (Uncle Leon) breaks from the group and climbs the steps and plays the saxophone. He will play this for the rest of the number. Tiresias continues to run through time as the Prologue Girls hold up signs through out the rest of the song as Tiresias is running that says, "600 B.C.", "900 A.D." "1500", "1800", "1950", "2000", "The Present". The Chorus continues to dance. They dance up and down the steps on each side of the stage. As the song ends five chorus members stay downstage to dance. Tiresias continues to run in place center with the Prologue Girls on each side of him and the rest of the chorus strikes both sets of steps. They begin to dance on with furniture pieces and set up a classroom on stage right with four desks and a teacher's desk with a fake tree next to it, they continue to dance doing this. Five chorus members who are in the next scene take off their cloaks and masks to reveal four students and a teacher. They continue to dance as they change. The students are dressed in nice clothes. They take a seat in their desks as the teacher sits on the desk. The rest of the chorus continues to dance and the Prologue Girls and Tiresias exit. The chorus dances throughout the whole song as they finish dancing downstage center the lights fade and fade up on the classroom stage right. Eddie Pius is sitting on his desk. His students are sitting in their seats. Class is already in session. Everyone is blind including Eddie and wearing black sun glasses.)*

Scene 2

EDDIE: So in conclusion we can say it was the Oracle and Apollo's prophecy that are to be blamed for Oedipus' demise. *(Jimmy rings a bell)* Yes Jimmy.

JIMMY: But sir, isn't it true that Oedipus lived under the illusion that he escaped his destiny of killing his father and marrying his mother, the queen. And It wasn't it that *illusion* which caused him to be blind to the truth?

EDDIE: Jimmy, Jimmy, Jimmy,...

JIMMY: But sir.

EDDIE: Shut up! We would probably never had a story if it wasn't for Apollo prophecy which really brought the problem to his mother and father in the first place which was that the child was to grow up and murder his father, the king, and marry his mother, the queen. *(Johnny rings his bell)* Yes Johnny.

JOHNNY: But sir isn't it true that Oedipus caused his own downfall by leaving a kingdom he was already established as heir and yet he decided still to go off to search for his real parents thus setting the prophecy in motion. *(Pause. Johnny stands and gives high fives to the class but misses his classmates hands due to the fact he's blind.)* Dude?

EDDIE: Sit down. Johnny, the prophecy was already in motion before the child was born. *(Johnny rings his bell again)* Who can blame a child who wants to know who is real parents are. Yes Johnny, you can stop ringing your bell.

JOHNNY: But sir, once Oedipus becomes King of Thebes he proclaimed to his subjects to bring him the murderer of King Laius only to find that he is himself, the murderer. Doesn't the twist of fate leads to his downfall? *(Eddie slams Johnny down into his chair)*

EDDIE: Thank you Johnny! We all know the story of Oedipus. All he was doing was protecting his kingdom from a flesh eating plague that was wiping out Thebes. If he finds King Laius killer then the plague is removed. Now you can't blame him for saving his city. They declared him King. *(Jamie rings his bell)* Yes Jamie!

JAMIE: But sir, If Oedipus wouldn't have insisted of finding the truth out about who killed King Laius then he wouldn't have learned the truth of his destiny, correct?

EDDIE: *(Losing patience)* You all are forgetting the man was dealing with a plague! You know what a plague is? It's like psoriasis, like what I have here on my elbows, see!! Because you get it when you're stressed and it itches like a bitch! *(He scratches himself all over)* Next question!

JIMMY: Sir… we can't see, we're all blind.

EDDIE: You watch your ass! What I'm trying say, if you would LISTEN, is Oedipus was dealing with a destiny that he himself never asked for, it was determined for him! *(Jimmy rings his bell)* JIMMY!

JIMMY: *(Nervous)* But sir...Oedipus himself called for his subjects to bring the blind seer, the carriage guard, and the sheppard to seek out the truth. He was under the impression he escaped his destiny thus he was living in the darkness of a lie. Wasn't he too proud to think he was the murderer of the King, his father, King Laius and too blind to see that he slept with his mother, the queen?

EDDIE: *(Losing it, grabbing Johnny)* Jimmy! The fact of the matter is that the Gods screwed with the guy, who the hells going to blame him I mean he's screwed at birth already that these things are going to happen to him. He has no free will, it's his destiny that he will grow up and do these things. Had his parents not given him away he might have been fine. *(Jamie rings a bell)* Jamie! Yes! Speak!

JAMIE: *(Very nervous, has a stuttering problem with his "w's")* But sir, your saying that Oedipus is completely innocent in his downfall wwwwhen it wwwwas his giant ego that lead him to be blind to the truth. His wwwwanting the knowledge destroyed him. Shouldn't he have left wwwwwell ...

EDDIE: Spit it out!

JAMIE: Wwwworking on it...enough alone but his pride would not let him?

EDDIE: *(Yelling)* His knowledge? His pride? The guy was set up! It's not every day your destined to wake up a kill your father and kill your father. *(Johnny rings his bell)* No more bells! *(He throws the bell out the door)* What Johnny?

JOHNNY: Well I don't want you to be mad if I make this next point.

EDDIE: *(Shouting. Moving to Jimmy)* Johnny...I will not be angry! This is just an open discussion on Oedipus Rex! Everyone has their own opinions on the story! Now go ahead!

JOHNNY: Well I just don't want to make you mad. You sound pissed off.

EDDIE: *(Disheveled, taking a breath and calming down.)* Listen to me very carefully everyone, pay very close attention; you will NOT make me mad. I will not be angry. Now out with it!

JOHNNY: Well sir it's just weird that you're defending Oedipus...

EDDIE: Go on...very calm...go on.

JIMMY: Well sir we just think it's weird that your name is Eddie Pius and you're making us read Oedipus. Like if you say your name real fast, it sounds sort of like Oedipus. *(He says it three times fast)*

EDDIE: Didn't know that...coincidences happen... continue...lets all breathe.

JAMIE: And the fact that you're blind like Oedipus and well sir acting impulsive, rash, and jumping to false conclusions with a big ego just like Oedipus did in the story.

EDDIE: Just like Oedipus did in the story...okay. *(Smiling)* Anything else?

JOHNNY: Oh and you do have his temper and anger.

EDDIE: Anything else...?

JAMIE: Oh and didn't you say you were adopted? The similarities are weird sir, really weird.

EDDIE: Adopted...right...right and weird. Great, great...anything else?

JIMMY: No I think that does it. *(They all agree.)*

EDDIE: Very good. Great. Oedipus? You think I'm like Oedipus? *(Laughing then switching on a dime to anger, he starts to choke Johnny as the other classmates try to pull him off)* Oedipus! Is that who you think I'm like? A LOSER like Oedipus? A big square? Not hip? A person who has no friends? Makes wrong decisions in his life? Is not good with the girls? Was adopted, has no clue who his parents were, are, all of the above! Is bitter about being blind at birth?

JIMMY: But sir, Oedipus wasn't blind at birth.

EDDIE: You shut up! Well maybe I'll just go out and look for my father. Find him *(grabs plant)* and kill him *(He strangles the plant and throws it)* and then when I locate my mother, I'll throw my arms around her and

31

welcome her home, because that's my destiny. Hiya Mommy (*He starts to hump his desk*) You want some of this Mommy? Huh Mommy? Mommy! Mommy! Mommy! OEDIPUS!! IS THAT WHO YOU'RE TRYING TO SAY I AM??

JIMMY: Sir, are you okay? You've really like... lost it!

EDDIE: (*Pounding his head on his desk after each word.*) PROPHECY! FATE! PROPHECY! FATE!

JIMMY: Sir? Should I go get help? Call 911? The psyche ward?

EDDIE: (*Turns around quickly and talks to his desk*) Alright you little bastard your suspended.

JIMMY: What the hell did I do?

EDDIE: Don't you talk back to me. (*He hits Jamie in the head with his blind stick that he takes out.*)

JAMIE: Ow! You hit me, you dickwad!

EDDIE: Dickwad, I'll give you a dickwad! (*He hits Johnny instead of Jamie*)

JOHNNY: Ow! Now you hit me. I'm telling my parents. They give a lot of money to this school and they make sure they fire your ass! (*A man in a cloak and mask (Tiresias) enters and listens from the back of the classroom. All the students hit Eddie.*)

EDDIE: Come here you little bastard I'll teach you. (*Eddie now hits all three boys with his blind stick.*

They get out their blind sticks and start hitting Eddie. Tiresias comes forward)

TIRESIAS: Excuse me; I'm looking for an Edward Pius?

EDDIE: Jesus!

TIRESIAS: Wrong God.

EDDIE: (*They all put their sticks away and quickly sit down in their seats)* Okay, good, good class boys, well pick it up here tomorrow. (*The boys exit. Jimmy puts a "kick me" sign on Eddie's back, Johnny kicks Eddie in the shin on his way out and Jamie throws a book which hits Eddie in the head. Eddie yells out the hall.)* Little bastards! (*He picks up the tree he threw and puts it next to his desk.)*

TIRESIAS: Are you Edward Pius?

EDDIE: (*Talking to the tree)* Eddie Pius, yes, yes, are you a parent, an administrator? (*Nervous laughter)* That class gets crazy sometimes. We were doing the big Oedipus battle at the crossroads from Oedipus Rex.

TIRESIAS: I am the blind prophet Tiresias, the son of the Shepard Everes and the nymph Charico, father of Manto and Daphne. I have come 2500 years, three months, fifty-two weeks, and seven episodes of Sanford and Son from the past to present you with the eyes of your great, great, great, great, great, well you get the idea, grandfather, King Oedipus Rex of Thebes. (*Thunder, they both look around. Long pause)*

EDDIE: Okay, Is this Jimmy? Johnny or Jamie's doing? (*Yelling out the door.*)That's cute but I really don't have time for this. *(Starts to leave.)*

TIRESIAS: *(Thunder)* Zeus' beard! You must not ignore the prophecy.

EDDIE: What was that about prophecy? What did you day? Prophecy?

TIRESIAS: It is the prophecy written down by the Gods and your destiny. Your family line is being threatened, and you Eddie Pius are the only one who can save it from distinction.

EDDIE: Do you really talk that way?

TIRESIAS: *(Geeky voice)* Which way? (*Powerful voice*) I mean which way?

EDDIE: Wait, no you just sounded different. Go back to that other way like you being all official and powerful.

TIRESIAS: Like this? You don't like this voice? *(Geeky Voice)*You like this voice better? Really? *(Powerful voice)* I use this voice for seer business and *(Geeky voice)* this voice for Grandma's birthday, get togethers, I really prefer it myself.

EDDIE: *(Feeling his face and clothes)* Let me guess, you're dressed in a mask and a gown? Oh my God you are dressed in a mask and a gown! They put a lot into this. I'm on Punk'd right?

TIRESIAS *(Feeling the tree by Eddie)* And you have very smooth skin.

EDDIE: Why thank you. You know I moisturize and I still get flaky skin.

TIRESIAS: I have the same trouble but I get it on my face, it's the real reason for the mask. I shed about a pound a skin a day. It's crazy. *(They both take a long pause and look straight out, then put their arms around each other and look at each other.)*

EDDIE: Look I'm sorry if I don't buy your story, it just seems far fetched that one day I'm going over Oedipus Rex with my class and all of a sudden out of the blue, Tiresias, the blind seer from the story decides to visit my class and present me the eyes of Oedipus. Sorry if that's hard to swallow. Good joke whoever you are but I'm late and I gotta go. See ya.

TIRESIAS: Maybe you'll believe this. *(He opens the box and the eyes glow inside)*Where the God's are you?

EDDIE: Hey, I can see! The light, it's so strong.

TIRESIAS: The eyes of Oedipus have great power, knowledge, strength, wisdom, sexual preference, pop culture, etc... all come from your ancestor, the great king Oedipus Rex.

EDDIE: Those eyes look like giant super balls. *(He tries to touch them.)*

TIRESIAS: *(Snaps the box shut)* We don't have much time. Creon and his goons might have followed me through the Portal of the Gods. Can we go someplace private to talk?

EDDIE: Portal of the Gods? Creon? The eyes of Oedipus? Oh this just keeps getting better. Okay, fine I'll play. You're good. Come on I'll invite you over for dinner, and then when you decide the jokes over and you've made an ass out of me long enough you can leave. It's the story of my life. I'm used to it. May I be struck by lightning if you're telling the truth.

TIRESIAS: How terrible it is to have wisdom when it does not benefit those who have it. We must go. This is hardly a joke. *(They leave in opposite directions. They come back together. Thunder again)*

EDDIE: *(Comes back. He has been struck by lighting. His face is black and his hair is standing on end.)* All of a sudden as I think about it, this seems possible as crazy as that may seem.

TIRESIAS: Which way?

EDDIE: This way. *(They leave again in opposite directions. They then come back together and leave stage right. Tiresias is now carrying the tree from the classroom.)* No, this way.

TIRESIAS: Can I keep the tree? *(Black out)*

Scene 3

(Lights come up center stage to reveal the home of Uncle Leon. The house is very minimal and only consists of a chair, a couch and some clutter. Uncle Leon dresses, looks and acts like Samuel L. Jackson's character, Jules Winnifield from Pulp Fiction. He stands in front of the couch pretending to play a saxophone he carries everywhere with him. China Baby sits on the chair pretending to play a synthesizer. Her hair is in pig tails. A boom box sits facing them on a table in front of them. They are pretending to play with instruments the theme from "Sanford and Son". Eddie and Tiresias enter.)

EDDIE: Uncle Leon didn't you see me. I've been standing in the doorway for the last couple of minutes.

UNCLE LEON: I saw you, we're not the blind one. Whose Foo Man Chu? That's hell of a get up he's wearing. We're a long way until Halloween. Look China Baby, Eddie brought home Foo Man Chu, you know the dude from the Chinese movies we watch.

EDDIE: This is Tiresias. He is a blind seer, a priest, and a prophet.

UNCLE LEON: *(Holds his hand to high five him but Tiresias is blind to it)* My brother, I too am a minister. Oh I see how it is. Too dark for you?

CHINA BABY: *(Looks at Tiresias and its love at first site)* Very nice to meet you. *(She bows to him)*

37

EDDIE: This here is China Baby, she's my sister. And this is our guardian who adopted us both, Uncle Leon.

UNCLE LEON: Alright Foo Man you can stop looking at my daughter like that.

TIRESIAS: Oh I cannot see, I'm blind.

UNCLE LEON: Well I'm an OBMF.

TIRESIAS: OBMF?

UNCLE LEON: One bad Mother Fu…

CHINA BABY: *(Cuts him off)* Uncle!

UNCLE LEON: God damn!

EDDIE: Uncle for the last time you're not Samuel L. Jackson and you don't even play the saxophone. I don't know why you insist on carrying it around everywhere you go.

UNCLE LEON: Hope is a hell of a thing Eddie and it sounds great. *(He plays a couple notes and it's awful.)*

CHINA BABY: Where you from?

EDDIE: Maybe you two should sit down before he tells you. It gets kind of weird from here.

TIRESIAS: Sort of a long story.

UNCLE LEON: Don't talk too long, I got your birthday dinner on the stove. I hope you like collard greens and chicken. I hope I got enough. I didn't expect Foo Man to invite himself.

CHINA BABY: What happened to face and hair? New look Eddie?

EDDIE: No I was struck by lightning today.

CHINA BABY: Well Happy Birthday anyways Eddie! *(She gives him a present.)*

EDDIE: What is it?

CHINA BABY: It's that Stevie Wonder CD you wanted. Greatest Hits!

EDDIE: Thanks!

UNCLE LEON: I got you the usual. Here's five dollars. *(It's actually a dollar bill)*

EDDIE: Thanks Uncle, it's probably a dollar. I appreciate the gifts but Tiresias why don't you tell them why you're here; you know what you told me.

TIRESIAS: Can they be trusted?

UNCLE LEON: What the hell does that mean? You trying to say you can't trust a black man and a Chinese girl. Baby girl go get my gun.

EDDIE: Uncle, he's blind remember, how does he know you're black and she's Chinese.

UNCLE LEON: Your ass just got saved on that one.

CHINA BABY: Uncle!

TIRESIAS: *(Runs into couch)* Damn that couch! I am the blind prophet Tiresias, the son of the Shepard Everes and the nymph Charico, father of Manto and Daphne. I have come 2500 years from the past to present Eddie with the eyes of his great, great, great, great, great, well you get the idea, grandfather, King Oedipus Rex of Thebes. *(Thunder, they all look around. Long pause as the lights flicker. Eddie falls to the floor)*

UNCLE LEON: God damn it! What the hell was that?

EDDIE: Whatever he says believe him. I got third degree burns on my ass from that lightning.

CHINA BABY: No God in damn uncle *(She hits him hard in the arm.)*

UNCLE LEON: God damn it China Baby!

CHINA BABY: Did you say Daphne? That's *my* real name.

TIRESIAS: I thought your name was China Baby?

EDDIE: It's a nickname Uncle gave her, don't get him started where it came from.

UNCLE LEON: It all started at the castle of the Great Emperor…

CHINA BABY: Not now uncle let him finish. *(Uncle Leon mumbles to himself pissed off.)*

TIRESIAS: I have come 2500 years from the past to take Eddie back to 432 B.C Thebes and stop King Creon from wiping out the Oedipus family line. *(Long pause)*

40

UNCLE LEON: So let me get this straight Foo Man, you want us to believe you have traveled from the past from Greece to present Eddie with a pair of eyes from his great grand pappy and now he needs to go back to Greece with you to stop this dude named King Creon?

TIRESIAS: Yes, you have listened very well.

UNCLE LEON: What the hell are you selling? *(Pushes Tiresias)*

TIRESIAS: Selling?

UNCLE LEON: China Baby, go in the closet and get me my gun. Its time me and Foo Man had a little talk with Smith and Wesson.

CHINA BABY: Uncle! Let him finish.

EDDIE: Go on Tiresias.

TIRESIAS: You see all this is my fault.

UNCLE LEON: Your dam skippy.

CHINA BABY: Uncle!

TIRESIAS: See, I'm not sure how much you all know, except Eddie, the story of Oedipus Rex, our King. Many stories by Sophocles I noticed since I came to your time have been written about him. Such as this one I hold in my hand. But now the pages are empty which means Creon is changing the future.

CHINA BABY: I know story very well. We read it in English class. He married mother and killed father.

UNCLE LEON: Well I don't know the damn story.

EDDIE: Later Uncle.

TIRESIAS: As you know the prophecy of Apollo about Oedipus killing his father and marrying his mother came true.

UNCLE LEON: Now that's some sick shit right there.

TIRESIAS: Oedipus in his guilt and being blind to the truth struck out his own eyes with his, mother, the queens, broaches after she hung herself after she found out she slept with her son.

EDDIE: She was also his wife.

TIRESIAS: Unfortunately yes. These are his eyes I hold in this box.

UNCLE LEON: That dudes eyes are in that box?

TIRESIAS: Yes.

UNCLE LEON: Get the hell out of here.

TIRESIAS: See for yourself. *(He opens the box and the eyes radiate a bright light. Everyone is hypnotized by the light. He quickly closes the box.)*

UNCLE LEON: You sick son of a bitch. What the hells wrong with you. You took that dudes eyes?

EDDIE: Uncle!

CHINA BABY: Uncle please! Let him finish! *(Hits him again)*

UNCLE LEON: God damn it China Baby. But the guy took the dudes eyes!

EDDIE: Go on Tiresias.

TIRESIAS: Well. Creon, Jocasta's brother, became King and banished Oedipus from Thebes to die a long and miserable life wandering the world blind and banished.

EDDIE: I still don't get how I fit into this?

TIRESIAS: In time. The Portal of the Gods is sort of a way to go back and forth in time. Only prophets, Gods, and seers can use it. Creon from the future discovered it, came back and told Creon of the past that Oedipus children would eventually lead to Creon's banishment and death.

UNCLE LEON: Can we eat, man I'm starving. I got a big chocolate cake in there also.

CHINA BABY: Uncle! Let him finish.

TIRESIAS: The only way to change this outcome is for Creon to kill Oedipus' children. Now that he's King that's exactly what he plans to do. He has Oedipus and his children locked up and he plans to kill them.

EDDIE: When?

TIRESIAS: He's waiting to hear from Zeus. He doesn't want to offend the Gods.

EDDIE: Won't this change the course of history?

TIRESIAS: Yes. You won't exist. Oedipus' family line will end with his death and the death of his four children.

CHINA BABY: How not Eddie exist?

TIRESIAS: He will vanish into thin air.

UNCLE LEON: Alright Foo Man Chu, You told a great story but now you're upsetting my baby girl, our dinner probably burnt, you messed up Eddie's birthday and on top of that I just missed the damn Chiefs on TV so now you got to go. *(He takes Tiresias and escorts him out.)*

EDDIE: *(Opening up the box with the eyes in them that Tiresias left on the table.)* Uncle wait. Leave him alone. I feel he's telling the truth. Don't you see, it all makes sense. That's why I was so angry today in class. I was defending Oedipus because…because…I am Oedipus, or a least related to him in some weird way.

CHINA BABY: I believe him too.

UNCLE LEON: Are you two out of your God damn minds? We're talking about some crazy shit with a guy that looks like Foo Man Chu and appeared out of the blue! What I'd like to know is what's in it for you?

TIRESIAS: In it for me?

UNCLE LEON: You so worried about that Oedipus dude and his kids getting whacked. Why? It has nothing to do with you, why should you care?

TIRESIAS: Because after he kills Oedipus and his children he plans to kill anyone associated with Oedipus which would mean me. I'm next, then maybe you or China Baby.

CHINA BABY: Uncle, he here to help Eddie, help us!

UNCLE LEON: If you're lying to us Foo Man then you is not only going to be wiped out by Creon but also by Uncle Leon.

EDDIE: What can I do? I can't fight a King of his power and army.

TIRESIAS: No, but you can stop him with these eyes. These eyes which are now infamous are claimed to hold secret powers, a claim spoken by the Gods. Whoever sees through the same eyes of Oedipus will gain Oedipus strength, power, and mind. In order for them to have their power the person who takes the eyes of Oedipus must be of family blood.

EDDIE: If I take these eyes whose to say I wouldn't kill my real father and sleep with my mother. I would have Oedipus' mind right?

UNCLE LEON: Not happening, you know your real parents died in a car accident. I told you that was in the note I found on you when I found you on my doorstep.

TIRESIAS: It would seem you would not experience his fate or destiny. You will create your own, his was determined for him by the Gods.

EDDIE: Why me. Why not go back in time and get someone else from Oedipus family line?

TIRESIAS: The portal brought me here. You are the chosen one.

CHINA BABY: *(Uncle Leon and China Baby laugh)* The chosen one.

UNCLE LEON: Hey if you think you're putting those eyes in his head and taking him to Greece you as crazy as you look.

CHINA BABY: Uncle, he must save his family.

UNCLE LEON: His family is right here baby girl.

EDDIE: Can't you look into the future at the outcome of all this?

TIRESIAS: My power of prophecy must be blocked from the portal. It is strange. I can see nothing.

UNCLE LEON: I can't let you do this Eddie. This shits just too weird to believe.

EDDIE: Uncle, I have to do this. This could be the most important thing I have ever done in my life. All my life I've needed someone and now someone needs me. No disrespect to you Uncle but you haven't been blind your entire life. With these eyes I can see, maybe make all my dreams come true. This would be the best birthday present a person could get, a fresh start at life.

UNCLE LEON: If this dudes telling the truth, you could also be killed. *(Smoke alarm goes off.)* Damn it, my dinner is burning.

EDDIE: Give me the eyes Tiresias. I'll do it. I will go back to Greece and help you save Oedipus and those children. For once in my life I have someone who needs me. I don't feel worthless.

CHINA BABY: I go too.

TIRESIAS: Behold the eyes of Oedipus. *(Thunder. They all duck. He opens the box and the light is glaring.)* All I need to do is touch your eyelids with the blood from the eyes and they will transform in your eye sockets. Are you ready? Once they are in, you cannot take them out unless you are in the presence of the one who they came from, Oedipus Rex.

CHINA BABY: This cool!

UNCLE LEON: *(Entering)* Well dinners burnt. Thanks to old Foo Man, hey what the hell are you doing? Whoa..whoa..whoa... back your Greek ass up away from my son.

TIRESIAS: He has decided to receive the eyes of his ancestor, Oedipus.

UNCLE LEON: I told you that ain't happening not on my watch. You're going to have to get past me to do your mumbo jumbo ritual on Eddie.

EDDIE: Uncle I'm taking the eyes.

CHINA BABY: He pretty square Uncle. He big loser. Sorry Eddie. He not very hip like you. Let him take eyes. Be powerful James Bond.

TIRESIAS: I must give him the eyes, it is his destiny. He must save Thebes from Creon.

UNCLE LEON: I got your destiny right in the chamber of this gun. Now you going to have to get past me Foo Man. *(He moves in front of Eddie.)*

TIRESIAS: Then so be it.

CHINA BABY: Uncle he blind, you not Samuel L. Jackson from Pulp Fiction!

UNCLE LEON: That ain't my fault; he'll fall just the same.

EDDIE: Uncle move!

UNCLE LEON: I tell you what Eddie, if he can get past me then you can have those eyes, if not, Foo Man goes out the door in a body bag

CHINA BABY: Uncle please!

TIRESIAS: Your move Mr. Miagi. *(Tiresias makes arm movements of grand style)*

UNCLE LEON: You want to play? Alright, you're getting ready to blow and I'm a mushroom cloud threshold for the abuse I'll take and you're abusing it. I'm Super Fly TNT. I'm the Guns of Navarone. I'm what Jimmy Walker used to talk about! *(Uncle Leon goes to hit Tiresias but Tiresias grabs Uncle Leon and throws him across the room)* Whoa...God Damn that was some divine intervention. How the hell did you throw me? You barely touched me.

EDDIE: Now do you believe him? It took lightning to convince me, you got off easy.

CHINA BABY: He not liar, he here to help Eddie.

UNCLE LEON: I aint blowin this shit off, what we have here isn't the failure to communicate, but a God Damn miracle.

CHINA BABY: No God in damn Uncle.

UNCLE LEON: You really who you say you are Foo Man?

TIRESIAS: You missed a foot ball game you call it, yes?

UNCLE LEON: The Chiefs game. Right, so.

TIRESIAS: Chiefs win 34-10

CHINA BABY: Let's see if he right, Uncle look game just ending *(She turns on the TV to hear the announcer say, "And the Chiefs win 34-10")*

UNCLE LEON: Now that kind of shit does not just happen. Can you do that for all sporting events?

TIRESIAS: Very easily. I can tell you the result of any event. I just for some reason cannot foresee Eddie's future. It's like its being blocked.

UNCLE LEON: How about say the lottery, Vegas…

TIRESIAS: Not even a challenge.

UNCLE LEON: Take the eyes Eddie. Foo Man Chu is alright. *(Puts arm around him.)*

TIRESIAS: If you say so. *(Turns to China Baby)*

UNCLE LEON: Just keep your blind eyes off my China Baby.

TIRESIAS: I can't make that promise.

EDDIE: Go ahead Tiresias, I'm ready. *(He takes his dark glasses off. The light change and thunder crashes down as Tiresias chants some Latin chant and then sings the theme song to Friends. He wipes a dot of blood on each of Eddie's eyelids. Eddie looks around.)*

CHINA BABY: You see me?

EDDIE: Clear as day! *(They hug and celebrate)* I can see! Hell of an afro Uncle.

UNCLE LEON: All my years at church and I ain't never seen shit like this ever. We got to celebrate. It's a damn miracle! This is a hell of a birthday.

TIRESIAS: We have time. The Gods will take a day to answer his request. Creon won't do anything without a sign from the Gods.

EDDIE: Check the book, are the pages still blank?

TIRESIAS: Still blank. You must stop Creon before everything is back the way it was.

EDDIE: Won't you change the past by talking to us, coming through the portal.

TIRESIAS: Prophets and seers only tell the future they don't change it.

UNCLE LEON: Look, I say we go out for Eddie's birthday dinner and celebration, go to the river boats, then do some gambling with our new buddy Foo Man Chu. Afterwards we can go to Greece save the children come back here and then go to the race tracks. Now who's with me?

TIRESIAS: We need to go back as soon as possible. We have one day and then it will be too late. Oedipus and his children will be killed.

CHINA: Let's go eat!

UNCLE LEON: Hey what about the boats and gambling?

EDDIE: It will be there when we get back.

CHINA BABY: We go eat Chinese food!!

UNCLE LEON: Again? Why all the time Chinese food?

EDDIE: Yeah why Chinese food again!

CHINA BABY: I China Baby?

UNCLE LEON: (*Arm around Tiresias*) You China Baby alright. Let me guess Foo Man, I'm buying your dinner also? You forgot your wallet in Greece? Well I'm getting one buffet and we share it. Until Foo

Man here becomes our sugar daddy, we all in the poor house. Oh and Foo Man, you're paying me back for this dinner with interest. We can pick up a lottery ticket on the way. Now what numbers you like Foo Man? *(They walk ahead.)*

CHINA BABY: You okay Eddie?

EDDIE: I'm a little scared but I haven't been happier. I can see!!!!

CHINA BABY: Your future so bright you better where shades, those eyes look scary.

EDDIE: *(Puts his sunglasses back on)* The question is, are these eyes my destiny or my downfall? *(Black out)*

Scene 3

(The Prologue Girls come out and Prologue Girl #1 holds up a sign that says "The plot thickens" Prologue Girl # 2 holds up a sign that says "This show is bitchin" As the Prologue girls are holding up their signs the chair is replaced with a desk and swivel chair. There is a stuffed beaver on the desk. A young woman enters the office.)

JOSIE: Hello?

DR. GENDER: *(Enters. He is a man dressed up like a woman, make-up and all and in a business suit. He has a twenty-four hour shadow and a blonde wig. He still talks like a man. He comes in pulling up his panty hose)* Yes, I'm sorry come in; I had to run to the bathroom in between sessions. You know panty hose they can be very tricky. I'm trying to hide a run.

JOSIE: Are you Dr. Gender, my psychiatrist?

DR. GENDER: Yes, you must be Josie my two o' clock. Have a seat. I've read the information you filled out. Very interesting… *(She sits on the couch and he sits at the desk.)*

DR. GENDER: Oh I'm sorry is my beaver in the way?

JOSIE: Excuse me?

DR. GENDER: My beaver. *(He shows her the stuffed animal)* Don't worry it stuffed, a gift from my ex-wife. She was a taxidermist. It's pretty old. My beavers pretty dry, needs more moisture or it starts to stink up the room. Once you got a smelly beaver no one want to be near you. If you want to pet my beaver later just ask. Many people like to pet my beaver, it relaxes patients, how can you not resist touching it, its right there for the taking. Enough about my beaver, now let's talk about why you're here.

JOSIE: Okay…um…I don't know if I can, I just ended a really serious relationship and it's hard to talk about it.

DR.GENDER: Just think of it as a couple of girls talking don't be shy. Is this your first visit to a psychiatrist?

JOSIE: Yes.

DR. GENDER: Well let's see how we can help. Why are you here?

JOSIE: I recently just went through a pretty rough divorce.

DR. GENDER: So did I… so I know how that can be.

JOSIE: My husband cheated on me and left me for another woman.

DR. GENDER: Men can be such bastards. I don't know how they walk around with those things between there legs. *(She looks at him, long pause)*

JOSIE: It… was… a bad divorce. I was devastated

DR. GENDER: The only way I felt better after my divorce was getting a breast augmentation. Do you think there too big?

JOSIE: No...they're… fine…I think.

DR. GENDER: I'm sorry go ahead with your story. I have a habit about it being about me all the time. You know talking about all I've done and never giving the other person a chance to talk.

JOSIE: Well my husband and I divorced after a tragic accident with our son.

DR. GENDER: Oh I'm sorry, did he die?

JOSIE: No he's still alive but...but… *(She starts to cry profusely as does Dr. Gender.)* I can't, I'm sorry, I can't, it's too hard. *(Dr. Gender comforts her on the couch.)*

DR. GENDER: *(Still crying)* Josie, I want you to look at me, now I know this is hard but you came here to get better right? Right?

JOSIE: Yes.

DR. GENDER: Now I want you to concentrate on this here lipstick, wait, let me put some of this on before we do this. I never put enough on.

JOSIE: What are we doing?

DR. GENDER: *(Putting on some lipstick)* I'm going to hypnotize you so you're able to talk about what pains you deep inside your psyche that you cannot let out. How's that look?

JOSIE: You've smeared it on your cheek.

DR. GENDER: *(Tries to wipe it off)* Did I get it yet?

JOSIE: Further on your cheek, up farther. *(He still doesn't get it.)*

DR.GENDER: How's that.

JOSIE: Here let me, if you don't mind. *(She wipes off the smear and reapplies his lipstick.)*

DR.GENDER: How's it looking?

JOSIE: Much better. Though I think you'd look better with red and not this pink. Pink doesn't show that well with your color of flesh tone.

DR. GENDER: That's what I thought. You are so smart! Now where were we...? Oh yes... I want you to watch the lipstick. I'm going to move it back and forth like this. (He moves it back and forth) You are getting sleep, your eyelids are getting heavy, heavy... you're asleep!

JOSIE: No, I'm not.

DR. GENDER: Is this doing anything for you?

JOSIE: No...it's not!

DR.GENDER: Damn. Okay..um *(moves lipstick in different direction)* keep watching, keep watching the lipstick...you are asleep!

JOSIE: I'm sorry, I'm not.

DR.GENDER. Wait. *(Goes to his desk, gets out a small bottle and opens it)* Smell this, *(She passes out)* maybe too strong. *(He slaps her face. She is barely awake but can still see)* Now watch the lipstick. When I count to three you will be asleep. One-two-three. *(She's asleep)* Josie, now I want you to wake up. Now, where did you buy your dress?

JOSIE: JCPENNY.

DR. GENDER: How much?

JOSIE: Clearance rack, five dollars.

DR. GENDER: How longs the sale?

JOSIE: Until Friday.

DR. GENDER: Now, I want you to tell me what happen that caused you to get a divorce from your husband and what happened to your child. Go back into your mind and tell me.

JOSIE: All of our problems started when we met the gypsy... *(The scene goes dark and switches to the other side of the stage. Josie is now with her husband Lionel. She is holding a baby. The Prologue Girls Hold up a sign, "Fortune Teller, fortunes read, $20")*

JOSIE: Think we should?

LIONEL: Let's see if our son is going to be a teacher like his father.

JOSIE: I'm so proud of you honey. *(She kisses him. They go in and sit at a table. There is a fish bowl on the table that is upside down. A woman dressed as a gypsy enters. She is carrying a stuffed cat. "Gypsies, Tramps and Thieves" by Cher plays in the background. She dances around the couple.)*

LIONEL: Excuse me but...

MELBA: Shhhhh. Cher! *(She dances spastically around them and notices that they are not impressed she speaks in a Transylvania accent.)* No good? Waaaait! Jimbo!...Track three, Eagles! *("Witchy Woman" by the Eagles plays. She dances around for awhile but again they are not impressed.)* Kill it! Alright, you don't like dance, you want fortune?

LIONEL: Well after all that I'm not sure?

JOSIE: Lionel! Yes, yes we do.

LIONEL: Pay up front twenty dollars; I take Visa, Master Card, Check, American Express, but NO DISCOVER! Who takes Discover these days, really?

JOSIE: Here you are. *(She hands her a twenty dollar bill. Melba sniffs it. She claps and does an arm movement in the air.)*

MELBA: I am the great Melba! *(She looks around. Josie and Lionel look all around trying to find what Melba is looking for.)* What do you wish to know?

LIONEL: Melba? As in melba toast? *(Laughs)* Give me a break. Let's get out of here this is such a scam.

MELBA: *(Looks into fish bowl)* Wait, wait, waaaait!

JOSIE: What? Whaaaaat?

MELBA: I see a spot on this glass. *(Cleans her bowl with Windex)*

LIONEL: That's it we're going.

JOSIE: Sit down.

MELBA: Wait! I would listen to what your wife tells you because the information I am about to share concerns your child *(Thunder.)* You see… *(Thunder again)* your child… *(Thunder, she yells behind her)* Pause the God damn thing, too much thunder! Can't get good help these days, geez! *(Turns back to Josie and Lionel, her cat falls to the floor.)* Taxi!

JOSIE: Your cats name is Taxi?

MELBA: You like my cat? I call her Taxi because she comes every time I call her and sometime she come when I don't call her and sometime she never come. Just like taxi. Taxi! *(Yelling off stage)* Somebody call a taxi! Oh there's mama's baby right there.

LIONEL: You realize that cat's dead and stuffed right.

MELBA: You... not... very... nice man. Taxi is deef thank God for you.

LIONEL: Deef. What's deef?

MELBA: You know deef. I can't hear you because I'm deef. I wear an ear piece because I'm deef.

LIONEL: I think you mean deaf.

MELBA: Is that how you say it. I always thought it was deef. *(Long pause. They stare at each other)*

LIONEL: I'm pretty sure it's pronounced "deaf". Look I'm outta here, come on.

JOSIE: Lionel sit! This is our child's future she discussing and I want to know.

LIONEL: Josie, that's not even a crystal ball it's an upside down fish bowl for Pete sakes.

MELBA: *(Looking into fish bowl)* Wait, wait, waaaaaait! I see a baby.

JOSIE: You do?

MELBA: I see two men taking baby away. They are from... SRS.

JOSIE: The SRS takes our baby away? Oh my God!

MELBA: No that's my baby. They say I'm too strange to be mother. I then blow them up with grenade. Sad story, very bad.

LIONEL: Seriously now, come on!

MELBA: Wait, waaait, waaaait! I...I...

JOSIE: Oh my God what is it?

MELBA: I....I...I gotta use bathroom. Be right back. Stay Taxi. *(She runs to bathroom)*

LIONEL: This is ridiculous. This is a total scam and I cannot believe your buying it. Her name is Melba? Stuffed cats named Taxi, this fish bowl? If that wasn't bad enough she played Cher for Pete sakes.

JOSIE: Look Lionel, if you want to leave go ahead but I'm sticking around to see what she says about our son. This is very important to me.

(Melba returns. "Gypsies, Tramps and Thieves" by Cher plays. She treats Lionel and Josie like new customers and dances around them.)

MELBA: Did I do that already?

LIONEL: Yes you just went to the bathroom.

MELBA: Played the Eagles? Melba, looked around, introduced Taxi?

LIONEL: Yes, we you did all that stuff. We met your stuffed dead cat.

MELBA: Twenty dollars.

LIONEL: We just gave you twenty dollars.

MELBA: I don't remember that.

JOSIE: Just give her another twenty.

LIONEL: *(Pays her)* This is highway robbery!

MELBA: *(Looks into fish bowl)* Wait, waaaait, waaaait. I see another baby. It is your baby!

JOSIE: What it doing?

MELBA: Crying, pooping, normal stuff a baby does.

LIONEL: Goodbye. *(He gets up)*

MELBA: You can leave but... beware of the child. *(Thunder)*

LIONEL: Why?

MELBA: Twenty more dollars.

LIONEL: For what?

MELBA: My rent? Car payment? How bout I don't like you! *(They both rise and make a growling sound to each other and sit down as Josie slaps another twenty in her hand.)*

JOSIE: Tell us please.

MELBA: How long since you gave birth to child?

JOSIE: Well see... we never...

LIONEL: Wait, first tell us why?

MELBA: You look good for just having baby. Pilates?

LIONEL: Why should we beware of our child?

MELBA: Because when the child grows up and… *(Yelling offstage.)* now Jimbo…thunder!..... he will kill you!

(Dramatic music and thunder is heard. They all look around.)

JOSIE: Oh my God. Will he kill me too?

MELBA: No. He will marry you! *(Dramatic music and thunder)* Nice wedding, lots of people.

LIONEL: Come on honey we don't need to listen to this!

MELBA: *(Lights grow dark)* Go then! But beware of the child. You must get rid of him. If you do not, he will wreak havoc on both of your lives and tragedy will befall you. Do not be blind to the truth or the child will be blind to your lies. Muhahahahahahahahaha… *(Thunder)* muhahahahahaha!

JOSIE: No!

LIONEL: Why are you laughing about that for?

MELBA: Affect? Too much maybe?

LIONEL: I hope you choke on your lies and your scams you fraud. *(They leave)*

MELBA: No it is you who will choke. *(She flips over her fish bowl and pours her fish back into it)* Look Taxi, Peanuts back. *(She claps and sings)*Thou shall have a fishy on a little dishy when the boat comes in. Dance to your daddy my little lady when the boat come in. *(The lights change back into the office with Dr. Gender and Josie.)*

DR. GENDER: What happened next? Go farther back Josie in your mind, don't stop. What happened to the child?

JOSIE: The gypsy was right we were blind to the truth. But we didn't listen. We were too much in love with that child.

(The lights change and Lionel and Josie are in the park center stage having a picnic. "Close to You" by Karen Carpenter plays in the background. Josie and Lionel play with the child and drink some wine. They laugh and have fun playing with their child. They then lift the child up and continue to play with him. They finish there wine and play a light toss with the child back and forth. They continue tossing the child but toss him from a farther distance from each other each time. Soon they are tossing the baby across the stage. The final throw is from Josie who, drunk like Lionel, throws the baby like a football to Lionel who catches it and forgets it's a baby and spikes it on the ground. Josie and Lionel celebrate the catch but then come to the realization of what happened and what Lionel just did. They both run to the baby. Josie picks up the baby crying while Lionel keeps mouthing "No!" really big and pounding his fists on the ground. Lights come

up on Melba laughing. She laughs but then chokes on something. The song and lights fade out and the action goes back to Dr. Gender's office.)

DR. GENDER: Did the child die?

JOSIE: No. He suffered severe damage to his optical nerve when Lionel…spiked him on the ground like a football and the doctors told us he would be permanently blind…forever. We were fearful about the rest of the gypsy's prophecy coming true since our child became blind because of our lies about the truth of his future just like she said. We decided to leave him on the doorstep of a man we read that had just lost his wife and son. After that we drifted…and then recently Lionel left me for a waitress that worked at a deli. I haven't seen him since.

DR. GENDER: What's the man's name you gave your child to?

JOSIE: I don't know. I don't even know where my son is. I'm so ashamed of what we did to him. It's been twenty years or so and I still have a hard time getting up in the morning and finding a reason to live. I just want love in my life again and then I know if I have that, I can make it.

DR. GENDER: Josie, now I'm going to help you forget all of this. When I count to three you will no longer remember the story you just told me, or anything about Lionel, the gypsy or your baby. You will start a fresh life. If anytime you try to think of you past instead of crying you will laugh and the more you try to think about it the harder you will laugh. Do you understand?

JOSIE: Yes.

DR. GENDER: Only I can break this hypnotic spell. The word that will break this spell is "pot pie".

JOSIE: Pot pie?

DR. GENDER: Pot pie. It must be said three times in precession in order for the spell to be broken. Do you understand?

JOSIE: Yes.

DR. GENDER: When I snap my fingers three times you will wake up and not even remember us talking. Whenever I say your name from this day on or whenever you see me you will always tell me that I'm looking damn fine today. Do you understand?

JOSIE: Yes. *(He snaps three times. She looks confused.)* I don't think you can hypnotize me, I'm still not asleep.

DR. GENDER: You know you're right. I think you're cured anyway. Our meeting is finished.

JOSIE: What the hell did I come here for? *(She tries to think and then she starts to laugh profusely)* Never mind I have to leave before I pee my pants. All of a sudden I got the giggles. *(She looks at Dr. Gender and laughs harder.)* I gotta go. See ya.

DR. GENDER: By Josie and good luck.

JOSIE: One more thing, you look damn fine today. *(She's rolling now)*

DR. GENDER: Why thank you. *(She exits. He goes to his phone.)* Sam, come in here a minute. *(A woman dressed like a man enters.)*

SAM: You look damn fine today!

DR. GENDER: Yes I know. Cancel the rest of my appointments for the day. *(She exits. He picks up the phone and dials)* Hey, it's me. You'll never guess who I saw today. Yeah, it's her alright. Get packed and get down here as quick as you can. *(He hangs up and fixes his hair in the mirror.)* You look so damn fine today! *(Smiles, black out)*

Scene 5

The Action switches to center stage. The Prologue Girls come in and carry in signs. Prologue Girl #1 has a sign that says, "Back in Greece, 432 B.C." The other Prologue Girl has a sign that says, "Call me, 555-1515" They leave as the lights come up behind them. Oedipus is in chains surrounded by four chorus members guarding him.

OEDIPUS: *(Singing)* Ain't no sunshine when she's gone. *(Pause)* It's not warm when she's away. *(Pause)* Ain't no sunshine when's she's gone, and she's always gone too long *(pause)* anytime she goes away. *(Long Pause)* Wonder this time where she's gone way, *(pause)* Wonder if she's gone to stay. *(Pause)* Ain't no sunshine when she's gone *(pause)* Ain't no sunshine when she gone and this house just ain't no home anytime she goes away.

CHORUS: *(Come in quickly around Oedipus singing)* And I know, I know.

OEDIPUS: *(Standing up and bringing in home)* Hey you ought to leave the young things alone, but ain't no sunshine when she's gone! *(Creon enters)*

CREON: What the hell is going on here? You're supposed to be guarding him not performing dithyrambs which I have to say Oedipus is another terrible thing you do, you've never won one contest in all the years I've known you. I on the other hand have won everyone I've competed in.

CHORUS: *(Spoken together)* Creon is dithyramb champion and a great King.

OEDIPUS: Out brainwashing? *(Chorus laughs)*

CREON: No actually at the axe grinders. I want to make sure those heads of your children roll right off their body when its time for their deaths and yours of course. Just waiting to hear from Zeus. *(He laughs, looks back.)*

OEDIPUS: Look, I'm sorry about your sister. I'm suffering too, all of Thebes is. Just banish me and leave my children be.

CREON: Can't do that, see had a little visitor from the future. My future self came to visit me and told me all about your son, Polynices going to war against me and then your daughter Antigone tries to turn Thebes against me for wanting to bury her brother. It results in not only my son's death but also my banishment and I can't have that happen since I plan to rule Thebes for a very long time after you're gone. And guess what, no more Oedipus family tree, cut down no longer able to sprout leaves for the future.

OEDIPUS: The Portal of the Gods is forbidden to mortals. If Zeus finds out you went through it and are trying to change the future, it will be you who will be banished.

CREON: No need to worry about me, you'll be dead already and the future will be altered. Come chorus, we must seek out mother to see if she wants to come to the executions tomorrow.

OEDIPUS: *(Laughs)*

CREON: What's so funny? Are you laughing at me?

OEDIPUS: No your mother, I mean yo mothers so fat she's on both sides of the family. (*The chorus rolls in laughter. Oedipus gets high fives. Creon turns to them and they are quiet.*)

CREON: Oh it's like that is it? Well yo mama's so stupid she stole free bread. (*The chorus laughs and celebrates with Creon.*)

OEDIPUS: Well... yo mama so ugly they pushed her face in the dough to make gorilla cookies. *(The chorus rolls in laughter giving Oedipus high fives but Creon stops them.)*

CREON: Yo mama so nasty she pours salt water down her pants to keep her crabs fresh. *(The chorus laughs and celebrates with Creon after he raises his axe towards them threatening. They all him high fives.)*

OEDIPUS: Your mama's so old she ran track with the dinosaurs. *(The chorus laughs and Creon stops them.)*

CREON: Yo mama is so nasty, just saying hi to her gave me the clap. *(The chorus celebrates with Creon as he raises axe again in a threatening manner towards them.)*

OEDIPUS: Well my mother was your sister and I fucked her. *(Long pause. Everyone is stunned then the chorus loses it. Creon is stunned)*...then, then, get this. The bitch hung herself. *(The chorus laughs harder and then they all stop. There is a long pause between everyone)* Oooh, that, that was a rough one. Snap Creon, snap!

CREON: It was, it was, good, but rough, that one hurt right here.

OEDIPUS: Hurt me too right here. *(They break back into action.)*

CREON: *(Waits for dramatic music)* You and your children will die a most painful death. I will rid the name Oedipus forever. Muhahahahahaha!! *(A chorus member runs in.)*

CHORUS MEMBER: Tiresias has left through the Portal of the Gods with Oedipus' eyes. He has gone to the future to find a relative of Oedipus' family line. He plans to bring him back here and defeat you and make Oedipus the King.

CREON: Who told you this? How do you know?

CHORUS MEMBER: Well it says it right here on page nineteen of this script, I Swear by the Eyes of Oedipus.

CREON: Let me see that. He's right. That's what he did and said. Oh by the way Oedipus, you messed up a line on page thirty. You said your mama is actually yo mama.

OEDIPUS: Let me see that. Damn I always mess that same line up.

CREON: Where did you get this?

CHORUS MEMBER: It was lying on the floor by the Portal of the Gods.

CREON: A Collection of Plays by Mark Frank Volume II...$21.95, someone's getting ripped off.

OEDIPUS: Did you read Volume I, what crap, you can get it for five dollars now I hear at your nearest used book store bargain bin.

CREON: We must go through the Portal of The Gods and bring this, what's his name? *(Looks through the script)* Eddie Pius! Yes we must bring Eddie Pius back to Greece and execute him with the rest of his long lost family. You stay here and wait for to hear from Zeus.

CHORUS MEMBER: Yes my King.

CREON: The rest of you let's get going. Find out in the script where this Eddie is in the next scene then grab the invisible cloak out of Pandora's box, we don't want to be seen looking like this ,we may bring about suspicious.

CHORUS MEMBER: You think? *(They all look at their robes and masks.)*

OEDIPUS: You won't win you know. You never do. You got dissed in *Oedipus*, Laughed at by the Gods in *Oedipus at Colonus*, Banished in *Antigone*, and burnt to death in *Medea*. What makes you think things will end in your favor this time?

CREON: Because this time I control the future. Muhhahahahahaha!

OEDIPUS: That's not funny.

CREON: No that wasn't, too much? To the Portal of the Gods! *(They exit.)*

OEDIPUS: *(Singing in a spot of light)* Anytime she goes away.

CHORUS MEMBER AND OEDIPUS: *(Look to see if Creon is gone. Both sing together face to face in spot of light)* Anytime…she…goes…away! *(Black out)*

71

Scene 6

(The Prologue Girls come out and hold up signs. Prologue Girl #1 holds up a sign that says, "Back to the Present" and Prologue Girl #2 sign says, " I'm drunk...really". As the Prologue Girls leave the set has now transformed center to a Chinese restaurant with three tables. The stage right table has a couple seated at it. You cannot see their faces as they are reading a paper. The center stage table slightly up center from the other two tables has Lionel seated at it looking at his watch and then looking around. The last table stage left has Eddie, China Baby, Uncle Leon, and Tiresias seated at it. The scene begins at their table.)

CHINA BABY: I want Moo Goo, I want Moo Goo!

UNCLE LEON: God damn China Baby, jus hold on a second. We got to get a waitress here first to wait on us.

EDDIE: I don't feel any different with these eyes. I mean I don't necessarily feel powerful or stronger but it's cool to see everything for the first time. I'm like a kid in a candy store with all this color and images.

TIRESIAS: Let's hope they live up to what the Gods say they are when we run into Creon. We will need all the power and strength to defeat him.

EDDIE: Uncle did you have to bring the saxophone, its jabbing my side.

UNCLE LEON: China Baby likes when I play.

EDDIE: But you don't know how to play.

CHINA BABY: He pretend play real good!

TIRESIAS: Why do you call her China Baby?

EDDIE: Here we go, remember we got to get back to Greece in a day Uncle so make the story short.

UNCLE LEON: Well... I DON"T SEE A GOD DAMN WAITRESS!!! So I tell you the story. You see I'm a widower and I also lost a child.

TIRESIAS: I'm sorry.

UNCLE LEON: Now don't be interrupting my story Foo Man, you want to hear the story or not?

TIRESIAS: My apologies go ahead.

CHINA BABY: This good story, about me!

UNCLE LEON: *(The story is reenacted on the right side of the stage)* After my loss of my wife and child I decided to adopt a child. On the back of the National Enquirer I noticed they had these China baby girls in China for adoption. I mean you have to wait forever to get a damn baby here in the states so I got my ass on a flight to China and they tell me they are all out of China babies. It seems everyone reads the Enquirer in China and they had tons of people come to China to adopt these babies. Well this lady tells me there is one child called the Chosen One. And she is the daughter of the great Chinese Emperor Kung Pau. She told me the secret to retrieving the child is to use the power of the child.

CHINA BABY: Spicy!

UNCLE LEON: But, in order to get this special China Baby I had to prove myself worthy and if I wanted the child I had to defeat the Brotherhood of Ninja Incorporated or as they like to call themselves the Bone Patrol.

TIRESIAS: Incorporated is with an "I" not an "E".

EDDIE: He's rolling let him go.

UNCLE LEON: Can I tell my God Damn story? So I climb up the emperor's castle which is twenty miles up on this huge slanted hill. I open the castle doors and there's China Baby sitting on a pillar in the middle of an empty room. So I just think I'll go in and grab her. But as soon as I do, four Ninja's surround me and let me tell you the battle was on. I was losing my ass pretty bad and they were handing it to me and then I remembered what the lady at the adoption agency said, she said, "use the power of the child". So I grabbed China Baby, she was so cute, couldn't of been but ten months old. *(When he grabs the baby off the pillar, "China Girl" by David Bowie plays in the background.)* All of a sudden China Baby starts battling the Ninja's a kicking ass and taking names. *(Uncle Leon is still telling the story as the battle scene of baby China Baby and Uncle Leon battling Ninja's continues to play stage right. We no longer can hear Uncle Leon talking even though he's still telling the story with grand gestures. The lights shift to China Baby looking at Tiresias and Tiresias, though blind, turns to the direction of China Baby. She touches his hand and while the song "China*

Girl" continues to play, a dream sequence between China Baby and Tiresias appears on the back wall in the form of a music video. In it there are many scenes with them together. The first scene is of them running through a field holding hands. The next scene is them feeding each other ice cream and ice cream is all over Tiresias mask, the next scene is them line dancing a bar together, the next scene is Tiresias playing quarters with a bunch of Chinese people, the next scene is Tiresias getting chased by Uncle Leon with a huge axe. The next scene is Tiresias and China Baby running to each other in a field. The dream sequence ends and the action and music continue onstage as Baby China Baby battles the Ninjas.) So after the battle was over, the emperor came out and said, "You have chosen... wisely." He told me anytime I needed a "Bone" that they would be at my service for taking care of China Baby. He was impressed I had the courage to come get China Baby and defeat his Ninja's. And the reason for that China Baby is...?

CHINA BABY: You OBMF*! (A waitress comes over to their table.)*

IPHEGENIA: *(In a fake Chinese accent.)* How we doing over here?

UNCLE LEON: It's about God damn time. We'll have one buffet, four plates and four waters.

CHINA BABY*: (Pissed off)* Uncle, she's poser, she not Chinese. She American.

IPHEGENIA: *(Bowing)* Very good, very good. Sorry for riducuwus wait.

UNCLE LEON: You think you're Chinese? You're going to insult my baby girl and pretend you Chinese?

IPHEGENIA: I Chinese.

CHINA BABY: You poser! I crush you!

EDDIE: Its fine, Iphigenia is it? Just please go get us the plates and water?

IPHEGENIA: *(Bursts into monologue. She is very dramatic, bitter and delivers monologue to them on their table)* You don't think I suffer? I don't love? No to you and you I'm just a piece of meat to be sacrificed. Like some goat to the Gods. But I have feelings. Oh yes I do! *(Acts out the story)* There I was strapped to the altar, my father, Agamemnon lurching over me with a sharp knife. He told me I was to come to Aulis to be married. What a liar! Because then he stuck the knife in, turned it, turned it, until I was dead. Sacrificed me? Just so his ships could sail to Troy to save Helen, Clytemnestra's sister. Who's to blame? She's to blame! She's to blame!!! *(She points to China Baby but then changes her mood on a dime and smiles and starts to off to get their plates and water.)* Konichiwa!

TIRESIAS: I think I know her she looks very familiar.

EDDIE: She's nuts!

CHINA BABY: She poser! *(The action shifts to the center table with Lionel. Josie, now a waitress, waits on him.)*

JOSIE: Are you going to have the buffet today?

LIONEL: Josie, I thought you worked here.

JOSIE: Do I know you? *(Laughs)*

LIONEL: Don't play stupid with me, you know who I am. Lionel?

JOSIE: *(Burst out laughing.)* I don't think so.

LIONEL: Alright, I'm sorry, that waitress meant nothing to me, it was a one time thing. I swear it will never happen again. Just come back home. We can rebuild our life.

JOSIE: *(Laughing harder at him.)* I'm sorry I just…

LIONEL: Is this funny to you? What about our child who I dropped on his head and caused him to be blind for the rest of his life, is that funny?

JOSIE: *(She is rolling now.)* Oh my God I'm going to pee myself.

LIONEL: I suppose its funny you gave our son away because you believed that crazy gypsy. *(Josie is on the floor laughing hysterically.)* You go ahead and laugh but I'm not taking all the responsibility for this, if you want a divorce, you got it lady!

JOSIE: *(Still laughing Hysterical)* I'll go get your plates and water. You're hilarious.

(The action shifts to stage right. Two people are reading papers, you cannot see their faces.)

DR. GENDER: *(Puts paper down looks around)* Alright, we now know she works here and that guy is her husband. It seems my little hypnotic spell worked. *(He raises his paper back up.)*

MELBA: *(Puts her paper down.)* Only you first could have found out more about this black man she gave the baby to before you hypnotized her. Here she comes. *(She puts her paper back up in front of her face)*

JOSIE: Here are your plates, water, and the ticket when you're done eating, oh and two fortune cookies.

MELBA: Thank you, nothing else.

DR. GENDER: Thank you Josie. Oops!

JOSIE: *(Leaves)* Comes back, by the way, you look damn fine today. *(She pauses and looks confused.)* Why did I say that? *(She exits.)*

MELBA: *(Puts paper down.)* You idiot, you almost blew our cover. *(Puts paper back up)*

DR. GENDER: *(Puts paper down.)* I'm sorry I forgot *(Puts paper up.)*

MELBA: *(Puts paper down.)* Tell me again what the detective you hired said this black man was or what he looked like? *(Puts paper up.)*

DR. GENDER: *(Puts paper down. He takes out a file folder, opens and reads from it.)* He's a minister at one of the Pentecostal church in the city. I guess he also dresses and acts like some sort of hit man. He carries a saxophone around his neck, but he doesn't know how to play it. This is the guy that adopted the child. *(He puts his paper up.)*

MELBA: *(Puts paper down.)* Pentecostal church? Now that's a church! *(Puts paper up.)*

DR. GENDER: *(Put paper down.)* I like when people talk in tongues and do flips in the air. *(Put paper up.)*

MELBA: *(Puts paper down, Lionel looks over and stares at Melba.)* Where the hell are we going to find someone of that description in such a big city as New York? *(She puts her paper back up. Uncle Leon comes over to their table.)*

UNCLE LEON: Excuse me but I couldn't help noticing you got a stack of plates here and since our waitress has never come back to our table I was wondering if I can have four of your plates, you'll still have two.

MELBA: *(Her paper is still up in front of her face.)* Take them all we're not hungry.

UNCLE LEON: Thank you very much and God bless you! Oh and if you're ever in the area I do sermons at the Pentecostal church, you two ought to stop by. *(He gives them his card and then goes back to his table.)*

MELBA: *(Puts paper down.)* It looks like we got a hell of a search ahead of us. Your wig's crooked. *(He fixes his wig. The action returns stage left with Uncle Leon.)*

UNCLE LEON: Come on everyone let's eat I got some plates. I'll try to get some water.

CHINA BABY: I stay here and talk to Tiresias. You get me Moo Goo.

TIRESIAS: I'm not hungry.

UNCLE LEON: Damn, I would have paid to see how you got food through that mask. Come on Eddie lets go get some food. I got a dollar; we can play the juke box.

EDDIE: I'll lead the way. They have a juke box at a Chinese restaurant?

UNCLE LEON: Hey Foo Man Chu now that we're all cool like Fonzee lets keep your hands off my China Baby.

TIRESIAS: *(He rises.)* I am a gentleman!

UNCLE LEON: Correctomundo, you best be *(He exits)*

TIRESIAS: Why does your Uncle Leon act so violent when he is a minister of faith?

CHINA BABY: He very protective of me and Eddie ever since he lost his wife and child.

TIRESIAS: Why does he carry around that saxophone? He doesn't even know how to play it.

CHINA BABY: It was a gift from wife, it was the last thing she gave him. He said she loved saxophone. He carries it everywhere with him. He good man, just a little confused with identity due to tragedy. Tell me about you.

TIRESIAS: What do you want to know?

CHINA BABY: Why you so worried what happens to Eddie's family?

TIRESIAS: Well I told you, after Creon wipes out the Oedipus family line, he's going to wipe all those associated with him which includes me.

CHINA BABY: *(Grabs his hand)* You didn't come for other reason. Maybe see love in your future with one China Baby? You could pick any Oedipus relative in future and you pick Eddie Pius? Why?

TIRESIAS: I think you already answered your own question.

CHINA BABY: You tricky, I flattered. *(She makes out with him really quick, kissing his mask.)* How we get out of this mess with Eddie?

TIRESIAS: *(Getting off the floor from the kiss.)* I'm counting on Zeus. He owes me big time. I sided with him on an argument he had with his wife and she mad him turn me into a woman for seven years because I sided with him. He owes me a favor. A BIG favor. Those periods are a bitch.

CHINA BABY: You so right. Look, you help us and I help you. *(She grabs him under the table.)*

TIRESIAS: China Baby, I don't know if we can be together, Uncle Leon would shoot me.

CHINA BABY: I tell you what, I take care of Uncle and you take care of me. *(She removes his mask and a good looking young stud is underneath it. She kisses him slowly this time and passionately. The action all of a sudden centers around on the whole restaurant.)*

LIONEL: *(Stands up)* Melba!

MELBA: *(Puts her paper down)* Oh shit!

JOSIE: *(See's Dr. Gender)* Dr. Gender?

DR. GENDER: Josie!

JOSIE: You are so Damn fine!

UNCLE LEON: *(See's China Baby kissing Tiresias, he has a ton of Chinese food piled up on a plate)* China Baby!

TIRESIAS: Uncle Leon!

EDDIE: *("Isn't She Lovely" by Stevie Wonder begins to Play)* Stevie! Good choice Uncle Leon. *(Eddie bumps into Lionel who was eating a fortune cooking. Eddie says excuse me to him but Lionel starts to choke on the cookie. Eddie begins to help Lionel but then sees Josie and its love at first site for the both of them as a spot hits them and a red wash surround them. He drops Lionel and starts to dance with Josie. Uncle Leon starts choking Tiresias at the table while China Baby tries to get him off of Tiresias. Melba sits and pets Taxi, her cat, while Dr. Gender replies his make-up. Iphigenia enters and tries to give Lionel the Heimlich Maneuver. He falls to the floor as Iphigenia starts to try CPR. Uncle Leon sees Eddie dancing with Josie and stops choking Tiresias. He wanders over to watch them as Melba and Dr. Gender get up and stand on each side of Leon studying him. Tiresias and China Baby start to dance. Two paramedics show up and bring out the paddles for Lionel. Iphigenia grabs the paddles and tries them on Lionel. She then, not thinking they work try them on each paramedic who she knocks out with the jolt. She gives herself a jolt and laughs and continues shocking herself and laughing. Lionel dies in front of her. He has choked to death on the fortune cookie. The Prologue Girls come on and pull the fortune from his mouth. Prologue Girl #1 sign says that she shows to the audience, "Today's fortune" Prologue Girl #2 sign reads: "You will have a great day!" The Prologue Girls start to dance. During the saxophone solo in the song, Uncle Leon pretends to plays his saxophone downstage. Iphigenia picks up a dead Lionel and dances with him. The song fades into a scene change. The tables are taken off by the cast while Eddie and Josie dance onstage in a spot. They kiss and take off each other's clothes. They crawl in bed stage left. End of Act I as the lights fade to black.*

Act II Scene 7

As the lights come back up from intermission, "Hip to Be Square" By Huey Lewis and the News begins to play as we see Eddie and Josie are having sex in grand fashion in the bed stage right. Stage right, China Baby, Uncle Leon and Tiresias are all gambling. They have a ton of cash in their hands. Center stage, with the time warp image on the back wall, we see Creon running in place with a huge Greek axe with three other chorus members. The Prologue Girls come out with a bunch of signs. "Here we go", ""The plot thickens" "Are you ready?" They move over to stage left as the lights spot stage left only as Josie and Eddie are still having sex under the sheets and hold up signs. "Eddie and Josie get to know each other" "Once", "Twice", "Seven times", "Fifteen times", "Twenty times", and "Lets leave them alone." The lights switch to center stage where Creon and his chorus are running in place with weapons. A time warp image continues on the back wall. The Prologue Girls hold up signs that say, "Creon is on his way to the future.", "He plans to take Eddie back to Greece to kill him and the rest of the Oedipus family.", "Creon's such a loser", "It's taking him forever to get here." The lights then switch over to stage right as The Prologue Girls hold up more signs. Uncle Leon, Tiresias and China Baby all come out and they have changed. Uncle Leon is dressed like a first class pimp, China Baby has a very seductive dress on, and Tiresias looks like a hip mobster. The signs from the Prologue Girls read, "Uncle Leon gets rich overnight", "He accepts the relationship between China Baby and Tiresias", "But he must be a chaperone on the dates", "They are all very rich and powerful", "Oops a saxophone solo", "Take it away Uncle Leon" Uncle Leon comes downstage to play the saxophone. All areas are lit and we see all the action at the same time. During the final chorus of the song, all the characters come together to form a kick line. As the song fades, the action shifts back into the bedroom where Josie and Eddie are in bed. The Prologue Girls hold up two last signs, "Back to the action" and "Your hot in the third row, seat J17."

EDDIE: *(Pulling the sheet off of him)* Mother of mercy! No more.

JOSIE: What did you say?

EDDIE: I can't do it anymore. Twenty times is my limit.

JOSIE: You seem to know my body so well, especially my breast.

EDDIE: Oh mama that was good!

JOSIE: What did you say?

EDDIE: I said that was good. I never had sex before, you were the first.

JOSIE: You're a virgin?

EDDIE: Yep! First time, but I feel like I've been inside you before. We were born to make love. How bout you?

JOSIE: *(Laughs)* First time I think? I can't remember. *(Laughs again)*

EDDIE: I feel like a little baby reborn.

JOSIE: Why do you say that?

EDDIE: I've never felt so alive so free!

JOSIE: Aww, do I make you feel this way?

EDDIE: Yes, I mean I'm head over heals for you. I've finally got someone who won't desert me… I mean I'm not alone anymore.

JOSIE: Well you have family don't you.

EDDIE: Yes. But I've never known true love. I mean I love China Baby and Uncle Leon but I never have been held in someone's arms like you hold me. You're so loving and nurturing. You're just what I needed.

JOSIE: Well… I need someone warm like you too Eddie.

EDDIE: It feels so great to be needed in life. I mean for once in my life I can say to the world, *(He holds Josie)* this is mine you can't take it and as long as I have love in my life I know I can make it.

JOSIE: You seem so happy, were you depressed before?

EDDIE: Let's just say I was blind to everything before and I woke up to reality.

JOSIE: Your eyes are amazing. It's like I can't keep from looking at you.

EDDIE: I look at you and for once in my life I can touch what my heart used to dream of long before I knew someone warm like you could make my dreams come true.

JOSIE: Eddie, that's beautiful.

EDDIE: That's Stevie Wonder.

JOSIE: You're so romantic. Tell me more about yourself, I love this.

EDDIE: Not much to tell. I'm adopted.

JOSIE: Adopted? *(She giggles)*

EDDIE: Yes, by my Uncle Leon, my parents died when I was very young.

JOSIE: *(Laughs)* I'm sorry.

EDDIE: That's not particularly funny.

JOSIE: I'm sorry I don't know what came over me. Go on, I'm sorry...really.

EDDIE: I used to teach for The School of the Blind but recently got these eyes and now I can see.

JOSIE: You used to be blind? *(Laughs)*

EDDIE: Is something funny about that?

JOSIE: No, no, not at all, I don't know why I'm laughing.

EDDIE: Listen, I've been made fun of my whole life and I would appreciate if you didn't laugh at me.

JOSIE: I'm sorry really...

EDDIE: Okay, tell me about yourself.

JOSIE: Okay...I....ah...well... I don't know?

EDDIE: You don't know about yourself? Have you been married? Have kids?

JOSIE: *(Looks at Eddie and starts to laugh hysterically)* Married…kids?

EDDIE: What did I say? I just asked if you were married. What? Are you divorced?*(Josie falls off the bed laughing; she looks under the bed and screams. Creon and his four chorus members crawl from underneath the bed.)* I've heard of the boogie man but give me a break. *(Melba and Dr. Gender enter.)*

JOSIE: Dr. Gender?

DR. GENDER: Josie!

JOSIE: You are so fine! *(Still laughing hysterically)*

CREON: Enough with introductions. Is this the boy you speak of?

MELBA: Yes, he is the one.

EDDIE: What the hell is going on? *(Creon grabs Eddie by the throat and lifts him from the bed.)*

CREON: I see you have the eyes of Oedipus. They suit you very well.

EDDIE: What do you mean?

CREON: Doctor, if you were to be so kind to un-hypnotize the girl so she shuts up.

DR. GENDER: Pot pie-pot-pie-pot pie.

ALL: Pot pie?

DR. GENDER: Their very delicious, you've got that crust and then all those vegetables and chicken with all that sauce.

EDDIE: I like the beef ones.

MELBA: I like my pot pie over rice.

CREON: Silence!

EDDIE: Looks like someone doesn't like pot pies....

CREON: Actually, I like the beef ones ...no...no!

JOSIE: *(She is broken out of the spell)* Dr. Gender? You are so fine!

DR.GENDER: Do you remember everything Josie.

JOSIE: Yes, what am I doing here in my slip? Why did you make me remember again?

CREON: That my dear was my request. I want you to meet your son.... Eddie Pius!

JOSIE: He's not my son.

EDDIE: Mother Fucker!

CREON: Pretty much.

JOSIE: He's not my son. I slept with him, he's not my... *(She passes out.)*

DR. GENDER: He's your step son.

EDDIE: So she's my step mother?

MELBA: Eddie! *(Goes to hug him)* I…I am your real mother.

DR. GENDER: And I used to be your real father, but now you can call me mom… also.

(He hugs him)

EDDIE: *(Goes over to Creon)* These are my real parents?

CREON: Yes. And I am King Creon.

EDDIE: You're King Creon?

CREON: Yes.

EDDIE: King Creon who has come to kill me?

CREON: Precisely.

EDDIE: Do it, please… now!*(Puts Creon's axe on his neck)* Use that axe, it will be quicker.

MELBA: Waaaait! You told us that if we lead you to our son we could have him back.

CREON: I lied.

MELBA: You lied?

CREON: I lied.

MELBA: You lied to Melba?

CREON: Yeeessss. *(Hold axe up against her chin.)*

MELBA: Alright, then we got that straight. *(Dr. Gender screams like a woman.)*

CREON: What was that?

DR. GENDER: It just felt right, too much?

CREON: Take them all to the Portal of the Gods. We will have a mass execution tomorrow, Gods permitting.

DR.GENDER: Why are you killing us Mr. Creon?

CREON: Didn't you say you were his real parents.

MELBA: Did we say that? No, no…we barely know the boy. We were just kidding. Little joke.

CREON: You lie! As hard as it to believe you could be spawned by such a King as Oedipus, you two must die with the rest of them.

MELBA: Why didn't I see this coming?

DR.GENDER: Because you're not really a fortune teller, you're a taxidermist.

MELBA: Yeeees, that could be the case.

CREON: When you are done take the other three and find Tiresias, this Uncle Leon, and China Baby. Kill them all, and then bring their bodies back to Greece. We'll burn them all together.

EDDIE: *(He hits Creon. It doesn't phase him)* Damn eyes.

Mark Frank

CREON: You have to believe in your destiny for those eyes to hold any power. You doubt it, it is written all over your face. You are weak like your ancestor Oedipus. It will be a pleasure killing you both.

MELBA: Can I bring my cat. Come Taxi! Taxi! Taxiiiiiiii! *(They all are taken away. Taxi, stuffed cat remains on stage in a spot. Black out.)*

Scene 8

(The lights switch from stage right to stage left. Tiresias, China Baby, and Uncle Leon are busy counting stacks of money at a table and all smoking cigars. They are still dressed up in their fancy clothes. They have an assortment of Chinese food surrounding them.)

CHINA BABY: More Kung Pao Uncle?

UNCLE LEON: China Baby, if I have anymore China food, I'm going to bust.

TIRESIAS: We probably need to find Eddie and get back to Greece. We have wasted enough time already.

UNCLE LEON: *(Counting stacks of money)* Hey, the boys in love. I told you to give him five minutes, is it my fault he releasing twenty three years of pent up stress and frustration. Hey, how'd this twenty get in here? *(Throws the twenty away.)*

CHINA BABY: We have nuff money to pay off house Uncle.

UNCLE LEON: And to get your eyes fixed.

92

CHINA BABY: This the way they are uncle, they not broke.

UNCLE LEON: God damn China Baby you can have anything you always wanted. We got enough money here to buy anything we want.

CHINA BABY: I'm happy just being with Tiresias.

UNCLE LEON: I was afraid of that. *(A chorus member comes running in.)*

TIRESIAS: I sense a messenger.

CHORUS MEMBER: King Creon! Where is King Creon?

UNCLE LEON: Looks like a friend of your Foo Man Chu.

TIRESIAS: What is it?

UNCLE LEON: *(Puts gun to his head)* You might want to tell him.

CHORUS MEMBER: Zeus has given his blessing for King Creon to execute Oedipus and his children.

TIRESIAS: We must go, now, we have no time to wait. We have to go get Eddie and leave through the Portal of the Gods. If we don't, Eddie will cease to exist. Oops, looks like we got company. *(Five more chorus members enter.)*

CHORUS LEADER: If you want to find Eddie you'll have to go back to Greece Tiresias. King Creon has taken Eddie and Josie back with him to execute them along with Oedipus and his children.

TIRESIAS: You must help us. King Creon is mad with power. If he destroys the Oedipus family, he will change history and possibly cause a cataclysmic reaction with the Portal of the Gods that could cause the destruction of the earth.

UNCLE LEON: Hey, that's the first time I heard that, I thought we were trying to save Eddie from vanishing, not the whole God damn world.

TIRESIAS: I must have left that part out.

UNCLE LEON: Left that part out? Shit! Now that would seem like an important thing to tell us.

TIRESIAS: Creon in the future went through the portal to visit the Creon in the past to warn him of his downfall. This is forbidden by the Gods because it disrupts the Gods power to interfere. If a mortal like Creon can change the outcome of the future disrupting the power of the Gods, then you're talking of a whole different future without the Gods leading to no direction of mortals, leading to death and destruction of everyone.

CHORUS LEADER: Your story seems very convincing but we have our orders from the King to execute the three of you.

TIRESIAS: Step aside. *(He tries to go, but the chorus member knocks down Tiresias.)*

UNCLE LEON: Man you okay? How come you didn't use that power shit with me earlier.

TIRESIAS: The eyes gave me power. I am weak without them.

CHINA BABY: You make big mistake. You not hit man I love. I tired of all this threat and meanness. You mess with wrong China Baby *(She goes at them and they push her down.)*

UNCLE LEON: You guys just messed up one hell of a way. You see that's my Baby Girl. You hit that blind dude over there and that just made me a little mad because I just started to like his ass because he made me some money. Money I can use for my family, my home, and my church. See I'm a pastor and I don't like violence. But I do believe that saying, what is it, spare the rod and spoil the child." You see my daddy taught me that, and his daddy before him. In fact when I was bad or disrespected him, kind of like you just disrespected me and my family he had a saying, he said, "Bend down and touch your toes." And then he would whip our ass black and blue. Now you six dudes don't read the bible because as I understand it your God is this dude named Zeus. In fact you got many Gods as I understand, but you see we have one God, JC and he's one bad ass mother. And we follow some of his ways to live your life on this earth through the book called the Bible. And there's a passage I got memorized, Ezekiel 25:17. "The path of the righteous man is beset on all sides by the inequities of the selfish and the tyranny of evil men. Blessed is he who, in the name of charity and good will, shepherds the weak through the valley of the darkness, for he is truly his brother's keeper and the finder of lost children. And I will strike down upon thee with great vengeance and furious anger those who attempt to poison and destroy my brothers. And you will know I am the Lord when I lay my vengeance upon you."

CHORUS LEADER: If it is your best intentions to fight us, then we will be forced to execute you with severe torture and pain. *(Uncle Leon shoots the chorus member in the leg.)*

UNCLE LEON: Oh, I'm sorry. Did that break your concentration? I didn't mean to do that. Please, continue. I believe you were saying something about, "best intentions."

CHORUS LEADER: What God are you?

UNCLE LEON: The God of bad ass.

CHORUS: What?

UNCLE LEON: What, what?

CHORUS: What? *(Uncle Leon shoots Chorus Leader in the other leg.)*

UNCLE LEON: Say *what* again, come on, one of you say *what* again. I dare ya mothers to say *what* again!

CHINA BABY: Uncle! Give me gun, we finish it fair. No more Jules Winnifield from movie, *Pulp Fiction*, you fight as Uncle Leon. *(She takes his gun.)*

TIRESIAS: Two bullets in his leg with five against three of us? I say shoot two more of them. Make them head shots.

CHINA BABY: No, now we finish it!

UNCLE LEON: Now you done it, you've pissed off China Baby. Foo Man, I suggest you just follow her lead because she is about to kick some serious Greek ass.

TIRESIAS: You mean…..

UNCLE LEON: That's right, member that story I told you, Power of the Chosen One. They about to see some of that power. You dudes in deep shit!

("Kung Fu Fighting" by Carl Douglas plays in the background as China Baby takes on five chorus members. Tiresias is back to back with China Baby as the five surround them. Uncle Leon wails away at the chorus leader who's been shot in both legs. The battle is on as they fight off the chorus members. An old Chinese movie of Bruce Lee plays on the back wall as China Baby and Tiresias mock it through out the song. Moves, sounds, and actions should be duplicated by Uncle Leon, China Baby, and Tiresias in the fight scene. When the song ends the six chorus members are defeated.)

TIRESIAS: We must take them back with us, they have seen too much of the future. We must get to the portal; hopefully we are not too late.

(China Baby comes on with a wagon. Uncle Leon starts to pick up the chorus members and put them into the wagon.)

UNCLE LEON: It's time for Leon and Creon round one and I'd put all of our winning on Leon.

CHINA BABY: *(Looks out at audience, pumps her fist in her hand.)* He next!

UNCLE LEON: Ding, ding! *(Black out)*

Scene 9

(The Prologue girls come out with signs that say, "Back in Greece" and "Home Stretch". They exit off and Eddie is tied up with Oedipus back to back. Melba and Dr. Gender are tied up next to them, and Jocasta is sitting in a chair passed out over by Creon. A chorus member stands next to Creon with an axe.)

CREON: Tough call, who should be first? Now I could go with Oedipus that started all this grief or I could go with the great grandson who thought he could defeat me with Oedipus' eyes. You fool, those eyes are powerless in Greece.

EDDIE: Now you tell me. I just bought into this destiny thing and now you tell me that? Great!

MELBA: Kill this guy tied behind me first. He's missed paying me my alimony check for twenty years.

DR. GENDER: You know I had to pay for that operation.

MELBA: Wait, waaait, waaaaaaaait. You cared more about yourself than your son, now look where you are. Kill him first, please.

OEDIPUS: How you two are related to me I'll never know.

JOSIE: *(Waking up.)* What happened? I had the most horrible dream...*(She looks around.)* ...and I'm still having it. Shit!

CREON: You have just woken up just in time to see your son die!

JOSIE: Oh my God Eddie, then it's true, you're really my son, I slept with my son!

ALL: Step-son.

JOSIE: That still doesn't make it right. I mean I am still your mother. Oh my God, that sounds horrible.

OEDIPUS: I had four kids with my mother, don't knock it. The sex was great.

EDDIE: I don't care what we are, I still love you.

JOSIE: Love, you don't even know what love is; you just met me. Do you think sex twenty times in one hour is love?

MELBA: Twenty times?

DR. GENDER: Twenty times?

OEDIPUS: Really? Twenty times?

CREON: I have to know before I kill you, did you really do it twenty times in one hour?

EDDIE: Yes! Since everyone has to know, I did it twenty times in an hour! Okay? I had years of pent up stress.

DR. GENDER: Oh my God, that's my boy!

MELBA: Ha! You be lucky if you could do it once.

JOSIE: Eddie, do you realize what we have done? It's so disgusting?

EDDIE: No, it's so beautiful. I'm not even blood related to you. I haven't known you my whole life. I'd like to know why you haven't been there before I die? I'd like to know how the hell these two are my real parents? How about some exposition?

OEDIPUS: Creon, could you hold our execution for a few minutes and humor me, I really got to hear this.

CREON: As do I.

MELBA: You are our son. The son of a gypsy and a cross dressing transsexual hermaphrodite

EDDIE: But how?

MELBA: We had sex, once! That's all it took. SRS took one look at our lives and took you away from us. They said we were weird. Yeah right. What do they know?

JOSIE: So he was put up for adoption by you, and then adopted by Lionel and me?

EDDIE: Who's Lionel?

JOSIE: Your step father, here's a picture of him. *(She shows him a picture of him.)*

EDDIE: Wait a second. This is the guy that choked to death on the fortune cookie at the Chinese restaurant after I bumped into him.

OEDIPUS: Our Greek plays were never this good.

CREON: I know. This is classic stuff.

MELBA: Wait, waaaaait, waaait! Do you know what this means?

ALL: What?

MELBA: I'm not sure. I thought you all knew?

JOSIE: What this means is the gypsy's prophecy came true. That you would grow up and sleep with your mother and kill your father.

OEDIPUS: Yeah I hate when that happens.

EDDIE: So then you left me on my Uncle's doorstep?

JOSIE: Not before we dropped you on your head causing you to be blind. I'm sorry Eddie.

EDDIE: You dropped me on my head?

JOSIE: We were drunk and Lionel scored a touchdown from a pass I threw to him and spiked the ball, only we didn't have a ball, we had a baby.

EDDIE: You used me as a football?

CREON: This keeps getting better.

EDDIE: I can't believe you used me as a football.

JOSIE: It was a friendly game of catch the baby.

EDDIE: But my parents died in a car crash. At least that's what Uncle…

(Uncle Leon, China Baby, and Tiresias enter with a wagon full of knocked out chorus members. Tiresias unties everyone.)

UNCLE LEON: Wait, hold the damn phone. I lied to you Eddie. Your parents never died in a car accident.

CHINA BABY: But Uncle Leon wife and child did, right uncle.

UNCLE LEON: Yeah, that's the truth Eddie.

EDDIE: Why, why did you lie? This all could have been prevented.

CREON: Everyone must die now! This is too weird.

UNCLE LEON: *(Pulls out gun and points it to Creon's head.)* You need to be cool, like Fonzie, now shut the hell up. Now we all gonna be cool like Fonzie's.

CREON: Kill them all! I have the worse sinus headache.

UNCLE LEON: Now Creon, I thought we were going to be cool? When you yell at me it makes me nervous. When I get nervous, I get scared and when I get scared, that's when people get accidently shot.

CHINA BABY: Uncle stop! For once and for all, you not Jules Winnifield, be self!

UNCLE LEON: China Baby's right. Now you're lucky I'm in a transitional period. I don't want to shoot you but I want to help the situation. Now there's a passage I got memorized. Ezekiel 25:17 and if I said it to you right now it means I would pop a cap in your ass and you'd be dead. But this is not who I am. *(He takes off his afro wig and gives China Baby his gun.)* I'm a pastor. I'm a man who lost his wife and child in a car accident. And when I hear you're going to kill innocent children when I lost mine, well that doesn't work with me. I'm trying to be a good Sheppard and look the other way but you making memories come back I don't want to deal with. I adopted these two because I wasn't man enough to protect my wife and child the first time around. We don't need to get into what happened with the car accident, that's between me and God. I became Jules Winnifield because I didn't like who I was for many years and no one was going to mess with him. But I no longer need his ass because I know now I can protect my family just as Leon, plain old pastor Leon, and I finally like who I am. And if I got to get my ass whipped by you just for being me, well so be it. But you ain't killing anyone here today, especially my kids or any other children, over my dead body.

DR, GENDER: You're now ready Leon to give up the saxophone, you don't know how to play, you never did, and you just pretend to play. Listen to Dr. Gender.

UNCLE LEON/CHINA BABY: You are so fine!

UNCLE LEON: I'm keeping the saxophone. My wife always wanted me to learn how to play and damn it I'm going to start taking lessons if we ever get out of this mess.

DR. GENDER: *(Crying.)* That story was so sad. He's made such a break through.

EDDIE: Have you been seeing Dr. Gender Uncle Leon? Have you China Baby?

UNCLE LEON: Nothing wrong with a little mental help.

CHINA BABY: She listen real well.

MELBA: There, there Gay. You gave treatment to this man we look for, for years. Yes? You sure you won't kill him first?

EDDIE: Wait, your name is Gay Gender?

DR. GENDER: Yes.

CREON: Melba and Gay Gender?

MELBA: Yes.

EDDIE: Okay, kill me now!

TIRESIAS: No, we have come to save you Eddie.

EDDIE: Oh really, If you hadn't come and given these eyes to me, none of this would of happened. Thanks for foreseeing me sleeping with my mother and killing my father. Oh and by the way these eyes have no power. They're useless.

TIRESIAS: Something was blocking me from seeing the truth.

MELBA: You a prophet?

TIRESIAS: Yes.

MELBA: Makes perfect sense then, I'm a gypsy. Two prophets cancel each other out.

TIRESIAS: Very true, Eddie, your true mother being a seer caused interference from me prophesying. That's why I didn't think Josie was a threat, had I known she was also your mother I could have prevented this.

CHINA BABY: Eddie, who your mother, Melba or Josie?

EDDIE: Both.

OEDIPUS: I only slept with one mother.

EDDIE: Hey, so did I, I never slept with Melba, did I?

MELBA: Wait, waaaait, waaaaait!

EDDIE: Oh shit.

DR. GENDER: Oh shit.

MELBA: No.

UNCLE LEON: What the hell is going on? You mean to tell me this gypsy is your real mother and this woman here that you slept with is also your mother?

EDDIE: Step-mother

UNCLE LEON: Hey Creon, use my gun, shoot them all.

EDDIE: Uncle Leon!

UNCLE LEON: I'm kidding but this some messed up shit. Look Creon dude, we want to take Eddie back home with us. We'll leave the eyes and you can still have Melba, this Gay guy, and Oedipus over there. I'll throw in Foo Man too.

CHINA BABY: Uncle! *(They all start to argue.)*

CREON: Silence! What is with you people? The only normal person here is me. Am I the only person who hasn't killed or slept with a loved one?

UNCLE LEON: Now wait a minute Creon, hold it right there. China Baby and Foo Man Chu haven't killed anyone or….

CHINA BABY: Uncle…I pregnant!

UNCLE LEON: What? Foo-man!

TIRESIAS: It was one time. She said she was on the pill!

UNCLE LEON: Alright, now kill us all.

JOSIE: Wait. What is wrong with all of us? Don't you see how much love is here? All of us here have sinned, killed, and procreated.

UNCLE LEON: Amen.

JOSIE: But does that necessarily make us bad people? Sure, okay I slept with my son, but you know what, it was the most alive I have felt in a long time. And for the first time I felt like somebody really loved me.

TIRESIAS: It was the eyes.

MELBA: Leave it go, she's on a roll.

JOSIE: All I know if you want to kill us Creon you go ahead but you will never take away the love that we all feel for each other. And as long as we all have love I know we can make it past all this. Because Eddie, as weird as it may seem, as sexually attractive I am to you, even though I'm your step mother, I am still in love with you.

EDDIE: And I love you. *(They kiss)*

DR. GENDER: Melba, I love you.

MELBA: Go To Hell!

CHINA BABY: You still love me Uncle?

UNCLE: I aint too happy, but I still love you. *(They hug.)*

TIRESIAS: I still love my King.

OEDIPUS: And I his servant. *(They hug.)*

UNCLE LEON: You two weird as hell but hell I love you. *(He hugs Melba and Dr. Gender)*

MELBA: And we love you too black man, we love you too.

DR. GENDER: Oh you are big. *(Uncle Leon lets go.)*

JOSIE: I love you three also. *(All of the parents join in a group hug. Uncle Leon stays clear of Dr. Gender)*

CREON: Oh so guess who is not loved me. Big surprise! Not even my own messenger will hug me. Want a hug?

Messenger: No!

CREON: See.

DR. GENDER: You know I love you. You want a hug? Here's my card. Did you want to schedule something? I'm available this Tuesday?

CREON: Enough. Get away from me! *(The chorus on the wagon has awakened and surrounds everyone.)* Now that we all said how we feel and made our peace with each other, its time to die.

TIRESIAS: No its time for the truth. Zeus! Zeus! Everyone yell quickly. *(They all yell. Thunder is heard. Zeus enters.)*

ALL: Zeus!

ZEUS: What in Hades is all that noise? What is more important than having my toga down at my ankles with five Trojan women?

TIRESIAS: Zeus, you have ordered the execution of Oedipus and his family without hearing all the facts.

CREON: Zeus, don't worry, we got your blessing. We were just about to begin. Go back to what you were doing. We're fine.

ZEUS: I'm going. Carry on.

MELBA: Wait, waaaait, waaait!

ZEUS: What is that? Hello little mama.

MELBA: Well my God, hello.

DR. GENDER: Hiya!

ZEUS: Oooh you're cute too, alright you got my attention. Lay it on me.

TIRESIAS: Creon from the future came through the Portal of the Gods to warn Creon about his dismal future and he plans to change our future by killing Oedipus. If he does then the works of Sophocles will be non-existent and he could disrupt the balance of the universe, your universe. His power may exceed your someday if he is given this decree of death for the Oedipus family.

ZEUS: That's bad right.

TIRESIAS: Really bad, like he could destroy even you.

ZEUS: Okay, you convinced me. Everyone lives. Oh and next time, call Apollo…let him deal with this shit. See ya! *(Melba and Dr .Gender wave and smile at Zeus.)*

CREON: That's not fair!

ZEUS: You were naughty Creon! Bad Creon! *(Zeus slaps Creons hands.)* No going through the Portal of the Gods only prophets and Gods.

OEDIPUS: I would like to remain King of Thebes Zeus with your blessing.

ZEUS: That's tough one. I mean you did kill your father and Creon's sister, also your wife, also your mother... the people want justice. What to do, what to do?

CHINA BABY: Decide by a dithyramb contest.

ZEUS: Who said that?

TIRESIAS: You did my great God, a great idea!

CREON: What's going on here?

OEDIPUS: What's going on? *(To China Baby.)* We've never won a dithyramb contest against Creon and his cronies.

UNCLE LEON: Trust China Baby. She knows what she's doing. She's on the dance team at her college.

ZEUS: Alright, for the kingdom and the right to rule Thebes. You both will pick your own chorus and present a dithyramb. May the best one win and the loser's fate is decided by the new King. Agreed? Oh and for those who don't know what a dithyramb is, it's a dance! *(He snaps.)*

CHINA BABY: We do it!

OEDIPUS: I hope you all know what you're doing.

CREON: I like this my great God, agreed. After I win, I kill all of you.

CHINA BABY: Don't sing it, bring it. You can even go first.

CREON: Why thank you.

ZEUS: Okay then, let's get jiggy with it.

(Creon goes first. It's a traditional dithyramb with Creon leading his chorus of six around in a circle chanting. They hold candles. The dithyramb continues with many unique movements and sounds and then ends dramatically.)

ZEUS: Very good Creon and hard to beat. You've never lost a contest and it shows!

CREON: That is correct my great God.

ZEUS: Oedipus, you and your group is up next. You al have got a lot to prove.

MELBA: Zeus, I move and groove for you.

DR. GENDER: Zeus, I move and groove for you too.

ZEUS: Oooohh, begin!

JOSIE: Eddie, if this is it, I do love you.

EDDIE: Marry me?

JOSIE What? Marry you? Oh crap we're starting.

UNCLE LEON: *(To Tiresias)* You better hope we win so I can kill you later for getting China Baby pregnant.

TIRESIAS: Now is that anyway to talk to your future son in law?

CHINA BABY: *(Goes up to Creon. She has two giant speakers and an IPod)* This IPod, this subwoofer speaker, Dolby surround sound. This rap, this where we finish it!

("Pon De Replay" by Rihanna plays. Three spots of lights are shown. Eddie, Tiresias, and Oedipus are spotted with a spot light. They dance in sequence together, then separately doing their own solo. The lights change to a wash and Josie, China Baby come down dancing in a spot. They then join Oedipus, Eddie and Tiresias dancing. There is a quick black out and the spot comes up on Melba and Dr. Gender getting down. They dance for awhile as the lights change back to a wash and Uncle Leon and the Prologue girls walk downstage into their spot. They dance for awhile and join everyone else dancing in sequence. The lights go black as the back wall is lit and a video of Zeus dancing to the song is shown. The song finishes with each person doing their own solo dance and finishing with them all dancing in sequence.)

ZEUS: What was that? That was orgasmic!

CHINA BABY: That was rap.

CREON: There that proves I won, it wasn't a dithyramb it was some sort of rap

TIRESIAS: It was music, dance and song, thus it was a dithyramb.

CREON: Well Zeus, who won?

MELBA: Yes Zeus, who won?

ZEUS: Um…let see…

CHINA BABY: Oh Zeus whatever you decide, I give you IPod still as gift, you like?

ZEUS: Does it have that song on it?

CHINA BABY: Two thousand songs, like it?

ZEUS: Winner! Right there! You are the winner.

CREON: She…she bribed you. That's not fair!

ZEUS: Well…okay what do you have to offer?

CREON: Only my leadership, my loyalty, and last but not least, my homage to you. *(He bows.)*

ZEUS: Boring! Sorry, get lost. Oedipus is King again!

OEDIPUS: Thank you my great God!

EDDIE: *(Hands him a box.)* These eyes are yours Oedipus. May you rule for a long time and always see the truth. I think I'm better off blind especially with my family. Plus they don't have any power.

TIRESIAS: But I thought when I threw Uncle Leon it was the power of the eyes.

OEDIPUS: Nope, just ordinary everyday eyes.

CHINA BABY: That all you stud! *(She grips Tiresias arm.)*

113

OEDIPUS: Well now that my mother and father are dead and I got my eyes back, looks like I'm back on the bachelor scene.

JOSIE: Now what did you ask me before we danced?

EDDIE: Uncle what do you think?

UNCLE LEON: Well we need a bigger house anyway for everyone, no reason we can't move to Arkansas. We got plenty of money. *(Pause, thinking.)* I say why not!

EDDIE: China Baby? What do you think?

CHINA BABY: I pregnant by a two thousand year old prophet, who am I to give advice.

TIRESIAS: My boys can swim!

EDDIE: Tiresias? Melba?

TIRESIAS/MELBA: *(They look into the future)* The future looks bright, I gotta wear shades...for now.

EDDIE: Dad?

DR. GENDER: Mom, remember, if you don't mind?

EDDIE: Okay, mom.

DR. GENDER: Oh I just think it's the best thing, *(Starts to cry.)* Damn it my make-up going to run.

EDDIE: Oedipus, what do you think?

OEDIPUS: I loved Jocasta. We had four beautiful children. Love can conquer all tragedies in life. As long as you truly love her it doesn't matter who she is.

EDDIE: Then Josie, *(Kneels facing the wrong way)* will you marry me?

JOSIE: Yes! *(Everyone celebrates)*

UNCLE LEON: Let's have us a wedding! Back to the future everyone to the Pentecostal church.

CREON: What am I supposed to do? Aren't you going to banish me?

OEDIPUS: What do you think Eddie? I'll leave it up to you.

EDDIE: He can be the flower girl.

CREON: Can I really? Oh I always wanted to be in a wedding.

DR. GENDER: Damn it, I was going to do that!

CREON: *(Puts arm around Dr. Gender.)* Now what days were you open for an appointment?

ZEUS: Well I better be invited.

EDDIE: What about Creon, Oedipus, and the chorus, they can't go through the Portal of the Gods, only Prophets and Gods.

TIRESIAS: You want to tell him or should I?

ZEUS: It's all good. Anyone can go through the portal. I lied.

CREON: Then this whole thing with Tiresias, Oedipus and you about the whole portal thing was a set up?

ZEUS: Yep, pretty much. We're even now Tiresias.

CHINA BABY: I don't get it?

TIRESIAS: Pay back for turning me into a woman for seven years. He owed me remember?

CHINA BABY: Hey, book by Sophocles has writing again. We did it! Everything back normal except....us. Won't we change future being together, me be pregnant with your child? Change future?

TIRESIAS: Your name is Daphne isn't it? They say in Greek history that Daphne came from a mysterious land. What's more mysterious then the future. *(They kiss.)*

CREON: Damn it, screwed again!

EDDIE: Do you know what a dumb as is? You had the script to this play, why didn't you just read the end of it so you could have seen your defeat once again?

CREON: *(Looks to end of script, to self.)* I wonder if the playwright wrote a back up copy, Muhhahahaha! *(Destroys script.)*

UNCLE LEON: Let's go everyone, through the portal!

116

EDDIE: Zeus, on that IPod is song number twenty-seven!.

CHINA BABY: Just hit the round dial in the front.

ZEUS: Got it.

UNCLE LEON: Sing it to her Eddie!

Scene 10

"For Once in My Life" by Stevie Wonder plays as Eddie sings it to Josie. Everyone runs through the Portal. The Prologue Girls hold up a sign that says. "The Present", and "The Wedding of Eddie and Josie". The cast gets choir robes on during the song and forms a choir around Josie and Eddie who change onstage into wedding clothes as Eddie continues to sing to Josie. Uncle Leon in his own gown has the Bible and pretends to read from it until the saxophone solo is heard in the song where he then busts into a saxophone solo. As the song ends Uncle Leon finishes up the wedding.

UNCLE LEON: Is there anyone here that does not want these two to join in holy matrimony speak now or forever hold their piece. *(Everyone looks at Creon.)*

CREON: What? I'm cool with it.

UNCLE LEON: Alright and now the vows.

EDDIE: I Eddie, take you, Josie, to be my wife, loving what I know of you, and trusting what I do not yet know. I eagerly anticipate the chance to grow together, getting to know the woman you will become, and falling in love a little more every day. I promise to love and cherish you through whatever life may bring us. This I swear by the eyes of Oedipus.

JOSIE: I Josie, take you, Eddie, to be my husband, loving what I know of you, and trusting what I do not yet know. I eagerly anticipate the chance to grow together, getting to know the man you will become, and falling in love a little more every day. I promise to love and cherish you through whatever life may bring us. This I swear by the eyes of Oedipus.

UNCLE LEON: Then Eddie do you take Josie to be your wife?

EDDIE: I do.

UNCLE LEON: Do you Josie take Eddie to be your husband?

JOSIE: I do.

UNCLE LEON: Then the power invested in me, I pronounce you husband and wife. You may kiss your bride Eddie. *(They kiss. She throws the bouquet and Creon catches it.)*

CHINA BABY: Now what Uncle the plays over?

TIRESIAS: How about another wedding?

UNCLE LEON: How about where's my gun?

EDDIE: How about a dithyramb?

ZEUS: Hot damn another dithyramb. So be it!

UNCLE LEON: Sing it Stevie!

118

Epilogue/Curtain Call

"Here I am Baby, Signed, Sealed, Delivered, I'm Yours" by Stevie Wonder plays in the background. The Prologue Girls come out with signs for curtain call for each character as they dance on. The first is the chorus. The Prologue Girls signs say, "The Greek chorus forms a rock group in Greece with extravagant make-up and costumes." And "Call themselves: "Kiss". The Chorus moves off to the side and Oedipus comes out dancing. Prologue Girls hold up signs that says, "Got his eyes back and can see again", and "Fell in love with a woman who ended up being his step mother." Creon comes dancing out, Prologue Girls hold up signs that say, "Loses Kingdom" and "Gets a job in the future as a dishwasher". Melba and Dr. Gender come in dancing. The Prologue Girls hold up signs, "They buy a camper and become swingers", and "They have their first threesome with Zeus". Tiresias and China Baby Come out dancing. The Prologue Girls hold up signs that say, "Tiresias doesn't change history, ends up marrying Daphne." And "Daphne children are black for some reason". Uncle Leon comes dancing out. The Prologue Girls hold up signs that say, "Uncle Leon is dating me." and "Me too". They hook arms with Uncle Leon. Eddie and Josie come dancing out and everyone throws rice on them. Josie holds up sign that says, "I'm pregnant!" Eddie holds up sign that says, "Oh no, sequel?" They all dance off the stage, Iphigenia comes dancing out, she holds up a sign that says, "You can leave now, but if you do, you'll miss this". She points to the back wall and a video plays of Zeus dancing to "Pon De Replay" by Rihanna with different members of the cast one at a time in a spot of light. The video ends and the play is over.

Hurricane Iphigenia
Category 5
Tragedy in Darfur

Cast of Characters

Iphigenia, A thirteen year old Greek princess
Tesfaye, An African refugee, mid twenties
Artemis, Goddess of the Hunt
Mr. Anon, United Nations monitor
Agamemnon, Greek King of Argos
Abadu, Chad Refugee
Rebel #4
Narrator #1/Refugee #2
Narrator #2/Extra Refugee
Narrator #3/Refugee #3
Narrator #4
Narrator #5
Narrator #6/Refugee Mother
Narrator #7 /Refugee #4
Narrator #8/Refugee #5
Refugee Woman/Woman #2
Refugee #1
Rebel #1, Janjaweed militia
Rebel #2, Janjaweed militia
Rebel#3, Janjaweed militia

Time: Present

Place: Sudan, Africa (Darfur region) \

Costumes: The costumes should be simple and uniform to create an ensemble feel for the cast. All cast members should look uniform with black pants and shoes and a shirt that says "Save Darfur" on it. Additional costume pieces can be added if needed.

Pictures: It's important to show pictures on the back wall of the conflict and atrocities of Darfur whenever it is called for during the play.

Ensemble: The actors are story tellers, and the "story" is more important than the color of the actor's skin. African accents are optional but not important.

Artemis: Artemis should be placed in a number of scenes walking upstage throughout the play but not stealing focus. Anytime she enters the sound of African drums can be heard in the distance.

SPECIAL NOTE ON SONGS AND RECORDINGS

For all performance songs, arrangements and recordings mentioned in this play that are protected by copyright, the permission of the copyright owners must be obtained; or other songs, arrangements and recordings in the public domain substituted.

Hurricane Iphigenia, Category 5, Tragedy in Darfur was first presented at Coffeyville Community College on September 28-30 2007 at the Spencer/Rounds Performing Arts Theatre. The Director was Mark Frank. The production stage manager was Cody Dunlap. The cast was as follows:

Artemis	Jacie Holtsclaw
Iphigenia	Samantha Cosby
Tesfaye	Tyrell Blue
Mr. Anon	Zade Lopez
Narrator #1/Refugee #2	Nicole Santorella
Narrator #2/Extra Refugee	Ashley Rowe
Narrator #3/Refugee #3	Dustin Morby
Agamemnon/Narrator #4	Chad Kimmons
Narrator #5/Refugee Woman	
Woman #2	Shayla Williams
Narrator #6/Refugee Mother	Chelsea Daniels
Refugee #1	Miwa Ishii
Rebel #1/Abadu	Cortez Carter
Rebel #2	Dakota Miller
Narrator #7/Refugee #4	Luci Spencer

A picture of a young African girl crying engulfs the stage in a blue wash before the play begins. An African Flag hangs down front the ceiling house left and on the other side house right a sign that reads, "A Call to your conscience" "www.savedarfur.org."

AT RISE:

In a blue wash downstage lights brighten on a grave marked in Greek lettering that read "Iphigenia" There is the sound of thunder and tribal African drums are heard in the distance. Artemis enters upstage dressed in a white flowing gown and crosses slowly downstage as the African drums get louder. She stops in front of the grave and kneels down. Her body writhes with outstretched arms over the grave as her eyes roll back as if she is possessed. Pictures appear rapidly on the back wall behind her of atrocities in Darfur, Africa and then stop. The tribal African drums get louder as a hand appear out of the dirt and a young girl, Iphigenia pulls herself out of the grave. She is wearing a white dress with a red sash. Her neck has blood on it from her throat being cut. She tries to scream as she comes out of the grave but can't. She gasps for air and retreats from Artemis in fear. She extends her hand to Iphigenia and she slowly crawls and rests at the feet of the Goddess. Artemis picks up Iphigenia and carries her off as the lights fade to black and the African drums fade out.

Scene 1

(Lights come up as each actor comes out one at a time on their line. The first picture on the back wall is that of a Hurricane.)

NARRATOR #5: We are not black.

NARRATOR #1: We are not white.

REFUGEE #1: We are not yellow.

REBEL #2: We are not red.

NARRATOR #3: We are colorless.

NARRATOR #4: We are storytellers.

NARRATOR #5: And this is our story.

NARRATOR: #6: About an-out-of control hurricane.

ALL: Category five.

TESFAYE: In Darfur, Africa. (*A map is shown on back wall of Africa and the Darfur region is highlighted.)*

NARRATOR #1: We begin in the Darfur region in Western Sudan, the largest country in Africa. (*Picture of a map of Sudan is seen on the back wall.)*

NARRATOR #2: Darfur is home to a predominantly population of six million people.*(Another map of Sudan is seen on the back wall with cities that surround it.)*

NARRATOR #3: Darfur is about the size of Texas. (*Picture of the Darfur region is seen on the back wall.)*

NARRATOR 4: The time is the present.

NARATOR #5: The location is the Darfur region.

REBEL #1: We are Janjaweed, a militia group recruited from the local Baggara tribes. (*Picture of a Janjaweed militia is shown on the back wall.*)

REFUGEE #2: We are the non-Baggara tribe; we are farmers in the regions. (*Picture of an African Farmer is shown on the back wall.*)

NARRATOR #4: We are the Sudanese government; we do *not* support either group. (*Picture of a government official of Sudan is shown on the back wall.*)

REBEL #1: The Sudanese Government supports the Janjaweed and supplies arms and assistance to them and has participated in attacks with the group. (*Pictures of Janjaweed militia are shown on the back wall.*)

IPHIGENIA: Ethnic cleansing. (*Pictures of dead bodies in Darfur are shown on back wall.*)

TESFAYE: Genocide. (*Pictures on hundreds of skulls are shown on the back wall.*)

REFUGEE #2: I am a non-Baggara African. (*Picture of an African man is shown on the back wall*)

REFUGEE #1: I am a Baggara Janjaweed African. (*Picture of Janjaweed troops are shown on the back wall.*)

REFUGEE #1: I am a Baggara victim. (*Picture of dead bodies are shown on the back wall.*)

REFUGEE #2: I am a non-Baggara perpetrator. (*Picture of soldiers with Africans is shown on the back wall.*)

REFUGEE #1: I am black in skin tone and I practice Islam. I am Arabic. Praise Allah! (*Picture of a Sudan Muslim is shown on the back wall.*)

REFUGEE #2: I am black in skin tone and I do not practice Islam. Praise God, Jesus Christ. (*A picture of an African woman in a shawl is shown on the back wall.*)

NARRATOR #3: The situation is under control. There is no genocide in Darfur. I repeat the situation is under control.

ALL: The situation is under control! (*More pictures on the back wall of death and destruction in Darfur, Africa. Black out to a blue wash. African drums are heard in the distance and Artemis crosses the stage, behind her is a picture of dead Africans who have been shot to death on the back wall. She crosses, stops center, and looks at the audience and exits.*)

Scene 2

Lights up. Iphigenia is walking with rebels who push her to the ground. One rebel has her by the arm and pushes her down. He is away from the other rebels. Iphigenia is covered in dirt and it's hard to tell with all the dirt on her if she is black or white. A picture of Janjaweed militia is shown on the back wall.

IPHIGENIA: (*Fearful*) Are you going to kill me?

TESFAYE: *(In a panic. He speaks with an African accent.)* Just shut up and be quiet. I can't help you if you speak, now shut up.

REBEL #1: You got anything?

REBEL #2: Get your own.

REBEL #3: I'm starving man.

REBEL #1: Here. *(He gives him a piece of jerky. The actors freeze as the lights switch to a blue wash.)*

REFUGEE #1: Hunger. *(A picture of a hungry African child is shown on the back wall.)*

REFUGEE #2: Malnutrition. *(A picture of a malnourished African child is shown on the back wall.)*

REFUGEE #3: Disease. *(A picture of a dead body is shown on the back wall.)*

REFUGEE #1: Rape. *(A picture of a sad African woman is shown on the back wall.)*

REFUGEE #2: AIDS. *(A picture of an ill African man is shown on the back wall.)*

REFUGEE #3: Murder. *(A picture of a dead African shot in the head is shown on the back wall. The action resumes.)*

TESFAYE: We should let the girl go man. We killed and rape enough today. She's no threat to us. *(A rebel slaps Tesfaye. He sticks his gun under his neck and holds Tesfaye. Two pictures of Janjaweed militia are shown on the back wall.)*

REBEL #1: *(Laughing with other guards.)* You scared like civilian, look at him, he messed in his trousers. *(The other rebels laugh.)* Get the girl. *(Rebel #2 tears Iphigenia's dress off her, pins her to ground and gets on top of her, tries to kiss her.)*

REBEL#1: Yeah man, give her the good stuff; pump it, man, into her.

TESFAYE: *(Pulling the rebel off Iphigenia.)* Man.... come on...we've done enough today. Let's move on to the next village. Let her be.

REBEL #1: *(Puts knife to Tesfaye throat.)* What's up man, you not jiving man, what going on? You not like what we do man, you don't like to get some, you never get some, you refuse to kill all da time man, me thinking man you not one of us but one of those Christian farmers we hang in the village, you a farmer man, let me hear you squeal. Squeal for me man and I let you live. *(They stare at each other.)* You Janja-weeeeeed or you nothing man. *(He pushes him down and spits on him.)*

TESFAYE: Praise to Allah and Jihad. *(The men laugh at Tesfaye.)*

REBEL #1: *(Joining the others in the rape of Iphigenia.)* Save me some man, get me a piece. *(Tesfaye shoots all three rebels and kills them. Tesfaye quickly checks each rebels pocket for food or ammunition. He collects all their weapons. Iphigenia moves far away from*

Tesfaye. He crawls over to her but she moves away from him in fear. She makes no sound but is fearful. A picture of an African woman hiding behind her scarf is shown on the back wall.)

TESFAYE: No...no! I'm not going to hurt you. I help you, I help you, stop. Quickly come with me, other will come. Here look take this rifle, see I'm with you not them. I don't kill or rape. I'm playing the role of a Janjaweed to survive. No Jihad I promise. No Jihad!

IPHIGENIA: *(Confused and scared)* Where am I! Who am I? *Who am I?*

TESFAYE: Shhhh....quiet now. More will come so you must not speak so loud. (*"Effigy" by Natalie Merchant plays in the back ground. He crosses over to her and she scurries in defense away from him.*) I won't hurt you, shhhh...You must go with me. (*She stares at him; she quiets down-still crying in fear.*) You want gun? Here. I'm not going to harm you. We talk later, first we must hide these bodies, bury them. Here, you put your dress back on. *(Iphigenia changes cautiously keeping her eyes on Tesfaye.)* We must go now quickly. Those men mean to rape you and then kill you. If you don't hurry more will return. *(Iphigenia just stares at Tesfaye after putting her dress on.)* Look we must go now. They probably heard my gun. (*He tries to grab Iphigenia but she moves away from him.*) Okay, okay, I won't touch but you follow me? Okay? (*He starts to leave. Iphigenia stands and stares at Tesfaye. Tesfaye stops and extends his hand to her. She takes his hand after a long pause as she follows very cautiously as the lights fade out. Fifteen pictures of devastation in*

Darfur are shown on the back wall which is followed by a black out and the music fades out.)

Scene 3

(Lights come up. Iphigenia and Tesfaye are sharing a can of beans. They eat in silence. Tesfaye keeps subtly staring at Iphigenia who catches him. They are silent for two minutes sneaking peaks at each other. It is obvious Iphigenia is hungry. A picture of African people crying is shown on the back wall.)

TESFAYE: I don't mean to stare, if you don't mind me asking, but we don't get many white women in the desert of Sudan, Africa, running around in a white dress. Can I ask you your name?

IPHIGENIA: *(Looking straight out.)* I... am Iphigenia.

TESFAYE: *(Trying to pronounce it.)* Iphi-genia?

IPHIGENIA: Iphigenia, yes, that I know for some reason is my name. For it is the name I found next to me on a piece of wood stuck in the ground. I was buried here for some reason.

TESFAYE: Perhaps left for dead?

IPHIGENIA: Perhaps, What I don't know is who I am and why I am here... As weird as it sounds I don't know how I got here. I have no memory of who I am.

TESFAYE: You seriously don't know where you come from, who your family is?

IPHIGENIA: (*Still not looking at Tesfaye but straight out.*) I...I don't know. I have tried to figure that out when I was captured by those men. As I was walking I was trying to recall but the only thing I remember is coming up from the ground in this desert. No... wait... (*African drums are heard in the distance. Artemis crosses the stage and stands behind Iphigenia for a moment then exits.*)...there was a woman in white and the smell of...flowers, tons of beautiful flowers...she saved me...but I think I was dreaming. She carried me.... It's all a blur.

TESFAYE: It sounds like you may have amnesia, maybe from stress or shock from the Janjaweed attack on you. Happens to many women they rape. We leave it alone for right now. With everything that has happened to you I am surprised you did not scream back there? (*Long pause. Iphigenia does not respond.*) We talk about it later.

IPHIGENIA: For some reason I cannot scream. I try but nothing comes out. Why did you help back there?

TESFAYE: You were in trouble. They mean to kill you. You would do the same for me?

IPHIGENIA: No...no...I don't think so...maybe...I don't...who are you?

TESFAYE: (*A picture of an African woman holding a baby is shown on the back wall.*)

My name is Tesfaye. I was displaced from my daughter and wife during the Janjaweed cleansing of villagers that were not in support of Sudanese government. My only method of survival was to put on this uniform or else I would have been shot. My family is somewhere in interior of Chad where they crossed over with thousands of other refugees. I have been trying to get to Chad but the rebels have a stronghold on the border into Chad. It can take almost three months to get to there trying to dodge the Janjaweed. We can get there in fifteen days if we travel by night and avoid any militia.

IPHIGENIA: Why is there all this killing? (*Picture of oil barrels are shown on the back wall.*)

TESFAYE: Yes, lots of killing…this war started in Sudan in early 2003, three years ago when the two allied rebel groups, the Sudan Liberation Movement Army and the Justice and Equality Movement attacked military installations of the government over money and revenues from oil. Sudan is rich in oil.

IPHIGENIA: This killing has been going on for three years now? Over… oil? (*A picture of a crying baby is shown on the back wall.*)

TESFAYE: Oh yes…five hundred million barrels of black gold in reserves, one million in revenues per day, which is funneled into Janjaweed arms, helicopters, and bombs. All the world thirst the rich black tea that's a drink of death for thousands of Africans.

IPHIGENIA: Why?

TESFAYE: (*A picture of a Janjaweed militia is shown on the back wall.*) Well non-Muslim rebels in Darfur, South Sudan, are tired of the region's chronic economic

---

Mark Frank

and political politics of the Sudanese government. They took up arms to protect their communities and villages against a twenty-year campaign by government-backed militias recruited among groups of Arab factions in Darfur, North Sudan and Chad.

IPHIGENIA: The Janjaweed? Is that what you called them?

TESFAYE: Yes these rebels, the "Janjaweed" militias have over the past year received government support and arms to clear civilians from areas considered disloyal to the Sudanese government and that do not practice Islam in the South. Militia attacks and government offensives have led to massive displacement, indiscriminate killings, looting and mass rape against black Christians. They want their farm land for drilling oil and pipelines.

IPHIGENIA: I'm confused by what many of your words mean but why is no one in the world stopping all this killing. (*A picture of the flag of Sudan is shown on the back wall.*)

TESFAYE: One would think so since it's all an infringement of the 1949 Geneva Convention that prohibits attacks on civilians. My father was a military man so I know this to be a fact. He loved Africa and would be holding his flag up high in defiance if he was still here.

IPHIGENIA: (*She is far away in her mind.*) Wait... I think my father too was a military man.

136

TESFAYE: Something must be done about this war, which risks inflicting irreparable damage on a delicate ethnic balance of seven million African people who are uniformly Muslim, and are involved in intertwined conflicts with those who are non-Muslim.

IPHIGENIA: I don't understand, I'm sorry, it's all very confusing.

TESFAYE: (*A series of pictures of groups of Africans are shown during the monologue on the back wall.*) Well let me speak clearer... one is between government-aligned forces, the Janjaweed and rebels, farmers over land for oil. A second entails indiscriminate attacks of the government-sponsored Janjaweed militia on civilians, Jihad; and a third involves a struggle among Darfur communities themselves to find identity. Its implications go far beyond Darfur's borders. This holy war indirectly threatens the regimes in both Sudan and Chad and has the potential to inspire insurgencies in other parts of Africa. Millions upon millions could die.

IPHIGENIA: Is there anyone to help stop this?

TESFAYE: Three years into the crisis, the Western Sudanese region of Darfur is acknowledged by the world to be a humanitarian and human rights tragedy but nobody is doing anything about it. No security and the atrocities continue, people are dying in large numbers of malnutrition, AIDS, and a new famine is feared. I heard the numbers of deaths are in the thousands. (*Lights down on Tesfaye and Iphigenia and a blue wash come up on Narrators.*)

NARRATOR #1: (*Picture of a crying African baby is shown on the back wall.*) Three and a half million people are now hungry.

NARATOR #2: (*A picture of women walking in the desert with their belongings is shown.*) Two and a half million have been displaced due to violence.

NARRATOR #3: (*More pictures of dead bodies in African are shown on the back wall.*) Four hundred thousand people have died in Darfur thus far. (*Lights back up on Tesfaye and Iphigenia. A picture of Africans living in a yellow tent is shown on the back wall.*)

TESFAYE: The international community is failing to protect civilians or to influence the Sudanese government to do so.

IPHIGENIA: Who is this international community?

TESFAYE: (*A picture of the United Nations building is shown on the back wall.*) The international community is the world deeply divided over politics...perhaps paralyzed is the better word because their money is invested in other wars in the world, other economic crisis, and according to the world Sudan sponsors terrorism. Do they want to help us in Darfur? No, because they don't care. Racism! Africa has always been ignored because Africans are viewed as jungle monkeys... shhhhh, quiet, I hear something. (*They both get on the ground. A woman appears wandering. "In the Ghetto" by Natalie Merchant plays in the background. A picture of an African woman is shown on the back wall.*)

REFUGEE #1: I'm looking for my baby have you seen him?

TESFAYE: No. We are alone

REFUGE #2: They shot my brothers in front of me, hung my family and took my baby. I think they threw it on the ground and beat it to death. I have nowhere to go. It does not matter I will be dead soon. Pray for me.

IPHIGENIA: She, like me, has no identity. She is lost with no family. You, come back, please.

REFUGE #2: Yes?

IPHIGENIA: (*Iphigenia lays her hands on her. A picture of a malnourished baby is shown on the back wall.*) If you look in that well over there your baby is alive sleeping in the well bucket.

REFUGE #2: God bless you.

TESFAYE: How did you know that?

IPHIGENIA: I don't know. I just did.

TESFAYE: I don't mean this in a bad way, but sometimes in Africa being dead is better then being alive. (*The lights fade. A spot captures a refuge woman alone. Pictures of an African woman, Saddam Hussein, Osama bin Laden, Kim Jong Il, Mahmud Ahmadinejad, and an African baby crying is shown on the back wall during the monologue.*)

REFUGE WOMAN #2: (*She holds her baby.*) Shhhh baby, you sleep you know your mama is here. Dats right baby the world holds a smoke screen in front of the genocide in Africa. Let's report on the conflict in Iraq, Afghanistan, North Korea, Nuclear missiles in Iran, the Israel-Lebanon War, Now you might ask why? Why would the world abandon Africa? Because we black? Dats right we's all black. Who cares about some black folk killing each other in Africa, it will resolve itself when they wipe each other out. Who cares about a bunch of sick niggers? I never thought I'd wake up and hate the color of my skin, because being black these days is being lost and no one cares. No one cares if another black baby dies. Population control, the less niggers in the world the better right? You think about dat when you go to sleep in your nice cozy bed as this nigger woman spends the night outside on the ground. (*Spot goes out and lights back up on Iphigenia and Tesfaye*)

IPHIGENIA: Being lost is being dead. This I know. (*Long pause. Tesfaye takes a long look at Iphigenia and starts to laugh.*) What, tell me why you laugh?

TESFAYE: No...no, no, it's too crazy.(*Still laughing*)

IPHIGENIA: Please tell me, you have a thought about me and I'd like to hear it.

TESFAYE: (*A picture of Iphigenia being sacrificed at Aulis is shown on the back wall.*)

Well, you in that dress...this is crazy but... "Iphigenia" If my memory serves me correctly and this is many years ago when I was young so... I could be mistaken but when I was in school, when my father could afford to send me, we read a Greek story with a thirteen year old girl named Iphigenia in it. I liked to read a lot when I was a child when books were available to us.

IPHIGENIA: Tell me more.

TESFAYE: Well... all I recall is this girl's father, a great King sacrificed her so his ships would sail to save one Helen of Troy considered by many to be the most beautiful woman in the world. The book I think, I recall was the, the... *Iliad* by the great Homer.

IPHIGENIA: Do you remember why she had to be sacrificed?

TESFAYE: Well I'm not sure if this is correct, but it seems that one Goddess got angry at her father for something and took away all wind for ships to sail so they could not go save Helen. In order to appease the Goddess Artemis, the father, Agamemnon, had to sacrifice something near and dear to his heart which was his daughter.

IPHIGENIA: Did he do it?

TESFAYE: I believe as the story goes is that he was just about to sacrifice her when the Goddess Artemis swooped down from the heavens and saved her and replaced her body with that of a deer for the sacrifice. Artemis, the Goddess of war, the Goddess of the hunt.

IPHIGENIA: Quite the story. Could it be possible…?

TESFAYE: *(Laughing)* Ah ah ah…quite the *story* indeed and let us remember the main word we are using, that being "story". Your memory will soon come back and you will know in time who you are and where you came from, but in the meantime you will be known as my Greek princess. (*He kisses her hand. She embraces him with urgency.*)

IPHIGENIA: You have done nothing but to protect me since I was captured and I appreciate it. I will help you for as long as it takes. We will get you back to your family, if that is what you truly want, that I promise.

TESFAYE: Then we must move by nightfall and hide and sleep during the day. You may want to put this on. This is Janjaweed military clothes. I took them off the dead militia. It will camouflage you better then that white dress that is badly torn. You best get rid of it as it will surely snag and rip more in the jungle.

IPHIGENIA: No! Please… I'll keep my dress on and take my chances. Please don't take my dress. It's all I know about myself.

TESFAYE: As you wish my princess, but now get some sleep, we have a lot of land to cover tonight and we will need our rest. (*Iphigenia uses her dress as a pillow. They both start to go to sleep. "My Skin" by Natalie Merchant plays in the background. A picture of an African baby sleeping by her father is shown on the back wall.*)

IPHIGENIA: Tesfaye.

TESFAYE: Yes my Greek Princess.

IPHIGENIA: I'm sorry this is happening in your country.

TESFAYE: Me too Princess, me too, go to sleep. (*Long pause*)

IPHIGENIA: Tesfaye?

TESFAYE: Yes princess.

IPHIGENIA: I'm sorry about your family.

TESFAYE: Go to sleep. (*Long pause*)

IPHIGENIA: Tesfaye?

TESFAYE: Princess...go...to...sleep. (*Pause*) What is it princess?

IPHIGENIA: Wake up and go to sleep. (*She covers his head with the blanket. They both laugh. Lights fade to a blue wash. A series of pictures of African life are shown on the back wall. The song fades out.*)

Scene 4

(*When the lights come back up six female refugees surround Iphigenia and Tesfaye. They have guns, a pitch fork, and a club. A picture of a group of African women with guns is shown on the back wall.*)

REFUGEE #1: Get up, you are now our prisoner.

REFUGEE #2: We should kill them. They have killed thousands-raped thousands of our people!

REFUGEE #3: Wait this girl is white, she is not Janjaweed.

TESFAYE: I am not either my sisters, I wear the military outfit to blend in, to hide, and to survive. Please I beg of you do not shoot, I tell you truth.

REFUGEE #1: Who is she?

TESFAYE: She is a woman I found in the desert. She is helping me cross the border into Chad to find my family.

REFUGEE #2: We are to believe them?

IPHIGENIA: We are not Janjaweed. Tesfaye is telling the truth.

REFUGEE #1: (*She stares into Iphigenia's eyes for a long time.*) I believe this girl is honest. Come follow us back to camp. We have lodging in an old school church and a man from the United Nations is staying with us and is monitoring the situation. He is collecting information to the UN that may bring in UN peace keepers to stop the Sudan Government from arming the Janjaweed. They have not attacked our camp because they fear this man from the United Nations. Come and rest a bit, we will try to give you more food and drink for your journey.

TESFAYE: You are very kind my sisters. Let us go. (*Black out.*)

Scene 5

(Pictures of the United Nations, Kofi Annan is shown on the back wall. The lights come up and Tesfaye, Iphigenia, and the other refugees sit with the United Nations monitor. He wears a suit coat. He has a briefcase and a bunch of folders in front of him.)

TESFAYE: I do not understand how the United Nations can sit and watch this happen.

MR. ANON: (Reading *a document. A picture of a Janjaweed militia is shown on the back wall.)* The situation on the ground shows a number of negative trends, which have been developing since the last quarter, deteriorating security; a credible threat of famine; mounting civilian casualties; the ceasefire in shambles; and increasing tensions between Sudan and Chad according from this report.

TESFAYE: Screw the report man what about humanitarian aid to help us refugees?

MR. ANON: (*A picture of an African woman with empty water jugs is shown on the back wall.)* The humanitarian situation remains catastrophic, due to ongoing state-sponsored violence, layers of aid obstruction, the lack of an overall humanitarian strategic plan, and the weakened state of displaced Sudanese. Refugees like yourself and internally displaced civilians have been displaced for long periods. They don't know how to solve the problem it's grown to epic proportions.

TESFAYE: (*A picture of an African woman is shown on the back wall.)* Look at us man we are in a terrible weakened state, our women and children are subject to sexual abuse and attack. We do not have adequate shelter, and a new famine is feared everyday. Take a look around man!

REFUGEE #1: (*A picture of a humanitarian doctor is shown on the back wall.*) Infectious diseases and dysentery has driven up the body counts rapidly into the millions. AIDS is out of control in this country and no one is doing anything about it. Africa is more heavily affected by HIV and AIDS than any other region of the world. An estimated twenty four and a half million people were living with HIV at the end of 2005 and approximately two and a half million new infections occurred during that year. In just the past year the epidemic has claimed the lives of an estimated two million people in this region. More than twelve million children have been orphaned by AIDS.

TESFAYE: Your so called "conventional responses" in the media are simply inadequate to prevent increasingly more deaths, and the current response by the UN will fail unless addressed by a number of bold and urgent actions. We need peace keeping forces from the UN to protect us from the Sudanese Government and the Janjaweed! (*The scene freezes and a spot comes up on Narrator #3. A picture of Sudan President, Omar al Bashir is on the back wall, followed by a picture of Adolph Hitler.*)

NARRATOR #3: I, President Omar al Bashir staunchly oppose the deployment of the twenty U.N. peacekeeping troops in remote, Western region to replace our seven thousand African Union-led forces

146

there now. "Everybody knows the American and British are scheming against Sudan. We shall not be the first country to be re-colonized in Africa…we are free and shall not be enslaved; the Americans and the British are not seeking peace but war and… oil. (*Narrator #3 exits. The action resumes. A picture of an African woman crying is shown on the back wall.*)

IPHIGENIA: Those animals tried to rape me.

REFUGEE: (*A picture of an African man lying dead is shown on the back wall.*) They murdered our husbands.

TESFAYE: (*A picture of an African family living in a straw hut is shown on the back wall.*) The Janjaweed drive the Darfurians from their homes but families must continue their daily living like everyday life.

REFUGEE #1: (*A picture of an African collecting wood is shown on the back wall.*) Like collecting wood.

REFUGEE #2: (*A picture of an African fetching water is shown on the back wall.*)

Fetching water.

REFUGEE #3: (*A picture of an African working in the fields is shown on the back wall.*)

Working in the fields.

TESFAYE: (*A picture of an Africans working is shown on the back wall.*) And by doing so, women put themselves or their own children at risk for rape, beatings or even worse, death. This happens as soon

147

as they wander from outside their village, towns or camps. Something has to be done.

MR. ANON: Yes, yes…we got some reports of rapes.

TESFAYE: (*A picture of an African woman being treated by a doctor is shown on the back wall.*) Listen to me man, they are too ashamed to come forward. Hundreds of women don't report it for fear they are to be killed.

REFUGEE #1: (*A picture of an African woman all alone in her village is shown on the back wall.*) If you are a rape victim you might as well be dead. In our society rape draws heavy social disgrace, victims are often ostracized by their own families and communities.

REFUGE #2: (*A picture of an African baby being treated by a doctor is shown on the back wall.*) These women and children, our women and children; are forced from their communities for illegal pregnancy as a result of being raped.

MR. ANON: (*Writing furiously. A picture of empty water tins is shown on the back wall.*) I'm getting this all down. Honest.

TESFAYE: (*Rips his pencil and paper from his hands.*) Stop writing and listen man, people are dying the main question is what are you…the United Nations, the United Sates, the world doing about it?

MR. ANON: (*Opening up his briefcase pulling out tons of documents. A picture of a UN hospital is shown on the back wall.*) Now just a second, we have made a lot of progress in the Darfur situation with many resolutions-Let's see…Oh yes here they are…

TESFAYE: (*A picture of an African man suffering is shown on the back wall.*) You have as many documents as the number of innocent civilians in Africa that were killed and raped just today.

MR. ANON: I'm sorry, you're right, you want the honest answer? This crisis is beyond the United Nations. Sometimes I feel they want the problem to solve itself like in Israel and Lebanon. Look, the need to millions of refugees is just too great to deliver aid. What can we do? The Janjaweed would just obstruct aid and humanitarian activities.

IPHIGENIA: (*A picture of Janjaweed militia is shown on the back wall.*) What about the army and police?

TESFAYE: They are all bought and paid for by the Janjaweed.

REFUGEE #1: If the Janjaweed don't kill us we will just simply starve. They have taken all our food.

MR. ANON: You'll just go back to your farms and plant in time for the planting season when this dies down, there will be food.

TESFAYE: Do you hear yourself, man? That will take months for that food to grow to be ready to eat. In May, the rain will make things worse so we will be unable to farm.

IPHIGENIA: It seems like no one is being charged with crimes and no one around the world is challenging the Janjaweed actions. There is no penalty for their actions. How can they be getting away with murder? (*A picture of Adolf Hitler is shown on the back wall.*)

TESFAYE: They brought down Hitler because of the death an annihilation of six million Jews but when the black race threatens to be annihilated over oil and religion no one does a damn thing.

MR. ANON: The U.N. Security Council just this month passed a resolution that would give the United Nations authority over peacekeepers in Darfur as soon as Sudan's government gives its consent, which so far refuses to do so. The resolution is meant to give more power to funding a force, now run by the African Union. The document passed 12-0 with Russia and China abstaining. African Union troops are set to be pulled out October 1st. (*Tesfaye gives Mr. Anon a disgusted look and rips up his documents.*) Now that's nor fair, we are doing…

TESFAYE: Black Africans are dieing by the hundreds per day, tell me you're doing something to stop it! Well go ahead. You can't because no one is coming to our aid.

IPHIGENIA: (*Staring off as she goes into a trance for a moment. African drums are heard in the distance. Artemis crosses the stage quietly in the background.*) Sacrifice.

TESFAYE: Now if you'll excuse me Mr. Anon, I and the princess need our sleep. We have many miles to travel to find my family that was misplaced from this as the United Nations would put it "small problem in Africa." Take this message back to them and ask them if one million deaths are not enough dead Africans to call it genocide? Ask them how many deaths it will take for them to realize we are facing an ethnic cleansing by the Muslims. You get back to me on that, okay?

MR. ANON: Listen sir, I got down everything you said word for word.

IPHIGENIA: But did you hear what he said, that's the question. Tell these displaced villagers their future. I'm sure their curious to know how you're going to help them. (*All of the refugee's have left except for one. She looks at Mr. Anon…there is a long uncomfortable pause.*)

MR. ANON: You wouldn't have by chance anymore of that delicious papaya juice? (*She gets up and leaves in disgust. Black out. More Darfur atrocity pictures are seen on the back wall. A spot goes up on a refugee.*)

Scene 6

REFUGEE #1: (*Pictures of American flag, attack on the World Trade Towers, George Bush, Condoleezza Rice and Colin Powell, and the American Flag are shown on the back wall during monologue. The National Anthem plays quietly in the back ground.*) Where are you America, most powerful nation in da world? Where is your mighty military, your fearless leader Mr.

Bush who is not afraid to walk into any country and start wars? Where are you red, white and blue? Where is your voice for democracy and freedom for all men? Where is dat constitution of yours that you wallpaper the globe with? Where are you America? Where are you Condoleezza Rice? Colin Powell? If at anytime I wish the Janjaweed had weapons, and then maybe now is the time for if they had weapons of mass destruction you may have come here to save us in Africa instead of Iraq. Where are you good ole U S of A? (*Black out.*)

Scene 7

(*Lights come up and Iphigenia and Tesfaye are in the church trying to sleep. Iphigenia wakes up from a nightmare. A Picture of an old brick African building is shown on the back wall.*)

IPHIGENIA: Father! Father!

TESFAYE: (*Goes over to her, holds her.*) Iphigenia, you okay princess?

IPHIGENIA: Tesfaye?

TESFAYE: Yes, I'm here.

IPHIGENIA: (*A picture of a dead rotting carcass is shown on the back wall.*) I had a horrible dream. I dreamed I was being killed, my throat cut as all these men stood around and cheered as it happened, thousands of them.

TESFAYE: It was only a dream. I have them too.

IPHIGENIA: What?

TESFAYE: Only I'm not being murdered but my family is...I fear them dead.

IPHIGENIA: Don't think like that, we are going to get to Chad and find them.

TESFAYE: I also ashamed of how I been thinking these days.

IPHIGENIA: What do you mean?

TESFAYE: That there is no God. I fear I have lost my faith.

IPHIGENIA: You mean Gods?

TESFAYE: What?

IPHIGENIA: I don't know...nothing...go on.

TESFAYE: There are so many things going on in Sudan. The main conflict is religion. A twenty-one year old Sudanese civil war continues to rage between North Arab Muslims and black African Christians. I am a black African Christian. It seems if you are not Arabic in Africa your life is also in jeopardy. Islam is taking over the word. The pro-government Arab militia, the Janjaweed will make sure of that at least in Africa. To them the Koran is the gospel and Abraham is the Messiah, but I am a follower of Jesus Christ, Our lord and savior. At least I was, but I'm not sure of my faith anymore.

IPHIGENIA: I'm sorry but I don't know who that is.

TESFAYE: He was a prophet who lived thousands of years ago and died on a cross for the sins of man. My faith in him is slowly disintegrating with all the lives lost. How could he let this genocide happen? African farmers vs. Arab nomads drive almost two million from our homes and seventy-five thousand die from hunger and disease. What God would let that happen? Let that many people die. (*The action freezes. A spot goes up on an African refugee woman. A series of pictures of Darfur burned and destroyed villages are shown on the back wall during her monologue.*)

REFUGEE WOMAN: Janjaweed burned, looted, and raped our women because our village of Tawilla was not Arabic. Tawilla was once full of people, but now it is empty. Most of us have scattered in the hills. I only came back to see if any food was left in my house. Now I'm heading back to my hiding place. Nobody spends the night in Tawilla anymore. The Janjaweed do this to villages all the time. They descend on a village to loot at night while police who come to protect Tawilla look the other way or they even loot the village themselves. Merchants robbed at gunpoint of tobacco, pots, clothes, and a bed. If we see any Arab women in our village we attack with stones, clubs and kill da women. An eye for an eye is what I say. We all from Tawilla participated in the killing. Was she Janjaweed? I don't know but they had it coming. (*Black out. The action resumes. Lights back up on Tesfaye and Iphigenia.*)

IPHIGENIA: I don't know?

TESFAYE: Six million Jews died due to ethnic cleansing from the Germans and the same thing is happening in Sudan. Where is God?

IPHIGENIA: I don't know.

TESFAYE: *(Crying)* A child is hung. Where is God? A woman is raped fifteen times in two hours. Where is God? Churches are burned. Where is God? WHERE IS GOD! (*He repeats the phrase screaming pounding his fists into the ground.*)

IPHIGENIA: (*Goes over to hold Tesfaye. "Breath" by Anna Nalick plays in the background.*)I don't know. I wish I could help. (*There is a long pause as Tesfaye stares at Iphigenia. Tesfaye touches Iphigenia face. He leans in and gently kisses her. They kiss more passionately until Tesfaye realizes what is happening and breaks away.*)

TESFAYE: (*A picture of an African woman and her baby is shown on the back wall.*)This is not right. I have wife. I am so ashamed.

IPHIGENIA: Look, you just need someone. You're scared. I'm scared. It's okay.

TESFAYE: I love my wife, my child, but I don't feel them anymore in here. Don't you understand? (*He pounds chest.*) I don't feel them anymore in here. I have to feel something. I have to feel something. I need something to feel. (*Iphigenia touches Tesfaye's face and leans in and kisses him. He angrily breaks away.*) What do you want from me? Why do you do this?

IPHIGENIA: I don't know. I just need someone also.

TESFAYE: *(He grabs Iphigenia violently.)* Who are you? Tell me who you are! Tell me who you are!

IPHIGENIA: I don't know! *(Crying)* I'm scared because I don't remember who I am and I'm in this strange place,, and all I have is my nightmare and this stupid dress *(She violently rips off the red sash that is attached to the dress.)* to figure out who I am and I can't...I can't... *(She breaks down.)*

TESFAYE: Wait...wait a minute, hold still. I didn't notice before but your neck has been cut and very badly. I guess it was hidden by all the dirt.

IPHIGENIA: My neck?

TESFAYE: The incision is closed now but under the dirt there is dried blood. *(He damps a cloth from his canteen he is wearing.)*

IPHIGENIA: Someone cut my throat? Like my dream.

TESFAYE: It appears with a very large knife. I better clean this wound. You don't remember who did this? I don't recall Janjaweed doing it.

IPHIGENIA: I didn't even know I was cut.

TESFAYE: Sit still why I clean the wound. *(Long pause, Iphigenia breaks the tension.)*

IPHIGENIA: Tesfaye...will you tell me about your family?

TESFAYE: (*A huge grin comes to his face.*) Oh…my family. Well my wife… her name is Abrihet, meaning, "she emanates light", and my daughter… Adama, which means, "beautiful child".

IPHIGENIA: Go on, you look so happy when you say their names.

TESFAYE: My family is my life. My wife, she is as beautiful as a sunset. She can make me feel so at peace when I am with her and then my baby girl Adama, she is five. She's daddy's girl and has a permanent seat right here on my lap. Where daddy goes, Adama follows, a real flower, a beautiful child. I'm ashamed that I never told them I loved them before they were taken

IPHIGENIA: They know, I'm sure of it.

TESFAYE: We take life for granted, it is so short we should speak from da heart and tell the people who we love……..we love them. (*He looks at Iphigenia. There is a long uncomfortable pause.*)

IPHIGENIA: What does Tesfaye mean?

TESFAYE: It means "my hope". My father named me that because his hope was I would get out of Africa and make a life for myself. He'd always say, "Tesfaye is my hope, our family's future." He loved Africa but could sense its future demise.

IPHIGENIA: What is it you do?

TESFAYE: I am a farmer. We had many acres until the Janjaweed… (*Screams are heard.*) Shhhh, be very quiet. (*Tesfaye slowly and quietly looks outside of the church. Three refugees and the United Nations monitor are on their knees. Janjaweed militias stand over them with guns to their head. One Janjaweed looks at the documents in Mr. Anon's briefcase. A picture of Janjaweed militia's is shown on the back wall.*)

MR. ANON: I am a United Nations monitor. I am protected by the United Nations. I have nothing to do with this conflict. I am merely a spectator of this conflict and I demand you let me go! (*He is shot in the head. The other Janjaweed militia shoots some of the refugees and cut some of their throats. They spot Tesfaye. A picture of dead bodies is shown on the back wall.*)

REBEL #1: You there... come here.

TESFAYE: Hey man. You got them. I got me own in the church. I was taking care of business inside (*Makes a pelvic thrust motion.*) before I got rid of them.

REBEL #1: Let's see what you got. (*Instructs a rebel.*) Go inside and bring them out.

TESFAYE: Hey man relax, there is enough shit in this village to satisfy us all. (*The rebel stares at Tesfaye, the other rebels bring Iphigenia out.*)

REBEL #2: She's white. (*The rebel crosses over to Iphigenia and rips her dress exposing her undergarments. They throw her to the ground in front of the dead refugee bodies.*)

REBEL#1: (*To Tesfaye)* Nice man, you got some white meat. Is she any good? *(Sound of African drums in the distance. The stage goes to a blue wash. Artemis appears behind Iphigenia on the ground. The action freezes. Iphigenia turns to see Artemis as she touches Iphigenia's hand. She looks at the dead refugee bodies and without speaking directs Iphigenia to lay her hand on each of their heads. As she crawls to do this the refugee's come back alive. Iphigenia looks back in shock at Artemis but she is gone. The action resumes. Iphigenia instructs the refugee's to lie still and act dead.)* Nice man, you got some white meat. Is she any good?

TESFAYE: Maybe I let you find out later. Let's bring her with.

IPHIGENIA: No! (*Struggles with Tesfaye's to play her role. The men laugh.*)

REBEL#1: Okay, bring her, pack up what we can use and let's move on. Torch all of this. (*Black out. Spot up on refugee. A series of pictures are shown of African villages that have been destroyed by bombs on the back wall.*)

Scene 8

REFUGEE (NARRATOR #3): There was a loud noise and then red dust, one of the houses was burning. There were craters all through out the village. You get used to the bombing and go about your daily life and hopefully you do not become a casualty. You burn the bodies or bury them in a mass grave because there are too many to identify. Sometimes there are just body parts to bury. You don't think about it, you can't, you just try to live another day and stay alive. That is the way of life, the way of life in Sudan, the way of life in Africa.

Scene 9

(Black out. Lights come back up and the militia is at another village. Three women are on their knees with their hands on their heads. Iphigenia is off to the side on her knees. Tesfaye is with the militia. They are drinking, laughing and touching the women inappropriately. They start to rip their close. Tesfaye does not participate. He goes over and pretends to rape Iphigenia. The women scream. Black out. Pictures of African women are shown on the back wall. A woman crosses downstage into a spot of light.)

REFUGEE WOMAN: *(Crying)* I am not smiling at the birth of my daughter with light skin, ebony eyes and curly black hair. My father looked at me but did not speak the whole day. He is angry for the Janjaweed and the government for giving me this baby. They have raped countless of women like myself. I was raped by ten different men in one day by pro-Sudanese government Arab militias because I am a black African Christian. After they rape me they do not kill me knowing my relatives will shun me. I try to kill my baby because I have loyalty to my tribe, but I cannot bring myself to do it because Janjaweed or not, I love my baby. My child will always be labeled and hated and I will be isolated by all who I love. *(She cradles her baby.)* I don't have a name yet, I show her to no

160

one. I am ashamed. (*Rebel #1 enters in another spot of light on the opposite side of the stage.*)

REBEL #1: (*Pictures of Janjaweed militia are shown on the back wall.*) The ten of us chased her down as she ran through the scabby terrain and dragged her into a hut. We ripped off her top and tore it apart, stuffing one piece in her mouth and wrapping the other over her eyes. (*He laughs.*)

REFUGEE WOMAN: (*A picture of an African woman and her baby is shown on the back wall.*) I kept it a secret for as long as I could. I finally told my father that ten Janjaweed militia raped me. The baby was Janjaweed. My father said, "If the child is from Janjaweed I don't want to see it. I'll remember these people, I can't accept this child." He then left to join his two wives and twelve children, and I haven't seen him in six months. When I was in the hut delivering the baby, no one came to see me or celebrate a fatherless baby born of hate. I finally named her. Her name is Menazel, In the Koran, Islam's holy book; it means "Houses of Stars" because the Janjaweed burned our villages. For her nickname I call her Juan which means Friday, the day I was raped. We give her Muslim name to know she came from Janjaweed. When she grows up we know our new enemies by their Muslim name. (*Refuge mother enters and stands next to the woman in another spot of light.*)

REFUGEE MOTHER: I am her mother and it will now be difficult to marry her off. Other women of who are raped by Janjaweed become prostitutes or commit suicide. She should kill the baby because it will grow up Janjaweed later and attack us again.

REFUGEE WOMAN: I have found myself hitting baby more, one time I tried to drown her. I may have to give her up so someone loves her, the way I can never. It will probably die as it suffers from malnutrition and diarrhea. That would be the best thing for this child in this world.

REFUGEE MOTHER/WOMAN: (*A picture of Janjaweed on horseback is shown on the back wall.*) Janjaweed: Evil men on horseback! (*Lights back up. The militia is sitting around eating. Iphigenia lies on the ground in front of the men. Tesfaye sits with them but doesn't eat.*)

REBEL: #1: She was one fine nigger. (*He starts to make humping gesture. The men laugh all except Tesfaye. Pictures of Janjaweed are shown on the back wall.*)

TESFAYE: You use the term nigger when we all niggers man. We niggers that steal, rape, yell ethnic slurs, shoot our rifles loud into the air. Stuffed wells with dead bodies and poisoned them and burned villages to the ground. What does the world now think of the nigger now man?

REBEL #1: What you saying?

TESFAYE: We African man, we play the role the world gives us. If we act inhumane then we everything the white man says we are, savages, hungry for respect man, and we get it by any means, including rape and murder.

REBEL #1: That is the Janjaweed way! *(They all laugh.)* We the police of the camps, we the security. We take care of the people of Africa!

TESFAYE: What picture does it paint of us man? How do you want the world to view us? We want freedom, equality, but this is not the way put the guns down man, go home to your family, kiss your wife, be at peace with God.

REBEL #1: No way you Janjaweed, you Christian man, but before I kill you let me tell you what is right and wrong with this black African. I am my brother like my other brother, Muslim, and when you, a black non-Muslim go against us then this is Jihad, this is "holy war." Or, by Sudanese definition: the legal, annihilation and termination of non-Muslims and land in effort to expand our territories and religion man. Our purpose is not with Jihad, to spread the Islamic faith but to extend sovereign Muslim power. Jihad is the goal man, of achieving Muslim domination over the entire African continent and then the entire globe.

NARRATOR #1: *(Crossing downstage the action freezes. A picture of a Muslim man is shown on the back wall.)* Wait, wait, wait! No Jihad! I will support these assertions with fact. But first, let's give Sudanese government officials in Khartoum their due. They prefer to explain the slaughter in Darfur as an ancient rivalry between nomadic herding tribes in the North and black African farmers in the South. They deny responsibility for the militias and claim they can't control them, even as they continue to train the militias, arm them, and pay them. They play down their Islamic ideology which supported Osama bin Laden and Al Qaeda and seek to impose Islamic fundamentalism in Sudan and elsewhere. Sudan does not sponsor terror as the US has listed us. Darfur, from their perspective, is an inconvenient anomaly that will go away, in time. Oil is to blame. Oil is driving the genocide in Darfur. Oil drives the Bush administration's policy toward Sudan and the rest of Africa. And oil is likely to topple Sudan and its neighbors into chaos, blood and oil man, blood and oil. (*Lights up on Tesfaye as he struggles as two men pin him to the ground. A picture of a Janjaweed militia is shown on the back wall.*)

REBEL #1: Listen to my lesson man before I castrate you, then shoot you in the head and kill you. We follow the Koran man and according to our holy book any Muslims or non-Muslim who interpret their faith differently are infidels and therefore legitimate targets of Jihad. This is why Algerians, Egyptians, Afghans, Americans and Israelis, must be annihilated. We will conquer Africa as we have conquered regions from Afghanistan to Spain. We will continue to rule the Arabian Peninsula just as we did when we came to rule at the time of Prophet Muhammad's deaths. We will continue to conquest the globe just as we did with India, Antaolia, the Balkans and now Sudan. Jihad, victory and martyrdom!

REBELS: Jihad, victory and martyrdom! Praise Allah!

TESFAYE: No brothers, you're wrong. Jihad is nothing but terrorism, In Sudan it has enslaved tens of thousands of females and children, forced them to convert to

Islam, sent them on forced marches, beat them and set them to hard labor. Our women and daughters also suffer ritual gang-rape, genital mutilation and a life of sexual servitude from your state-sponsored Jihad which has caused about two million Sudanese deaths and the displacement of another four million. That is the reality of Jihad.

NARRATOR #1: (*They freeze and a woman walks into a spot of light. She wears a Muslim scarf. A picture of an old Muslim man is shown on the back wall.*) No Jihad! No Jihad. I am a good Muslim and the Koran contains many moral attempts of persuasion, forming the basis of Islamic law. It lays down generosity and fairness and the one is invited or becomes a Muslim by declaring there is only one God and Mohammed is his messenger. We pray five times a day, pay a tax to help the needy, fast during the month of Ramadan, and make a pilgrimage to Mecca if we are able, abstinence during daylight hours in the month of Ramadan. Suicide bombings and ethnic cleansing of Christians are condemned by Muslims. The vast majority believe that political grievances should be resolved with demonstrations and fair fights which do not harm the innocent. Muslims see terror as sabotage of their just causes. We are not terrorist but good people. Muslims are good people. We denounce Osama Bin Laden, al Qaeda, and all terror as it relates to Jihad. We are not Janjaweed. (*Black out on spot. The action resumes. A picture of a Janjaweed militia is shown on the back wall.*)

REBEL #2: Kill him man, what you wait for?

REBEL#1: No-no man, the girl over there, the one he cares for is the girl. Here, you shoot her or I shoot you, you choose. You want to be hero to your people? (*He brings Iphigenia over.*) Kill her. (*Puts gun in his hand.*) Save yourself. You kill her I let you live.

TESFAYE: I just want to see my wife and child again.

REBEL #1: And you will man, praise be to Allah, in the name of Mohammed. You kill her and we let you live. (*The rebel puts the gun in Tesfaye's hand. He points the gun at Iphigenia's head. Tesfaye turns to shoot the rebels only his gun is empty. The Rebel #1 opens his hands and drops the bullets on the ground. The men laugh. They take Tesfaye and knock him to the ground. They rip off his shirt and start to whip him. African drums are heard in the distance.*)

IPHIGENIA: Hey over here. Come on. All of you come here. (*Yelling*) DON'T YOU UNDERSTAND? DAMN YOU, COME HERE! YOU WANT SOME, THEN COME GET SOME YOU PIGS!

TESFAYE: Iphigenia no, don't. I will be okay. Leave her alone. (*One of the rebels moves over to Iphigenia to knock her out with the butt of his gun but he is stopped when Artemis appears. She touches him and the action freezes. Iphigenia does not see her. She is standing in front of the Goddess. Lighting and thunder is seen and heard. Iphigenia goes into a meditated dark state as the men approach her. She looks possessed and in a deep trance. A picture of an African girl crying is shown on the back wall. More thunder is heard.*)

IPHIGENIA: Do not destroy me before my time, for it is sweet to look upon the light, and do not force me to visit the world below ... Why is Helen's kidnapping to prove my ruin, father? Look upon me; bestow one glance, one kiss that this at least I may carry to my death as a memorial of you, though you do not heed my pleading. To gaze upon the light is man's most cherished gift; that life below is nothingness, and whoever longs for death is mad. Better live a life of woe than die a death of glory. If Artemis has decided to take my body, am I, a mortal, to thwart the Goddess?....a dreadful ill is death. (*The action continues, Artemis is gone and the rebel knocks out Iphigenia with his gun.*)

TESFAYE: Iphigenia NO!!! (*They knock Tesfaye out with the butt of the gun and all descend on Iphigenia.*)

REBEL #1: Get her dress off, hurry up man, spread her legs. (*They begin to rape her as she lies unconscious. Artemis watches. The lights fade to black. A picture of a Janjaweed militia can be seen on the back wall.*)

Scene 10

(*The lights come back up and Iphigenia and Tesfaye are lying on the ground. Iphigenia's dress has been ripped off of her and she is in her slip with blood running down her legs. She is crying. Tesfaye is lying, bleeding with his shirt next to him. "Chasing Cars" by the Snow Patrol plays quietly in the background. A picture on the back wall of an African woman crying is seen on the back wall.*)

IPHIGENIA: Tesfaye, are you awake? (*Pause*)

TESFAYE: Yes. *(Pause)*

IPHIGENIA: Are we dead? *(Pause)*

TESFAYE: No.

IPHIGENIA: Did they rape me? *(Pause)*

TESFAYE: Yes.

IPHIGENIA: Many times? *(Pause)*

TESFAYE: Yes.

IPHIGENIA: I feel something running down my legs...I think its blood. I'm bleeding Tesfaye.

TESFAYE: *(Trying to hide from her that he's crying)* Try to sleep. Don't think about it.

IPHIGENIA: I'm scared Tesfaye.

TESFAYE: Rest.

IPHIGENIA: I hurt Tesfaye.

TESFAYE: Rest my princess.

IPHIGENIA: Will you just lie close to me...please.

TESFAYE: Sleep princess...sleep.

IPHIGENIA: Why is there so much pain in your world? Why is it I can heal others but I cannot heal myself?

TESFAYE: Shhhh, sleep. *(Tesfaye moves near Iphigenia and puts his head near hers. She touches his hand. The lights slowly black out.)*

168

Scene 11

(Lights up. Tesfaye and Iphigenia still lay on ground.)

IPHIGENIA: It's raining. I smell flowers.

TESFAYE: They are gone.

IPHIGENIA: Why didn't they kill us?

TESFAYE: Because of you.

IPHIGENIA: Me?

TESFAYE: They hit me with their gun, but right before I went out I saw this beautiful woman, she was standing over you.

IPHIGENIA: Who was it?

TESFAYE: I don't know. You mentioned the name Artemis before they raped you.

IPHIGENIA: Artemis, why does that name sound familiar?

TESFAYE: *(Stares at Iphigenia in disbelief and shock.)* She is the Greek Goddess I mentioned before to you in that story. You may be a Greek princess after all.

IPHIGENIA: Back at that camp I touched those that were shot and…

TESFAYE…and what?

IPHIGENIA: …and…they… *(Iphigenia stares at Tesfaye as a group of three refugees run in. A picture of African women is shown on the back wall.)*

169

REFUGEE #1: Are you alright man?

TESFAYE: Yes, help the girl first. (*They help Iphigenia and Tesfaye up.*)

REFUGEE #2: I'm surprised they didn't kill you.

TESFAYE: *(A picture of an African woman and her baby is shown on the back wall.)* Listen to me; I have been lying here all night thinking how selfish I was trying to just find my wife and child. We must not only find them but save as many refugees as possible and get them across the border into Chad.

IPHIGENIA: How can we fight an entire army protected and supplied by the government?

REFUGEE #3: *(A picture of African soldiers is shown on the back wall.)* We do have help. The Alliance of Revolutionary Forces of West Sudan was formed in January 2006 when the Justice and Equality Movement and the Sudan Liberation Movement merged to form a single rebel alliance. The JEM and the SLM used to fight the Janjaweed for many months, now they are one force. They will help us.

TESFAYE: We must be quick there are Janjaweed militias everywhere. Grab as many weapons as you can and contact the alliance, let them know we are coming by the hundreds, no by the thousands, to take any survivors as we can to the camps in Chad.

REFUGEE #1: They will just die in the camps; there are hundreds and thousands without food and dieing.

TESFAYE: Brother, help me, we can't think about that right now, we must take it one step at a time. We will battle to open the roads that the Janjaweed are blocking from the humanitarian workers, we will get food, and we will find a way.

IPHIGENIA: What can I do to help?

TESFAYE: *(Putting his hands in her hands. A picture of many Africans in a group is shown on the back wall.)* You must stay here. I cannot afford to lose you. *(He kisses' her forehead and stares into her eyes.)* Come someone and take her to repair her dress.

IPHIGENIA: *(A picture of African villagers with guns is shown on the back wall.)*

Give me a rifle; I want to fight along side of you.

TESFAYE: No!

IPHIGENIA: If not for you then for Africa, let me decide my own destiny.

TESFAYE: *(Holds Iphigenia.)* I have been so selfish not to think of my people but just my own family. My father was right in my name; I am my people's hope for survival. If I die, then I will die for my people. This is what my father would have wanted.

IPHIGENIA: But what of your wife and daughter?

TESFAYE: I trust in my God, and the faith I question. I see them in heaven if not in person first. *(He kisses Iphigenia. Artemis enters upstage.)* Stay here and rest, I will return for you. The rest of you, Let us go find our people and take them home. (*He exits. Iphigenia stays behind. She feels Artemis standing behind her.*)

IPHIGENIA: (*She is by herself and looks out. African drums can be heard in the distance along with intense wind blowing. She sits for awhile and then suddenly remembers something, she goes into another trance. She walks downstage and takes a knife and cuts both of her hands. She raises her hands as blood pours out. She looks possessed and the evilness of war has flown into her body. A picture of an African girl with a tear in her eye is seen on the back wall.*) Altar...Aulis...may the winds blow...let them blow! (*Black out.*)

Scene 12

(Lights come up again as Tesfaye takes villagers from a remote village with him in a vignette of different scenes by crossing back and forth to each side of the stage with Janjaweed militia in pursuit. "What's Going On" by Marvin Gaye plays in the background during the vignette as a series of pictures of villagers leaving Sudan and trying to cross the border into Chad are shown on the back wall. Artemis crosses the stage and walk among the Janjaweed hunting refugees in the jungles of Africa. Black out.)

Scene 13

(A raging battle is heard as more pictures on the back wall depict the three year old battle between the Janjaweed and the Alliance of Revolutionary Forces of West Sudan is shown on the back wall. The lights come

172

up as Tesfaye and Iphigenia on the ground with six other refugees as the bloody battle rages on. Tesfaye continually fires his weapon at the Janjaweed militia who are attacking while Iphigenia holds her gun in confusion.)

TESFAYE: (*Yelling over the gunfire.*) The interior of Chad is over that hill one hundred feet away but the Janjaweed have it secured with the Sudanese army. We need a diversion if we can get these people through. How many do we have you think?

REFUGEE #1: (*Crawls over to him*) You have a thousand strong but not all are armed and the alliance is taking many casualties. The Janjaweed have better weapons.

TESFAYE: They are supplied by the Sudanese government. No way would they have those type of weapons on their own. We have to figure a way to get these people across.

IPHIGENIA: (*The fighting is intense, Iphigenia stops fighting and stares at Tesfaye. Something he said has triggered a memory in her. Lighting and thunder is seen and heard and the light now is only on Iphigenia. Lightning flashes, she sees Artemis in the distance, it flashes again and she sees King Agamemnon holding a knife over Iphigenia on an altar. The lights flash again and the King Agamemnon is seen cutting her throat. She screams a horrific scream. Iphigenia looks out in a trance and touches her cut neck as Tesfaye grabs her out of harms way and down by him as she snaps out of her trance).*

173

TESFAYE: What are you doing, are you crazy, you could have been killed.

IPHIGENIA: I am... dead Tesfaye. I...remember it all.

TESFAYE: Pull yourself together princess, we need every weapon firing.

IPHIGENIA: (*She sits looking in the opposite direction of where Tesfaye is firing. The song "Ophelia" by Natalie Merchant plays in the background. Gun fire and exploding bombs continue to be heard in the background.*) Tesfaye, what do you think death is like?

TESFAYE: (*He continues to fire as he talks.*) What do you mean?

IPHIGENIA: What do you think happens when you die?

TESFAYE: You go to heaven, if you believe in God. That is Christian belief. (*A picture of Jesus Christ is shown on the back wall.*)

IPHIGENIA: I don't know Jesus Christ.

TESFAYE: He's in your heart. You feel him. You know.

IPHIGENIA: But you said you didn't believe him anymore, you lost your faith. (*A picture of the Bible is shown on the back wall.*)

TESFAYE: I was wrong. He's with us now. He will help us across.

IPHIGENIA: This war is over religion? Islam vs. Christianity?

TESFAYE: Yes, among other things.

IPHIGENIA: It seems as if religion is root of all evil. People are being killed because of it. Why?

TESFAYE: Two prophets, two beliefs. We believe in Jesus Christ and the Bible, they believe in Abraham and the Koran. (*A picture of Abraham and the Koran are shown on the back wall.*)

IPHIGENIA: I do not believe in either... what will happen to me?

TESFAYE: I do not know, but God is merciful and take pity on you because you are a lost soul with no identity...no memory.

IPHIGENIA: What if you die and there is no God, just darkness?

TESFAYE: You have to have faith that something is there after death Iphigenia, if not then we become afraid of death.

IPHIGENIA: (*In a trance again.*) I have died once. I am dead now. I saw and smelled flowers, and when I awoke I was lying in a sea of them. Artemis saved me, saved me so I could heal the wounds of the sick and dying.

TESFAYE: (*Lost in the battle, ignoring Iphigenia.*) You did not die but cut very badly. Keep firing!

IPHIGENIA: No. I died, Tesfaye. I remember. (*Crying, gunfire can still be heard.*) I died in the arms of my father so other men could fight to save another. I died so thousands wouldn't die; the winds must blow. Don't you understand? Listen to me! Artemis will save me; she always saves me and brings me back every time there is genocide. I am a healer of pain.

TESFAYE: (*Yelling*) They're advancing, pull everyone back. Pull back! (*All the refugees leave the stage.*)

IPHIGENIA: (*With tears in her eyes.*) Reborn, reincarnated over and over again to play my role given to me wherever there is sacrifice. We all are reborn to live again, except for me; Artemis brings me back each time whenever I'm needed to heal the pain, to save a soul. The Holocaust, Bosnia, Rwanda, I was there. Don't you understand…time never stops for those who sacrifice their lives for the good of others; they are wrapped in a cloak of immortality. I am a princess. Your princess! (*Artemis enters and crosses upstage and watches the action. African drums are heard in the distance.*)

TESFAYE: Keep firing!

IPHIGENIA: (*Grabbing Tesfaye, smiling and crying*) Don't you hear me, don't you understand? I remember! I know who I am; I know why I'm here! I'm here to save you! I'm here to sacrifice my life for you and your people!

TESFAYE: Keep firing, keep firing!

IPHIGENIA: Who do you want to save, Tesfaye, these refugees or your family? For some strange reason I have the ability to…

TESFAYE: Not now Iphigenia, keep firing!

IPHIGENIA: *(Grabs him and shakes him.)* Listen to me!!! YOU MUST TELL ME AND CHOOSE, WHO DO YOU SAVE? WHO DO YOU SACRIFICE?

TESFAYE: Let go of me, I must get these people across! *(He continues to fire, caught up in the moment of battle, ignoring Iphigenia.)*

IPHIGENIA: *(Kisses Tesfaye)* I know what I must do. *(She runs out in the middle of the battle, her dress flowing in the wind.)*

TESFAYE: Iphigenia no! Get back!

IPHIGENIA: *(Stretches out her arms wide.)* O my father, here I am; willingly I offer my body for my country and for Helen of Troy that you may lead me to the altar of the Goddess and sacrifice me, since this is Heaven's ordinance. May good luck be yours for any help that I afford and may you obtain the victor's gift and come again to the land of your fathers. So then let none of the Argives lay hands on me, for I will bravely yield my neck without a word. *(She is shot many times.)*

TESFAYE: Iphigenia no! NO!!!!! *(Screaming, he runs to her.)* NO! *(There is a pause in the gunfire, pictures on the back wall show casualties of the Sudan war.)*

IPHIGENIA: Go, they're free...free... Tesfaye...get them across...my sacrifice is my destiny and my love for you like it was for my father and your love for your father. *(She touches his face and then dies. Everything moves in slow motion. The rebels run across the border celebrating. Tesfaye runs to Iphigenia. He is crying, shaking her. Rebels continue to run across shooting Janjaweed in their path, the action resumes.)*

TESFAYE: *(Cradling Iphigenia in his arms, and crying.)* I love you my Greek Princess. You have gotten us through. We made it and you have saved thousands of people through your sacrifice. God speed Iphigenia and may you find your heaven of flowers and sleep only to return again one day to save others with your sacrifice. *(Artemis appears right behind Tesfaye, he see's her and they share a long stare with each other, Tesfaye takes Iphigenia in his arms and gives her to Artemis who carries her in her arms. She looks over to Tesfaye and smiles. She slowly vanishes. A refugee runs towards Tesfaye.)*

REFUGEE (ABUDU): Tesfaye is that you?

TESFAYE: Abudu! Give me hug. We made it man, we made it! We are here in Chad. Look at all the refugees and all the camps, there must be thousands of them. *(They embrace. Pictures continue on the back wall of refugee's fleeing Sudan.)* Where is Abrihet? Adama? *(Abudu is silent and stares at Tesfaye. A*

178

picture of saints is shown on the back wall.) Where are they, man? Come on.

REFUGEE ABUDU: They didn't make it Tesfaye. They were hanged and burnt with the village. Your wife saved your fathers flag from the village. She had it when she died. I'm sorry Tesfaye. (*He hands him a flag of Sudan, Africa that is old and tattered. Tesfaye embraces it as if it were his wife.*)

TESFAYE: No. no...no...! (*Tesfaye screams cries of anguish on his knees. As he cries the lights gets fainter and fainter on him until it goes black. Lights come up one at time on the Narrators as pictures of the Darfur conflict are shown on the back wall throughout the last scene. Adagio for Strings by Samuel Barber plays in the background during the scene.*)

Scene 14

(*Lights come up. A series of pictures of Darfur atrocities are shown on the back wall during the scene. Narrators enter one at a time delivering their lines.*)

REBEL #1: We are not black.

NARRATOR #2: We are not white.

REFUGEE #1: We are not yellow.

REBEL #2: We are not red.

NARRATOR #3: We are colorless.

NARRATOR #4: We are storytellers.

NARRATOR #5: And this is our story.

TESFAYE: About an out of control hurricane in Darfur Africa.

ALL: Category five.

IPHIGENIA: (*A picture of an African woman is shown on the back wall.*)
Sacrifice.

ALL: (*A picture of a starving African baby is shown on the back wall.*)
Genocide.

TESFAYE: (*A picture of the flag of Sudan is shown on the back wall.*)
Hope.

ARTEMIS: (*A picture of two African politicians shaking hands is shown on the back wall.*)
Peace.

IPHIGENIA: (*A picture of green Darfur wrist band is shown on the back wall.*)

Save Darfur. As of November 2009, the atrocities continue in the Darfur region of Africa and have spread into Chad. (*Sound of an intense wind. A series of pictures of African children are shown on the back wall. The song, "King of May" by Natalie Merchant plays in the background. The cast exits the stage and joins the audience to watch the pictures in the aisles. As the last picture of a crying child is shown on the back wall,* Artemis *steps into the light and addresses the audience.)*

ARTEMIS: Please join us outside for a candle light vigil to remember those innocent lives lost in Africa. *(Once outside the audiences candles are lit by the actors. They stand on a platform facing the audience. Each cast member reads a line at a time of the poem.)* A poem, "Vigil for Darfur" by Sabrina Carlson.

CAST:

Hold up your candle if you are an angel.
Hold up your candle if the light of hope
dances and curls about your spine
like the breath of light
about the wick.
Or blow out your candle if you believe
that when
these flames flicker out
we will forget
the faces we now see before us:
the faces
of the hopeful,
and the memory of the abused.
Hold up your candle
if the people standing along side you
have become your wings,
and that
side by side
we fly
to a better place and time.
hold up your candle if you know that sound does not travel

through air and wires but rather through the chords
of our hearts and that we will never
be able to claim
that we could not hear
a single cry
because a deafening ocean
stood between us.
Hold up your candle if you remember
how the world forgot 800
thousand Rwandans,
hold up your candle if you have a hole
burnt into your heart
by the Shoah, the Great Fire,
the Holocaust
and hold up your candle if you can still see
the smoke
and taste the ashes.
hold up your candle
you know
that tears
if only feed
that fire.
and hold up your candle
if you refuse to let the world
sob itself to sleep, waiting for a wish,
because we did not listen to them,
because we did not burn with them,
because we did not tell them
I am going
to save you.
Here.

ARTEMIS:

I am your miracle.
For who
dares to say that miracles are simply
the dusted spines
of Bibles?
Friends, look
at the crying wings you stand
side by side with, listen to the heavenly
psalms of hope and hurt, feel your heart rise
through the halo above your head
to join with a hundred thousand others
who will heal
this world.
hold up your candle
if you are an angel.

And now a moment of silence for the four hundred and fifty thousand lives lost so far in Darfur, Africa.*(After the moment of silence, Artemis instructs the audience to blow out their candles and go in peace. The cast greets the audience with warm embraces as the play ends. *NOTE: The Darfur conflict is far from over as this play is published. Information about the conflict can be added to the ending narration in the play for those that produce the play as it becomes available.*

The Rock of Troy
Based off the Iliad by Homer

Characters:

The Achaeans

Achilles: The son Peleus and the sea-nymph, Thetis. He is the most powerful warrior in the *Iliad*.

Agamemnon: King of Mycenae and leader of the Achaean army; brother of King Menelaus of Sparta.

Patroclus: Achilles' beloved friend, companion, and advisor.

Odysseus: A fine warrior and the cleverest of the Achaean commanders.

Diomedes: The youngest of the Achaean commanders who is bold and fearless.

Iphigenia: Daughter to Agamemnon who was sacrificed at Aulis so the ships could sail to save Helen of Troy.

Giant Ajax: An Achaean commander who is the second mightiest Achaean warrior after Achilles.

Little Ajax: An Achaean commander with great speed, small in size.

Nestor: The oldest Achaean commander.

Menelaus: King of Sparta; the younger brother of Agamemnon.

Calchas: An important soothsayer.

Peleus: Achilles' father and the grandson of Zeus.

The Trojans

Hector: A son of King Priam and Queen Hecuba, he is the mightiest warrior in the Trojan army.

Priam: King of Troy and husband of Hecuba. He is the father of fifty Trojan warriors, including Hector and Paris.

Hecuba: Queen of Troy, wife of Priam, and mother of Hector and Paris.

Paris: A son of Priam and Hecuba and brother of Hector.

Helen: The most beautiful woman in the ancient world and Menalaus' wife.

Aeneas - A Trojan nobleman, the son of Aphrodite, and a mighty warrior.

Andromache: Hector's loving wife.

Astyanax: Hector and Andromache's infant son.

Polydamas: A young Trojan commander.

Patroclus: A powerful Trojan warrior, friend to Achilles.

Agenor: A Trojan warrior who attempts to fight Achilles.

Dolon: A Trojan sent to spy on the Achaean camp.

Pandarus: A Trojan archer.

Antenor: A Trojan nobleman, advisor to King Priam, and father of many Trojan warriors.

Sarpedon: One of Zeus's sons.

Chrysies: Chryses's daughter, a priest of Apollo.

Briseis: A war prize of Achilles.

Chryses: A priest of Apollo, the father of Chrysies.

The Gods and Immortals

Zeus: King of the Gods and husband of Hera.

Hera: Queen of the Gods and Zeus's wife.

Athena: The Goddess of wisdom, purposeful battle, and the womanly arts; Zeus's daughter.

Thetis: A sea-nymph and the devoted mother of Achilles.

Apollo: A son of Zeus and twin brother to the Goddess Artemis, Apollo is God of the arts and
archery.

Aphrodite: Goddess of love and daughter of Zeus.

Poseidon: The brother of Zeus and God of the sea.

Hephaestus: God of fire and husband of Aphrodite.

Artemis: Goddess of the hunt, daughter of Zeus, and twin sister of Apollo.

Ares: God of war and lover of Aphrodite.

Hermes: The messenger of the Gods.

Iris: Zeus's messenger.

SPECIAL NOTE ON SONGS AND RECORDINGS

The Rock of Troy was first presented at Coffeyville Community College on April 10-12 2008 at the Spencer/Rounds Performing Arts Theatre. The Director was Mark Frank. The production stage managers were Thorr Miller, Melissa Bowman, and Rebekah Rose. The cast was as follows:

The Achaeans

Achilles:	Justin Wilson
Agamemnon:	Chad Kimmons
Clytamnestra/Antilochos:	Hannah Carter
Patroclus Odysseus:	Kortlyn Forrester
Diomedes:	Caitie Almond
Iphigenia/Calchas:	Samantha Cosby
Giant Ajax:	Valerie Thomison
Little Ajax:	Matt Gardner
Nestor:	Ashley Rowe
Menelaus:	Zander West
Helen:	Sarah McConnell
Automedon:	Brandon Jackson

The Trojans

Hector:	Gavin wells
Priam:	Tyler Mackie
Hecuba:	Tara O' Brien
Paris:	Nick Rush
Aeneas/Chryses:	Dakota Miller
Andromache:	Lyndsey Cranor
Polydamas:	Jeff Johnstone
Dolon:	Amanda Tharp
Chrysies:	Kerri Davis
Briseis:	Lindsey Golden
Glaukos:	Nicole Santorella

Mark Frank

The Gods and Immortals

Zeus:	Anthony Hill
Hera:	Chelsea Daniel
Athena:	Venessa Freeman
Thetis:	Bethanie Frank
Apollo:	Alec Rigdon
Aphrodite:	Milena Barone
Poseidon:	James Hart
Hephaestus:	Griffin Wright
Artemis:	Sam Quackenbush
Ares:	Ryan Fuller
Hermes:	Crystal Laiosa
Iris:	Amanda Spencer

AT RISE: The setting is an empty stage except for three large scaffolds. One is six feet tall and the other two are four feet. They are all three on castors. Eight black chairs are set upstage of the set. There is one red chair placed in the middle. A dozen ropes hang from the ceiling scattered out to the floor. Actors will be able to slide down these ropes or swing to scaffolding when needed. The play is underscored with classic rock music from the 1970s and 1980s. The lyrics to the songs tell the story of the Iliad along with actions from the Greek and Trojan characters and from the Gods on video and projected on a white wall or white screen upstage during the course of the play. Some Gods take mortal form and appear in the play and on video. There is no dialogue from the characters as their story should be told through their action, movements, and lyrics from the rock song that is playing. The twenty Greek and Trojan actors in the play should all wear an identical costume which consists of women in black corsets and gladiator skirts with leather wrist bands. The Trojans wear blue capes, the Greeks wear red capes. The men also wear black gladiator skirts and have leather wristbands. Both armies have helmets, shields, swords and spears. The Trojans have red face paint and the Greeks have blue face paint. Tattoos and piercing should cover both armies and hairstyles should be as creative as possible. The Gods should be different colors and have an "alien" feel to them and each be unique in their own way. Their costumes should be extravagant and not of this world. The lights should capture the feeling of being at a rock concert. Suggested pre-show music should be The "Stroke" by Billy Squier, "Paranoid" by

Black Sabbath, "We Will Rock You" by Queen, "Misty Mountain Top" by ZZ Top, "Baba O Reilly" by the Who, "Tale of Ulysses" by Cream, and "In The White Room" by Eric Clapton.

Prologue: How It All Began.

("Lagrange" by ZZ Top plays in the background. The play begins with Paris who sneaks into the camp of Menelaus of Sparta. He looks around with sword drawn. It is quiet, empty and dangerous. A woman enters. Her face is covered and she slowly sneaks very carefully looking around to meet Paris center. The woman is Helen, the most beautiful woman in the world. She takes off her scarf that hides her face and she kisses Paris passionately. Thirty-five seconds into the song, both Greek and Trojan armies advance and battle center stage. Paris runs off with Helen as the battle intensifies. Zeus' face appears on the back wall laughing. Running off, Helen looks at Zeus and laughs. Menelaus grabs his brother, Agamemnon, and pleads with him to help him get Helen back. The Trojans exit as the Greeks assemble at Agamemnon's command. He stands on top of the six foot platform with Menelaus. The men chant and raise their swords to both men pledging their allegiance to get Helen back. The wind blows strong and then stops. The men seize the scaffolding ready to sail and just as they are all ready the wind dies down. Artemis' face is now on the back wall and she is laughing. Men start to drop from the plague, sickness lurks inside the camp. Agamemnon looks at Menelaus and back at Artemis. He knows he needs a sacrifice for his ships to sail.

He grabs his daughter Iphigenia's hand and his best warrior, Achilles' hand and he readies to marry them. He joins their hands, they kiss, and then Agamemnon signals for his men to hold Achilles. He tries to break free but he is overwhelmed. Agamemnon takes his daughter and bounds her hands and legs. Screams are heard. He puts her on the altar and Artemis smiles. Frantically, Clytemnestra tries to stop Agamemnon, but he just pushes her to the ground and his men take her off. Agamemnon picks up a huge battle axe and aims at the throat of his daughter. He sacrifices her to the Gods as the ritual is performed. He throws back the axe in great sorrow, looks at Menelaus and lowers the ax. The lights go dark for a second, and when they return up, Iphigenia is gone. Artemis laughs again. The wind blows and the men board the ships (scaffolding). Achilles pulls a sword on Agamemnon once his men let him go. Agamemnon's men surround Achilles ready to kill him. Agamemnon waves them off. He crosses up to Achilles and stares at him, he hands him a shield and his sword and boards the eight foot scaffolding. Achilles stares up at Agamemnon. The ships (scaffolding) move off to the wings. Achilles picks up the veil worn by Iphigenia rips it and ties it around his arm. Before he exits he sees Clytemnestra on the ground crying, he kneels to her and puts Iphigenia mask in her hand and exits. She gets up, holds the mask tight in her hand. She looks up at Agamemnon sailing off. She is intense and furious. She will have her revenge. The ten year war begins... The scene and song should run three minutes and thirty-two seconds.)

Mark Frank

Ten Years Later...

A Poem about Troy-*The Iliad*

("TNT" by ACDC plays in the background. Both armies come out on opposite ends of the stage. The Greeks are on one side and the Trojans are the other side. They pound their swords ready for battle, a battle they have fought for the last ten years. They are wounded, dirty, and still dangerous. They all face-off with Zeus' face in the middle on the back wall on video. The scaffolding is pushed in as they circle each other while switching. They are ready to pounce. Fifty-five seconds into the song they attack on the ground. Once every Greek and Trojan fighter reaches the ground, the fight changes into slow motion with strobe lights while using sword and fight combat.. This plays out three minutes and thirty-three seconds into the next song as...)

Book 1: The Rage of Achilles

("Helter Skelter" by the Beatles plays in the background as the Greeks kill a few guards and then proceed to capture two beautiful enemy maidens, Chryseis and Briseis. The two warrior maidens fight to escape but are over matched by the three powerful Greek men who take them by force. They deliver them on top of the four foot scaffolding where Agamemnon sits. They are thrown to the ground and whipped. Agamemnon looks over the two girls and he chooses Chryseis. The other girl is taken to Achilles whose camp is below the scaffolding. The girl is thrown in front of the feet of Achilles who is reminded of Iphigenia whenever a woman appears in front of him. He sees Iphigenia covered in blood in

the distance, but she disappears into the darkness. This brings about rage in Achilles as he dismisses Briseis and exits. As she leaves they both share a look for one another, it is obvious there is an attraction. The father of Chryseis pleads for the return of his daughter. He is thrown out by Agamemnon's guards. Chrysies prays to the God, Apollo, who appears on the back wall. Apollo nods in acceptance. Thunder. Greeks begin to fall in sickness. Many die. Achilles searches out for the answers from a soothsayer who performs a ritual in front of Apollo. A soothsayer has Apollo's answer. The soothsayer has a private moment with Apollo, he then returns to give Achilles his answer. Achilles marches into Agamemnon's tent and grabs Chryseis by the hair and drags her with him. He is greeted with swords surrounding him. They are Agamemnon's guards. He looks around, frees himself with pure force and lands his sword under Agamemnon's throat. They have a stare down again and Agamemnon frees Chryseis to Achilles. He smiles at Achilles and claps his hands, and Briseis is brought in. She runs to Achilles and kisses him passionately as Achilles continues to stare at Agamemnon. He breaks the kiss with Briseis and will take both women with him. Achilles men come in to guard Achilles. Achilles stands tall and gets nose to nose with Agamemnon. He throws down his sword at Agamemnon's feet and spits at the ground. The men follow and throw their swords down. Achilles is done fighting and will no longer fight alongside of Agamemnon. He and his men are leaving. Achilles returns Chryseis to her father. Chryseis runs to Achilles and kisses him passionately. She has him pull her hair.

Achilles touches his veil on his arm and walks Chryseis over to her father as they leave. Achilles makes love to Briseis only to be interrupted by Agamemnon's men who take her out. She is topless and covers herself with her arm as they lead her out. Achilles is silent, the men take her. He is filled with rage. Achilles summons his mother, Thetis, the sea goddess. She appears on the back wall. He throws his cape and helmet to the ground. He kneels before her. He stares over at Agamemnon and makes a cutting motion with a knife to his mother. He asks her to let the Trojans prevail over the Greek army, he will not fight. She smiles and nods. Achilles stands on top of the six foot scaffolding and stares down at Agamemnon. Agamemnon kisses Briseis by force and smiles down at Agamemnon. Briseis cries and sinks to Agamemnon's feet. She cannot bear to look at Achilles. A cold death stare is shared between Agamemnon and Achilles. Thetis appears in mortal form and holds her son. Zeus appears on the back wall. Thetis cries, prays, and kneels before Zeus. She gestures to her son and to Agamemnon who has Briseis by the hair fondling her. Zeus thrashes a bolt of thunder. He will give victory to the Trojans for this misconduct by Agamemnon. The song and scene plays out to four minutes and twenty-eight seconds.)

Book 2: Agamemnon's Dream

("Dream On" by Aerosmith plays in the background as Agamemnon is sleeping and he awakes in his dream to see his daughter Iphigenia wandering towards him. He unsheathes his sword. Her bloody gown blows in the distance. She goes towards Agamemnon, and as she

tries to speak a gust of wind is heard. Blood pours out of her mouth as Agamemnon drops to his knees, throws down his sword, and puts his arms around Iphigenia's waste. He is a broken man. She grabs a pitcher of water and pours it over Agamemnon's head cleansing him, but the water is bloody. She kisses him on the forehead and leaves upstage and fades out of sight. Agamemnon rubs his face as though he has awakened from a terrible dream. He summons his army as they wait for his instructions. He climbs the six foot scaffolding and looks down on his men. He points over to Zeus who appears on the back wall and in disgust throws his sword, shield, spear and helmet to the ground. With his scepter raised, he motions that Zeus has betrayed all of them. The men celebrate enthusiastically for they are finally going home after ten years of fighting. Fear, panic, and jubilation hit the troops as some celebrate and some cry. They remove their swords, helmets and shield and pile them up alongside Agamemnon's. Athena appears on the six foot platform and throws thunder bolts to get the men to re-consider. Odysseus with the help of Athena gets up on the four foot scaffolding and stops the men dead in their tracks as they prepare to leave on their ships. Nestor and Odysseus enter and stand on the six foot platform and give war cries. Athena shows the Greeks an image of Paris seducing Helen. Menelaus wounded, battered, can barely stand. He raises his sword and shield in the air. The army slowly picks up their stuff and agrees to stay and fight. They are fired up and ready to bring Helen home and destroy Troy! The test worked, the Greeks are ready. Zeus appears on the back wall and Greeks kneel down to offer libations to him. Agamemnon makes a sacrifice to Zeus as the men put on war paint and prepare for battle. The men cheer Menelaus and Agamemnon who are ready for battle. The lights fade up on the other side of the stage and Hector receives a message from a messenger, the messenger is Achilles. He removes his helmet to reveal himself. They stare at each other in respect. Achilles motions to see Hectors sword. He obliges as Achilles gives Hector his sword to view. They both take a couple practice swings and are impressed. Chryseis comes out and both Achilles and Chrysies stare at each other. Hector steps aside as Achilles dismisses Chryseis who kisses him. He is in love with Briseis. Chryseis senses this and runs off. He then bows in Hectors direction who bows back. They exchange smiles. There is a mutual respect between them. The message is Menelaus challenges Paris to fight him. Hector summons Paris who is with Helen. Hector prepares Paris for battle as Helen tries to stop him. Hector pushes Helen to the ground. Paris grabs Hector and he easily takes him down. He grabs Paris' head and pulls him over to Helen and forces him to kiss her passionately. He is angered and upset by his brother who is the cause of the war. Hera is present on the back wall enjoying the feud between Trojans. King Priam watches from a distance and fears his sons defeat at the hands of the goliath Menelaus. Helen holds Paris tightly as Paris stays on the ground rocking in fear. The song and scene play out to four minutes and twenty-seven seconds.)

Book 3: The Cowardness of Paris

("Thunderstruck" by ACDC plays in the background as the Greek and the Trojans advance two at a time

and face off in a mist of fog, Greeks on the left and Trojans on the right. The Trojans advance banging their shields and screaming battle cries. The Greeks move silently, hard faced and solemn. Both sides line up pounding their swords on the ground to the music. Paris comes to the front of the line standing center. Agamemnon and Hector are in the front of their lines. Helen, Priam, Andromache stand on the four foot scaffolding on the side of the Trojans. Achilles stands on the opposite side of the Greeks. Paris shows off his skill walking arrogantly up and down the Greek line with a bow and arrow on his back, a sword at his hip, and a spear in each hand. He challenges any Greek to fight him. Menelaus steps forward and accepts the offer. Paris is overcome with fear and hides behind Hector who picks him up and gives him a tongue lashing. He then strides along the battle line with his brother and his sword horizontal to show he means no harm. The Greeks start pelting Hector with rocks and Agamemnon signals them to stop. Paris agrees to save face and fight Menelaus so not to embarrass his Trojan brothers. Agamemnon comes forward and points to Helen and Hector nods in agreement. Menelaus and Paris look up at Helen and agree whoever wins the fight wins Helen and the war is over. All bow down and pay homage to Zeus and offer a sacrifice of a lamb. Zeus appears on the back wall and approves of the agreement. The fight begins with the Greeks and Trojans whooping and yelling; the two men prowl each other shaking their spears, each trying to scare the other. Paris strikes first and hits Menelaus' shield. Menelaus shakes his spear in the air and screams to the Gods and then drives

201

it into Paris' shoulder. He then draws his sword and brings it crashing down on his helmet. He then seizes the chin strap of the helmet and chokes Paris with it. He drags Paris lifeless body over to the Greek side. Aphrodite appears on the back wall and she fills the area with fog. Menelaus is suddenly writhing in pain on the ground. Paris disappears, and when the fog dissipates, Paris is on the four foot scaffolding with Helen and King Priam. Helen, furious at Aphrodite interference, faces off with her. Thunder knocks Helen backwards. Paris helps Helen, looks at Aphrodite, and kisses Helen passionately which causes Aphrodite to leave. Agamemnon furiously declares Menelaus the winner which brings an uproar of applause from the Greeks. Menelaus points at Helen to come down as he has rightfully won her back. She stares at him and then leaves with Paris and King Priam. Hector and his men slowly back away from the battle grounds as a truce is recognized by both armies as they exit off. As they exit, Achilles applauds Hector. He, in return, gives Achilles a half smile which is noticed by Agamemnon. He looks up at Achilles and he is gone. The song and scene play out to four minutes and fifty-two seconds.)

Book 4: The Truce is Broken

("Rebel Yell" by Billy Idol plays in the background as Paris is making love to Helen as Aphrodite watches on the back wall in video form. Paris stops and looks at Aphrodite as Helen leaves in anger. He flashes back to the wedding of Thetis and Peleus. Thetis goes up to Paris and gives him a golden apple. He wants him to present it to the feet of Hera, Aphrodite or Athena. Hera

*and Athena are all over Paris with sexual pleasures, but
Aphrodite grabs Paris' hand and shows him Helen who
is naked behind a sheet on the eight foot scaffold. She
takes the sheet down to cover her body and he sees her
face. In a trance he drops the golden apple of the feet
of Aphrodite who then kisses Paris passionately. The
flashback is over and Aphrodite whose face is still on
the back wall smiles at Paris. He leaves in a rage. On a
four foot scaffolding Achilles is making love to Briseis,
who has snuck into the Greek camp to be with Achilles.
He is unaware of the battle that is about to take place.
Hera's face is seen on the back wall and she is slowly
killing Trojan soldiers with a wave of her hand. Zeus
is seen on the back wall and he revives the Trojans
as Hera and Zeus have a stare down. Hera wins and
Hera convinces Athena to break the truce. Athena on
the back wall looks to Pandaros who stands on the
four foot scaffolding and sees Menelaus standing on
the four foot scaffolding stage left. He draws his bow
and pierces Menelaus in the side as Athena looks
on. This brings the Greek and Trojan soldiers out as
Menelaus screams in pain. Odysseus then runs into full
view of both armies and cuts the throat of Democon,
killing him. Both armies are enraged. Agamemnon and
Hector call on their troops to fight. The two armies
clash violently and many men are killed on both sides.
Hera is seen with Athena on the back wall, watching
them fight. Hera is very pleased, she has broken the
truce and still hopes for the destruction of Troy. Paris
grabs Helen and assures her the he loves her, he then
proceeds to seduce her again. The song and scene play
out at four minutes and forty-seven seconds.)*

Book 5: The Heroics of Diomedes

("Crazy Train" by Black Sabbath plays in the background as Athena is on the back wall. Diomedes is looking up at her as he kills six Trojans. He looks up at the four foot scaffolding where Pandoros stands. He goes down on his knees and begs Athena for aid. She raises her hand, and he starts to glow. She has given him power to tell gods from men and great strength. He feels the strength rip through his body. He is a changed warrior. She shows him a picture of Aphrodite, and she rips it in half. He shows Athena that he will cut her neck and kill her for Athena. With renewed strength Diomades climbs the four foot scaffolding after he fends off four more Trojans, he kills Pandoros. He then picks up Aeneas and wounds him. Aphrodite appears on the back wall and pleads for his life, but Diomedes means to kill him. Aphrodite transforms from the back wall to the battlefield. Aphrodite protects her son and stands over him and gives Diomedes a blast with a wave of her hand. She continues to blast Diomedes with flashes of thunder as he writhes on the ground. Athena appears behind Aphrodite and they clash. As Aphrodite has her back turned to battle Athena, Diomades drives his sword into Aphrodite and cuts her hand. She screams a deadly scream. Zeus appears on the back wall and freezes the action. With a bolt of thunder both Athena and Aphrodite are again on the back wall with him. He chastises them both as Aphrodite shows him her wound. As Zeus, Athena, and Aphrodite disappear from the back wall; Apollo appears and protects the wounded Aeneas. As Apollo freezes Diomades, Aeneas with the help of Apollo, walks off the battlefield to his

wounds. As Apollo disappears from the back wall, Ares appears. Hector and the Trojans surround Diomades who is still frozen in place. Ares lifts his hand and Diomades is unfrozen and starts to battle Hector and the Trojans. More Greek warriors arrive, but Hector and his men drive Diomades and his men back. As the Greeks are driven back and Diomades is almost killed, Athena and Hera appear in human form and blast the Trojans back with their super natural powers. Ares appears in human form and now battles Athena and Hera who stand opposite of him with a wounded Diomades on the ground. Just as Ares is attacking the two goddesses are getting the best of them by driving them back with his powers. Diomades then stands up and drives a spear into the belly of Ares. Zeus appears on the back wall and Ares shows him the wound caused by the two goddesses. Zeus heals Ares' wound and in a fury he sends out a bolt of lighting and thunder. Ares, Hera, and Athena are back on the back wall with him. He chastises them again. Diomades is also healed by Zeus as the Greeks and Trojans enter from opposite sides comes running into battle. The battle becomes fierce. The scene and song play out at four minutes and fifty seconds.)

Book 6: Hector and Andromache

("Another One Bites The Dust" by Queen plays in the background. The two armies continue to battle with neither side gaining the advantage. Ajax takes out Acamax with his spear. Odysseus and Agamemnon continue their killing spree slaughtering many Trojans. Menelaus is about to kill Adrestus, a Trojan who had

fallen, but Adrestus grabs Menelaus around the knees and begs for his life. He offers Menelaus a satchel full of gold which he's about to take until Agamemnon slaps Menelaus, who in turn, kicks Adrestus off of him as Agamemnon cuts his throat. On the other side of the stage Hector is in conference with Aeneas and Helenus. He tries to tell them that the Greeks are causing the Trojans to retreat. Hector gathers all the women and gets them to kneel in prayer to Athena on the back wall. He takes a beautiful robe which is his mother, Hecuba, and places it on an altar for Athena so she will help the Trojan army. Athena smiles and looks up to the four foot platform where Diomades stands. He comes down center to challenge a Trojan that calls him out. He stands facing the Trojan, it is Glaucus. They notice they both have family lockets on and exchange them to look at them. They discover they have ties to each others' families. Diomades throws his spear on the ground a hugs his Trojan friend. They exchange shields and swords. Diomades turns to his fellow Greeks and warns them not to kill Glaucus. Glaucus does the same to his fellow Trojan fighters. Hector discovers his brother, on top of the other four foot scaffolding making love to Helen. He pulls him out of bed and drags him to the edge of the scaffolding to view the fighting. He throws down a shield, a sword, a spear, and helmet in front of Paris. As he goes to hit Paris, Helen intercepts and hugs Hector to stop. Hector pushes Helen down and leaves in disgust. He goes and visits his own wife and child and he is panicked when he can't find them. Andromache spots Hector and runs to him. She embraces him and breaks down. They share a long passionate kiss. He holds her face in his hands and then holds his baby son up in the air. Andromache looks across the battlefield and Achilles watches both of them smiling sharpening his sword. Achilles has killed all Andromache's brothers and father. Hector readies to meet Achilles on the battlefield. He kisses Andromache and his son and climbs down the scaffolding. Andromache tries to stop him but can't; she collapse in tears on the ground holding her baby. Hector is moving to the battle when Paris arrives at his side ready for battle. Hector hugs Paris in respect as the two men join the battle. The song and scene play out at three minutes and thirty-seven seconds.)

Book 7: Ajax takes on Hector

("Bang Your Head, Mental Health" by Quiet Riot plays in the background as Paris and Hector burst into the battle and start to slaughter the Greeks left and right. Athena appears on the back wall concerned about all the Greek losses. Apollo appears on the back wall and stops Hector from fighting. He sends Priam's son, Helenus, to him to pick out the biggest Greek to fight in a single battle. He backs his Trojans off and Agamemnon does the same as both armies sit on the ground facing each other. Hector stands up and points down the row of Greeks for someone to challenge him for his sword and shield. No one takes the offer, they are ashamed to refuse his challenge but also afraid to accept it until Menalaus rises and prepares to go against Hector in battle. The Greeks jump up and pull Menalaus back down to a sitting position as Agamemnon sees that Hector is more powerful than him. Achilles stands

alone on the four foot platform. He's not ready to fight Hector, but acknowledges him with a slight nod. Ajax, Diomades, and Agamemnon draw lots and Ajax claims the fight. He is ready and blood thirsty to prove he is better than Hector, better than Achilles, and the most powerful Greek in the army. The battle is set but before they battle both armies fall on their knees to pray to Zeus on the back wall. Ajax and Hector hold their shields and weapons high in the air. Hector starts the battle and strikes Ajax's shield with his spear. Ajax does the same and penetrates Hectors' shield. Both me are evenly matched. The Trojans and Greeks encircle the fight and cheer on their warrior. Both men retrieve their spear and fight each other hand-to-hand. Ajax manages to pierce Hectors' shield and cut his neck open. Hector throws dirt in Ajax's face and blinds him. In a rage, Ajax blindly goes towards Hector and clotheslines him down to the ground. As Ajax is about to drive his sword into Hector, Apollo appears on the back wall and stops Ajax in his tracks. The Greeks and Trojans break up the fight. The fight is considered a draw. Hector knowing he was bested by Ajax gives him his cape and Ajax returns the favor as both men shake hands. The Greeks celebrate by drinking and having a huge feast. A Greek and Trojan meet center for a truce as the dead are picked up and are burned. The Trojans, unhappy on how the war is going, grab Helen from Paris and are going to deliver her to Menalaus. Paris stops the men and throws down gold and treasures to be returned to Menalaus instead of Helen. The men agree and take the treasure to the Greeks. A Trojan messenger takes the treasure to Diomades but Diomades knocks the treasure from his hands and threatens his life unless he leaves the Greek army. Idaeus, the messenger, takes the treasure back to Paris who is disappointed the Greeks did not accept the peace offering. Both armies stand on the four foot scaffolding to pay honor to their dead. Torches flame on each corner of the scaffolding as the Greeks and Trojans kneel in prayer to Zeus on the back wall. Thunder is heard from Zeus. Wine and ashes of the dead from both armies is spilled to the ground as libation to the gods. The song and scene play out at five minutes and eighteen seconds.)

Book 8: Zeus Favors the Trojans

("Black Dog" by Led Zeppelin plays in the background as the Greeks continue to drink wine, eat, and polish their weapons as do the Trojans in the opposite camp. As dawn breaks, they go back to battling, with shields slamming, spears and swords clashing against each other, men screaming in death and victory. The battle rages with great losses on both sides and Zeus watching the entire battle on the back wall. He promises Thetis a Trojan victory, so he throws down a thunderbolt that rocks the Greeks, knocking them over. Many of their valiant warriors run for cover. Nestor holds tough and refuses to go down; Hector strikes him, but Diomades comes to his rescue and blocks Hectors' spear with his shield. This angers Zeus, and with one wave of his hand throws Diomades across the battlefield and leaves him defenseless. Nestor tries to get Diomades to safety, but he knocks down the old Greek and charges again at Hector in defiance of Zeus to prove he is no coward. Each time he charges at Hector, Zeus throws a

thunderbolt down and knocks Diomades to the ground and burns his flesh. Hector realizes that he was helping the Trojans win as his men race on the battlefield and celebrates in joy. Hector charges fearlessly towards Nestor and a wounded, burned Diomades, and he intends to kill them both with Zeus at his side and take their weapons as a war prize. Just as Hector is to kill both Greeks, Hera shows up in mortal form and knocks Hector across the battlefield. An army of Trojans surround Hera but she laughs and wipes them all out with a wave of her hand. She looks up at Zeus who is furious. She gets down on her knees as all the gods' faces appear on the back wall. Agamemnon, in a panic, climbs the six foot platform and prays to Zeus for help. He then gets up and rallies his troops to come out and pray to Zeus for protection while fighting the Trojans. Zeus feels guilty, and seeing his wife defy him, he stops the Greeks from being massacred by the Trojans. Hera climbs to a four foot platform as the battle continues. Diomades takes out many Trojans, even though he is wounded. Again, Achilles watches in interest but does not fight. He does throw Hector a spear from the four foot platform to help him during the fight. The Trojans, led by Hector, are still winning the battle and driving the Greeks back. Hera, in shear anger, summons Athena and begs her to help. Together, with each one on the four foot platform, they start plowing through the Trojans killing them with a wave of their hands. Zeus appears on the back wall and sends Iris out in the middle of the battle. When she reaches center stage both armies freeze in place. She looks at Hera and Athena and points to Zeus who summons them both back to Olympus with a look. The two are once again on the back wall with Zeus chastising them. They disappear, and the battle unfreezes with Hector driving the Greeks back to their ships. The Trojans celebrate and offer prayer to Zeus. Achilles, alone from the four foot platform, applauds Hector. Hector throws Achilles a bottle. He breaks it and both men toast each other and drink to another day of mutual respect for each other. The song and scene play out at four minutes and fifty-five seconds.)

Book 9: Pleading With Achilles

("Tom Sawyer" by Rush plays in the background as the Achaean army is badly wounded with soldiers in a panic and alarmed by Zeus' betrayal of the Greeks. Agamemnon commands his men to stand as they gather in a line badly wounded. He walks up and down the line and throws down his sword and shield and goes to his knees and weeps. There is a long pause and no one speaks until Diomades steps out of line and picks up Agamemnon with the help of old Nestor. He puts the shield in Agamemnon's hand and a sword and a spear. He climbs the four foot scaffolding. He pours blood on his face and gives a war cry which the men repeat. Nestor runs up and down the line quieting the men and lowering their arms. The Trojan army is surrounding them on the other scaffolding. Zeus appears on the back wall. Hector is paying homage to Zeus. Diomades comes down from the four foot platform and challenges Nestor to a fight to win the support of the troops but Nestor points to the four foot platform to show him where Achilles now stands. They

all look up at Achilles. Agamemnon pulls Odysseus, Ajax, and Phoenix forward to go and talk to Achilles. He gives them gold, and he pulls Briseis forward and throws her at the men. He looks up at Achilles and offers him a sword, spear, and shield, but Achilles spits towards Agamemnon and turns his back to him. The men are sent with the offerings and climb the four foot scaffolding to convince Achilles to fight and save the Greek army from destruction. Achilles greets the three men as they arrive on the scaffolding. He embraces Briseis. They drink wine and feast a little. They offer Achilles his shield, sword, and spear, but he throws them down as he points down to Agamemnon in anger. Below, Agamemnon and the men are on their knees praying to Zeus on the back wall to change his favor to the Trojans. The three men offer Achilles the gold which he throws back at them. He takes Briseis, kisses her, and then gives her back to the men. He turns his back on them. They leave, except Phoenix, who stays and tries to convince Achilles to fight. Phoenix shows Achilles their matching childhood medallions. They embrace but Achilles throws down the shield, spear, and sword again. He will not fight. Diomades is offended by Achilles' actions; he rounds up the men and starts a war cry with them. He pushes Agamemnon forward and, sticks a sword in his hand as the men bow to Agamemnon. He is renewed by the men's faith in him. The men chant around him as he looks up at Achilles who is with Phoenix. They share a long hateful stare. The Trojan's who have surrounded the Greeks, wait patiently for Hector's orders who is watching the Greeks' every move. He is ready to attack. The song

and scene play out at four minutes and thirty-four
seconds.)

Book 10: Spies and Night Raiders

*("Paint It Black" by the Rolling Stones plays in the
background as Agamemnon can't sleep. He keeps
staring at the Trojan army that surrounding his camp,
pacing, and cursing his situation. He wakes his two
bothers, Odysseus and Menalaus for council. They
also wake up Nestor, Diomades and Ajax. They decide
that Diomades and Odysseus are going to go into the
Trojan armies' camp to spy on their next plan of attack.
As the men arm themselves and put on dark cloaks,
Hector, on the other side of the stage, tries to find a
man to spy on the Greeks. One weak, warrior, Dolon,
steps forward to volunteer. Hector grants him to go but
sees he is not as good as the sharp-eyed Odysseus and
Diomades who sees the Trojans trying to sneak in the
Greek camp. They corner him. Dolon pleads for his
life as the two Greeks trap him. He offers them gold as
Diomades and Odysseus laugh and then torture Dolon
for information. Dolon points to Hector as the guilty
party for sending him. The two Greeks look up at Hector
and cut Dolon's neck in front of him. Hector, in a fury,
runs to get his army to kill the two men. Diomades and
Odysseus pray to the goddess Athena for protection.
Athena appears on the back wall and with a wave of
her hand puts all the Trojans to sleep that were about to
advance on Diomades and Odysseus. The two Greeks
storm into the Trojan army and kill many while they
sleep. They walk out a bloody mess. Apollo appears on
the back wall and is furious that Athena got involved.*

Apollo tells Hector of the slaughter, and all the men killed are brought back to life by Apollo. As they chase after Diomades and Odysseus who are now are long gone with the Trojans treasure. This deeply upsets Hector. Diomades and Odysseus enter the Greek camp and throw gold coins into the air as the men welcome them home with a victory feast of wine and food. The Greek army pays homage to Athena who had protected the two Greeks from slaughter. Apollo rages on the back wall as Athena turns to look at him and laughs. The Trojans finally feel pain. The song and scene play out at four minutes and ten seconds.)

Book 11: Agamemnon in Glory

("All Along the Watchtower" by Jimmy Hendrix plays in the background as the goddess of strife, Eris, stands on the highest scaffolding giving a war cry to the Greeks to fight on. Zeus appears on the back wall behind Eris. Agamemnon leads the way grabbing his shield, sword and spear and shouting orders to prepare his troops for battle. On the other side of the stage Hector is barking orders assembling his troops to prepare for their battle. Both sides leap into attack mode. The fighting is fierce and long. Agamemnon breaks through the Trojan line and takes out Trojans left and right who are no match for him. Hector, who has a green glow around him is protected by Zeus and matches Agamemnon in his onslaught of the Greeks. Agamemnon continues to advance to the Trojan wall and Zeus sends down Iris in a thunderbolt. Iris tells Hector she was sent by Zeus and tells him to keep fighting because if he defeats Agamemnon he

will be victorious. The battle continues as Greeks and Trojans die in a blood bath battle. Agamemnon is wounded by a Trojan. He is losing strength and retreats as he signals his army to keep fighting. The Trojans rush the Greeks feeling victory at the loss of their best warrior. Agamemnon, Diomades and Odysseus battle back and take the lead and drive the Trojans back. Hector and Paris size up their competition. Diomades knocks Hector to the ground with his spear. Hector retreats. As Diomades yells after him, Paris wounds Diomades in the foot with an arrow. He continues to fight until Odysseus pushes him back and saves Diomades from being killed as the Trojans advance. Odysseus is then wounded between the shoulder blades and falls, but is taken to safety by Giant Ajax who cuts down Trojans left and right. Giant Ajax is outnumbered and falls back as the Trojans advance on him. Little Ajax comes running in to help Giant Ajax survive the onslaught and get him back to the ships. In camp Nestor points to Achilles who is watching the action and instructs Patroclus to persuade Achilles to return to battle. Achilles again is defiant and sends Patroclus away. Nestor and Patroclus look at the wounded around them which consists of, Agamemnon, Diomades, Odysseus, Giant Ajax, Little Ajax, and Menalaus. Patroclus grabs Achilles' shield, spear, sword and helmet. He will pretend to be Achilles to scare the Trojans in retreat. Achilles stares down at the wounded Greeks and gives a smile to Agamemnon who passes out from pain. The song and scene play out at four minutes.)

Book 12: Hector Reaches the Wall

("Break on Through To the Other Side" by the Doors plays in the background as the Greeks take refuge behind their wall of shields. The two Ajax's stand guard and bring the Greeks to guard their wall. Zeus on the back wall, blows a mighty wind that knocks down the Greeks so that the Trojans led by Polydamas and Hector can advance. Cassandra appears with snakes in her hand on the top of the tallest scaffolding freezing the Trojans from advancing. Polydamas grabs Hector to retreat but Hector pushes him away in disgust. Thunder and lighting are seen as the Trojans advance despite the bad omen sent by Cassandra. The fighting is intense with both Greeks and Trojans fighting to a stalemate. With Zeus protecting him, Hector breaks through the Greek wall as the Greeks retreat. Hector and his men stand victorious upon the four foot scaffolding. They have once again made the Greek forces retreat. The song and scene play out at two minutes and twenty-six minutes. Suggested Intermission music is," Come On Feel the Noise" by Quiet Riot, "A Little Piece of My Heart" by Janice Joplin, and "You Really Got Me" by the Kinks.)

ACT II Book 13: Poseidon Rises

("We're not going To Take It" by Twisted Sister plays in the background as the Trojans continue to slaughter the Greeks and almost conquer them all. Zeus appears on the back wall and signals to Hector that his job is done. When Zeus vanishes from the back wall, his brother, Poseidon, appears on the back wall in a fury and strikes an earthquake that topples the Trojans.

Poseidon appears in mortal form on top of the six foot scaffolding with triton in his hand and strikes the two Ajax's with immense god-like power. The Ajax's start plowing through the Trojans and make a heroic comeback. Hector is not threatened by Poseidon as he feels Zeus is still on his side. He rallies his troops, but Poseidon strikes Hector down and immobilizes him on the ground so he can't get up. Menelaus joins the Ajax's and continues to make a comeback against the Trojan army. The battle is fierce and bloody, even as the Trojans and Greeks are again equally matched. Zeus reappears on the back wall and with a lighting strike releases Hector from Poseidon's powers. Paris helps his brother up and goes head to head with the Ajax's. It is a stalemate as both armies suffer casualties. Hector has lost many warriors while he is incapacitated by Poseidon. Zeus, in a thunderbolt, warns Poseidon to return to Olympus with a great war cry and a thunderous hurricane. Both armies are knocked down by Poseidon. They both gather to their feet and charge at each other, Hector and Paris for the Trojans and the Ajax's for the Greeks. The scene and song play out at three minutes and thirty-nine seconds.)

Book 14: Hera Seduces Zeus

("Won't Get Fooled Again" by The Who plays in the background as Nestor finds himself on top of the six foot scaffolding surrounded by Trojan fighters. Many of his Greek brothers lay on the ground below him hacked to pieces. From the other side of the stage three wounded warriors limp on stage from their ships, Agamemnon, Odysseus and Diomades. They want a better view of the

battle. They see their Greek brothers being demolished by Hector and the Trojans. It is too much to bear for a leader. Agamemnon drops to his knees and cries out. He throws down his sword, shield and spear. He has quit and is ready to go back home. Odysseus, in shock, slaps Agamemnon across the face as Diomades picks Agamemnon up on his two feet and draws a blade underneath his chin. Agamemnon pushes Diomades off him and picks up his sword to defend himself. Odysseus throws his sword up at Agamemnon. As all three men are about to go at it, Poseidon appears in a thunderbolt strike and separates the men. Poseidon quickly heals the three warriors' wounds. They feel the strength of the gods as Poseidon touches them with his triton. They grab their weapons and climb the six foot scaffolding to save their brother, Nestor, who is surrounded by Trojans. They start to slaughter the Trojans left and right until Zeus appears on the back wall. Hector rallies his troops and prepares to kill Nestor. The two Ajax's prevent this. Hector then looks to Zeus and is ready to receive his strength to defeat the three healed Greeks approaching him. Before Zeus can do anything, Hera appears next to him and kisses him. Aphrodite appears in the middle of them causing Zeus to lose his focus on Hector. Hector is struck unconscious by the two Ajax's. Giant Ajax gets Hector in a bear hug and tries to squeeze the life out of him. Paris hits Ajax from behind as he lets go of Hector long enough for Paris to take Hector to safety. The Greeks renew their attacks and demolish the Trojans and save Nestor. The Greeks stop fighting. Agamemnon, Odysseus, Nestor, Diomades, and the two Ajax's from the top of the six foot scaffolding look down at all the dead Trojans. They all look back at Poseidon who is laughing with Hera. The Greeks give a war cry in their honor. The war has now shifted in favor of the Greeks. The song and scene play out at three minutes and fifty-two minutes.)

Book 15: Zeus Regroups

("Back in Black" and "Dirty Deeds" by ACDC plays in the background as the Greeks are driving the Trojans back, hacking them to pieces by the dozens. Zeus appears on the back wall. He is shocked by the Trojan defeat. Poseidon is leading the charge for the Greeks and Hector has been knocked unconscious. Zeus turns to Hera, who is behind him, and gives her a threatening look. She had taken Zeus' eye off the war through luscious sex. Hera shrinks back in fear from Zeus. He knows he must stop his brother, Poseidon, or the Greeks will win and he would break his promise to Achilles' mother, Thetis. Thunder strikes and Iris and Apollo are sent by Zeus to the battlefield to stop Poseidon and bring him back to Olympus. Iris and Apollo surround Poseidon and prepare to stop him. It is a showdown of the gods. Zeus appears on the back wall to let Poseidon know he has ordered Iris and Apollo to stop him from helping the Greeks. Poseidon looks at his brother and gives him a wicked smile. He will not stop. The gods are about to do battle. Apollo and Iris freeze the Trojans and Greeks around them. They strike first and blast Apollo from both sides with flashes of light and electric shock from their hands. Poseidon is down. He raises his hands and brings Apollo and Iris to their knees. It is obvious the brother of Zeus is more

powerful and could kill both Iris and Apollo. But Zeus looks at his brother and shakes his head no. Athena and Aphrodite appear in mortal form on the six foot platform and summon Poseidon to stop. They must all return to Olympus. Zeus has denied the Greeks' victory by Poseidon's hand. As Poseidon puts down his hands, so do Iris and Apollo. Zeus drops a sacred storm shield down from the sky. It belongs to Zeus and it will be used to fix what is wrong in the war. Apollo grabs the shield as Iris runs to Hector who is wounded and unconscious. Iris put his hands on Hector's face and he leaps up in full strength. Poseidon climbs the six foot scaffolding to be with Hera and Aphrodite. Achilles comes from the edge and stands across from the three gods, smirking. Zeus unfreezes the armies with a flash of lighting and the Greeks see Apollo with the storm shield along with a renewed powerful Hector behind him ready to take back his position as the victor of the war. The Greeks build a wall with their shields once again. Apollo throws Zeus' shield at the formed wall and it knocks it down and mortally wounds them all. Poseidon is beside himself and glares at Zeus who is smiling. He must make the sides even again. The Greek and Trojans resort to hand-to-hand combat. The Trojans lay corpses left and right and have so much momentum against the Greek army with Apollo leading the way. The Greeks are in a great panic as Nestor kneels and begs Zeus for mercy. Zeus hears his cries and sends a thunderbolt down to slow the Trojans down, but it does the opposite, it makes them more powerful as more Greeks die. Patroclus runs up to Achilles and begs him to fight as the Trojans are almost at the Greek ships. Hector is close to the ships but Giant Ajax stands in his way. Hector tries a war cry for victory, but Giant Ajax gives a war cry back in anger. The slaughter continues between Trojans and Greeks. Giant Ajax has the Greeks build another wall with their shields. Zeus is determined to do one last thing to give the Trojans the advantage and punish his brother Poseidon for helping the Greeks. He drives Hector on with great power and speed. Apollo tosses Zeus' shield to Hector and he blows apart the Greek wall killing many but not Giant Ajax. The Greeks are minutes from defeat until Athena swoops down and creates a huge fog. Giant Ajax seizes the moment as Poseidon throws his triton to Ajax who has wiped out two dozen Trojans with it. Ajax is now being powered by Poseidon. Hector is being powered by Zeus as the two men meet center. Ajax strikes first with his triton which is blocked by Hector using Zeus' shield. A great explosion takes place blowing both men backwards. Ajax gets back up, and he and Nestor cry out to save their ships and save the war. Both armies continue to do fierce battle. All the gods on the ground disappear in the fog. Hector still has the upper hand but he must get past Giant Ajax first to get to the ships. Zeus looks on for he has done enough for the Trojans today. The Trojans are back on top and that is good enough for now. Zeus vanishes from the back wall. Achilles stares down at Hector; he waits patiently for their fight, it is not the right time yet. Both men know this, and Hector, looking up at Achilles senses his own death is upon him. 'Back in Black" plays out at four minutes and fourteen seconds and is followed by "Dirty Deeds", which plays out at four minutes and ten seconds.)

Book 16: The Death of Patroclus

("Black Betty" by Cream plays in the background as Patroclus meets Achilles on the six foot scaffolding and weeps at Achilles' feet. Achilles just stares at the Greek destruction below him. Patroclus, angry at Achilles' ignorance, starts to fight him as Achilles quickly has a sword to Patroclus' throat. Patroclus' apologizes and begs for Achilles helmet, spear, shield, and sword so he can disguise himself as Achilles to scare the Trojans since Achilles won't fight. Below, Agamemnon continues to shout orders, and Giant Ajax still has the Trojans at a stand still. Achilles hugs his friend. He then pours libations to Zeus and prays for the protection of Patroclus from the Trojans. Zeus, who appears on the back wall, looks at Achilles, and he decides he will not interfere with this battle. Patroclus rallies the Greek troops and asks them to win for Achilles which may drive Achilles into battle for the Greeks. He also exhorts the troops to recognize the disrespect Agamemnon has given Achilles. Agamemnon walks away in anger and prepares for another battle. When the Trojans see Patroclus with Achilles' helmet, cape, sword, spear and shield they begin to retreat in fear. As this happens, the Greeks attack with Nestor and Giant Ajax killing many Trojans. Zeus takes no action in the battle. He just watches until Patroclus kills Zeus mortal son, Sarpedon. Zeus, in anger, still does not interfere, but sends Apollo down in disguise to do his bidding. Zeus

continues to stay out of favor as Patroclus drives the Trojans back. Hector retreats sensing a new energy in the Greeks from Achilles and he must now regroup and plan a better way to attack the Greeks. Patroclus gets all the way to the great Trojan wall but each time he scales the six foot scaffolding, Apollo on top, knocks him down as a favor to Zeus. Apollo now goes and whispers to Hector to take Patroclus out and tells him that Zeus is on his side. The Greeks continue to battle and gain the upper hand and drive the Trojans back. This angers Apollo who comes over to Patroclus and knocks him down. Apollo discovers is not Achilles who he knocked down. Feeling duped, Apollo lashes into him and tortures him while Patroclus retreats from Apollo and runs towards the Greek army. Hector comes from behind him and cuts his throat still thinking its Achilles. Both armies stop in silence and shock as they think Achilles has been killed. Hector walks in the middle of both armies and spits down on Achilles in front of the Greeks who almost attack him, but the Trojan armies are ready to battle again. Hector turns the body over and sees its Patroclus. He bends down as Patroclus points to Apollo and Zeus on the back wall and blames them for his death, not Hector. He embraces Hector who is in shock and dies. Achilles looks down from the six foot platform at his dead best friend. He is seething. Hector stares up at Achilles and to show him he's next as he drives his sword into the dead Patroclus for effect. Hector is scared for the first time in his life. Achilles is not amused. Both armies are at a standstill. Achilles will get his revenge. The song and scene play out at three minutes and thirty-one second.)

Book 17: Struggling Over the Body

("Achilles Last Stand" by Led Zeppelin plays in the background as Menelaus rushes over to protect the dead body of Patroclus with his spear and sword. A Trojan sneaks up behind him to try to claim Patroclus' armor and Menalaus turns to block a spear strike with his shields. He kills the Trojan and continues to protect the body. Apollo urges Hector to return to the battle field and claim Achilles' armor. He charges at Menalaus. Menalaus at first readies for the charge but thinks again since Zeus is protecting Hector. Menalaus abandons Patroclus and retreats back to the ships. Hector has stripped the armor from Patroclus' body and is ready to chop his head off until Ajax comes on the scene to protect the body. Hector is afraid of Ajax and makes his way back to his city. When he gets to his city he put on Achilles' armor and feels the power of fifty men. Zeus, who appears on the back wall, is sad because he realizes Hector does not have a long time left to live. Feeling strong, Hector makes his way back to the battlefield to drag Patroclus' body back. Andromache tries to stop him but he is determined. Ajax and Menalaus go on a slaughtering spree of the Trojans. Giant Ajax worries he and Menalaus could survive the onslaught of Trojans attacking by themselves. He calls a war cry and Little Ajax and more Greeks join the fight. The Greeks are pushed back by the great Trojan forces. Giant Ajax rallies the Greeks with a war cry. Apollo, disguised as Aeneas, scolds Hector and the Trojans for

being cowards. He leads them through the Greeks. The two Ajax's, holding Patroclus' dead body, and fight off many Greeks. Giant Ajax continues to protect the body. The fighting rages fiercely. Athena intervenes and tells Menelaus not to give up and gives him more power for praying to her. Apollo whispers in Hector's ear about fulfilling revenge. Just then, Hector appears wearing the armor of Achilles. The Greeks are sickened. A thunderbolt sent from Zeus is heard. This shows the Trojans the tide has turned. Menelaus, thinking all is lost, gets on his knees and prays to Zeus. To return the favor, Zeus creates a mist to help the Greeks fight so they do not go down in defeat by the Trojans. A Trojan, Antilochus, meets with Achilles and begs him to come and fight. He shares with him the death of Patroclus. Achilles is devastated and climbs to the six foot scaffolding. Back to the battle, the two Ajax's and Menalaus stand firm protecting Patroclus body. They continue to battle the Trojans, pick up Patroclus body, and take it back to their ships. Hector celebrates with his Trojans in Achilles armor. Achilles stares down at Hector. He points to him. He breaks a spear in half. Hectors death is coming. This Zeus and Achilles both know. Hector is too lost in power to realize that his days are numbered. He holds Achilles' helmet up and celebrates another Trojan victory. His men cheer. The song and scene play out at three minutes and eleven seconds.)

Book 18: Achilles in Anguish

("Stairway to Heaven" by Led Zeppelin plays in the background as everything moves in slow motion during

this scene. Achilles, standing on the six foot scaffolding leans over the body of Patroclus and wails as the entire Greek army pays their respects to the brave hero on their knees. Achilles picks dust from the ground and pours it over his head. The Greeks leave Achilles to his mourning as the Trojans are attacking below with Hector still trying to get the body of Patroclus. Achilles begins to smear his face and clothes with dirt and Patroclus' blood. He lies on the ground clawing at his hair, bathing himself in his best friends' blood. His mind is not right. Briseis enters. She stops Achilles from killing himself and holds his hands tightly. They embrace with a passionate kiss. Achilles breaks away and screams in anguish. His mother, Thetis, appears on the back wall. Achilles points down to Hector in a rage. He prays to his mother to give the Greeks strength and takes back his wish for them to be destroyed. He wants to join the battlefield. Thetis smiles and nods, but insists he waits. Briseis gives him a new shield, armor, spear, sword and helmet, but it is thrown out of Achilles' hands by his mother's powers. She will make him new armor and weapons from a god. He cannot fight until they are ready. Briseis kisses Achilles, and they make love. The two Ajax's continue to battle the Trojans below and protect Patroclus' body from Hector. The Trojans get past the Ajax's and climb the six foot platform. They have Briseis and Achilles surrounded. He is unarmed. Athena appears, and engulfs Briseis and Achilles in a beam of light that the Trojans cannot penetrate. Iris appears and places weapons in his hands. The Trojans retreat as Achilles kills seven Trojans with one swing. Briseis kills three Trojans herself. As the Trojans leave,

the Greeks finally place Patroclus body on the funeral
brier and place coins on his eyes. All the Greeks join
Achilles in a prayer to Zeus around the body. On
the other side of the stage on the four foot platform,
Andromache celebrates her husband being home while
Paris celebrates with Helen. They all begin to feast and
drink as Hector holds Achilles armor and weapons high
over his head in celebration. Cassandra enters and
knocks them out of his hand. She points to Hector as
blood pours out of her mouth. Hector's not amused and
he beats Cassandra by whipping her and throws her
off the scaffolding. Cassandra leaves the Trojans and
heads to the Greek camp. Achilles lays his hands on
Patroclus' chest and gives a huge cry out. Achilles slices
his hand and drips his blood over his fallen friend's
body. He then cuts Patroclus' hand and wipes his blood
on his own face. The Greeks then wipe the blood off of
Patroclus and wrap his body in linen clothes after they
anoint it with oil and ointment. The Greeks continue to
pay their respects. Agamemnon sees Achilles. The two
men stare at each other. Agamemnon touches Achilles'
shoulder as Achilles walks away. Below, Cassandra is
entering the Greek camp. Iphigenia stops her and puts
a knife to her throat. The two women look at each other
and Iphigenia smiles and let's her go. Hera and Zeus
appear on the back wall. Achilles new armor appears
from the sky in a beam of light and is lowered down with
his new weapons. The armor is smoking and powerful.
Thetis appears in mortal form and gathers up the new
armor and weapons. She looks at Hephaestus, the
blacksmith of the gods. She embraces him. Achilles is

now ready to destroy the Trojans. The song and scene play out at eight minutes and two seconds.)

Book 19: Achilles Takes Up Arms

("Knights in White Satin" by the Moody Blues plays in the background. Achilles, still on the ground, weeps with Patroclus' body in his arms. Around him stands an army of mourning Greeks. Thetis crouches down by Achilles and leads him to the gift she has brought him. Achilles' grief turns to joy. Thetis motions the Greeks to take Patroculus' body, but Achilles sees them taking his friend and pulls a sword on the Greek soldiers ready for battle. His mother lowers his sword and the men take the rotting body away. Achilles gives one last cry for Patroclus and then calls a meeting of all Greeks. Odysseus and Diomades limp to the call as does the wounded Agamemnon. Achilles climbs the six foot platform and addresses his troops. Thetis returns to Olympus and is now on the back wall. Achilles looks down at Agamemnon and lifts his spear and yells out a war cry. The men cheer and yell back. Agamemnon must make amends with Achilles to protect his investment. He is still jealous at the cheering Achilles receives and silences the men. Agamemnon climbs the six foot platform. He faces off with Achilles who stares a hole right through him. The men below are nervous. Agamemnon claps twice and men bring treasures to Achilles. He kicks the treasures off the platform and raises his spear in a war chant. This makes Agamemnon mad but Odysseus intervenes quickly and separates the men. Achilles then brings out Briseis and takes her over to Agamemnon. He lifts up her skirt and throws

her at Agamemnon. Agamemnon goes over and kneels next to Achilles and presents him with his sword and swears he never touched Briseis. He even calls on Zeus who appears on the back wall and nods with approval that Agamemnon is telling the truth. Achilles last test is grabbing Briseis and putting a sword under her neck. Agamemnon looks away and bows his head. Achilles accepts Agamemnon's oath and passionately kisses Briseis. He presents her with the locket he had given to Iphigenia. They are to be married after the war. Hector stands on the four foot scaffolding staring at Achilles and wondering when their battle will take place. Achilles throws bottles of wine down at the men. He then returns to weeping for Patroclus. Athena appears and places her hands on Achilles' head and takes his sorrow away. Agamemnon comes over and embraces Achilles. They have had their differences, but now it is time for Achilles to dress for war. "Sharp Dressed Man" by ZZ Top plays in the background as Agamemnon takes off Achilles' old cape. He holds up Achilles' new armor, cape, helmet, and weapons. The men cheer below. Briseis and Agamemnon slowly dress Achilles for war. Thetis appears on the back wall watching intuitively. They first put on his armor, then his helmet, and last his cape. They then present him with his weapons. When he is ready, he scales down to the ground. The men crowd around him. Odysseus and Diomades present Achilles with his new shield, sword and spear. Briseis kisses Achilles as the Greek soldiers get ready for battle with their gear and weapons. Finally, they are ready. Achilles and the men do some sword play to tune up for battle. Now Achilles stands side by side with Agamemnon ready to conquer the Trojans. They bang on each other shoulders, they are ready. Achilles gives a battle cry and then they run towards the Trojans. This is now Achilles' army. Achilles is ready to fight and the balance of the war shifts. The Greeks form a wall with their shields and storm towards Troy. Both songs and the scene play out at eight minutes and three seconds.)

Book 20: The Gods of War

("I Want to Rock and Roll All Night" by Kiss plays in the background as the Greeks form for battle behind Achilles and face the Trojan line across from them. Zeus appears on the back wall. The fighters on both sides are at a standstill. The gods arrive in a huge thunderbolt and choose sides. Hera, Athena and Poseidon stand on the four foot scaffolding on the side of the Greeks along with Hermes and Hephaestus. On the side of the Trojans stand Ares, Apollo, Artemis, and Leto with Aphrodite and Xanthus. Before the gods arrive, the Greeks are defeating the Trojans led by Achilles and his powerful armor. Athena gives a battle cry and blasts Ares with her supernatural powers as the battle begins. Poseidon takes out many Trojans with his powerful triton. Zeus answers back with a thunderous thunderbolt. Apollo takes on Poseidon with his golden arrows in his hand. War crazed Ares confronts wild-eyed Athena; Artemis, goes against Hera, Leto takes on Hermes; and Xanthus battles Hephaestus. Their super natural powers ablaze and cause a bright light that blinds both armies. Apollo leaves his fight with Poseidon and fetches Aeneas to fight Achilles. Athena

has been protecting Achilles by placing a force field around him. With Aphrodite and Apollo protecting him, Aeneas goes up and down the Greek lines looking for Achilles. Zeus throws down a thunderbolt telling the gods to back away from Achilles and Aeneas. Both armies and the gods stop fighting as Achilles and Aeneas face off and circle each other. Both are ready to fight. Aeneas strikes first and goes at Achilles with his spear which Achilles blocks with his powerful shield. Achilles strikes next and wounds Aeneas in the shoulder by thrusting his spear forward. Aeneas then comes at Achilles with his sword; it is obvious Achilles is the better fighter. Poseidon knows this and tries to stop the fight by blasting Achilles with his triton, but Achilles blocks the supernatural blast. He then casts a mist in Achilles' eyes. He pulls Aeneas aside and tries to get him to leave so he won't be killed. The mist clears and Achilles finds himself staring at Poseidon. He decides to turn his back on Aeneas and propels his Greek army forward. Poseidon smiles at Achilles. This is exactly what Poseidon wants. Hector is trying to get his Trojans to advance, but they are fearful of the mighty Achilles. Apollo appears to Hector to warn him that Achilles is coming to kill him. Achilles kills Priam's youngest son and continues in the slaughter. Seeing this, Hector ignores Apollo and charges madly at Achilles. Achilles sees Hector running towards him and urging him on. Hector comes at Achilles with his sword and almost cuts Achilles' head off, but Athena blows Hector backwards in a great wind. Achilles then charges Hector but Apollo throws a thick mist in the air and takes Hector away. Achilles on his knees, screams to the skies and becomes enraged in madness. The dead stack up around Achilles. The Trojans retreat and the Greeks celebrate with prayers to the gods who protected them. The gods come center and face off with each other. Zeus appears on the back wall and sends a thunderbolt down. The gods vanished. Zeus knows the time has come to leave the fighting to the mortals and keep the gods as spectators at least for the time being. Troy is days from falling. The song and scene play out at four minutes and five seconds.)

Book 21: Achilles and the River

("Fly by Night" by Rush plays in the background as Xanthus is upset at all the Trojans that Achilles killed in the river. He blasts Achilles and with his supernatural powers over and over almost killing him. Zeus appears on the back wall and Achilles crawls to pray to him for mercy. Zeus sends Poseidon and Athena to jolt him with power so he can stand up to Xanthus. Xanthus summoned his brother Simon to assist. Again Xanthus throws a bolt of electricity at Achilles but Hera intercepts it. She summons her son, Hephaestus to battle Xanthus. This triggers other gods to start fighting again as the earth roars with another god battle and Zeus just watches on with amusement. He loves to see the gods fight each other. Ares charges at Athena who strikes back a powerful blow from her hand. Aphrodite rushes down to help him up and leads him away from the fighting, but Hera sees her and calls to Athena to go after her. Athena pounces joyfully onto Aphrodite, pummeling her breasts with her fists. Aphrodite and Ares both collapse as Athena celebrates

her victory and is ready to strike anyone else that supports Troy. Poseidon and Apollo face off but do not battle. They greet each other and turn away. Artemis comes in and slaps her brother, Apollo, for letting Poseidon win. Apollo ignores her, but Hera flies into a rage. Hera boxes Athena all over with her weapons and Athena returns to Olympus to get comfort from Zeus who is just watching and laughing. Priam stands on top of the six foot scaffolding watching Achilles rise within the ranks. Apollo sticks around to assure Priam's safety. Andromache looks at Priam and then looks down at Achilles. She is worried about Hector's fate. Apollo follows Achilles to the front gate but not before he taunts him disguised as a mortal. He blows a mist so Achilles can't see. Finally, Achilles reaches the gates of Troy. The Trojans open the gate and many Trojans soldiers surround Achilles who doesn't care. He wants Hector, and with a war cry, shouts at the top of his lungs "HECTOR!" Hector appears on top of the six foot platform with Paris and Helen. He looks at his father, Priam, his wife, Andromache, and runs to them and cries. It is time for Hector to test the fate of the gods and see if the prophesy of his death is true. He readies himself for battle. The battle he has waited all of his life to fight. The song and scene play out at three minutes and twenty-one seconds.)

Book 22: The Death of Hector

("Four Sticks" by Led Zeppelin plays in the background as the exhausted Trojans sink back into their castle on the four foot scaffolding as the Greek army advances. Achilles leads the Greeks straight towards the gates.

Priam watches Achilles as he gets closer to the gate. Priam hugs his son and hands him a spear, a sword and a shield. He hugs his son to say goodbye as he senses Achilles will kill him. Hector kisses Andromache passionately, hugs Paris, and before he leaves, he gives a cold stare to Helen. Hector meets Achilles at the gate. As Achilles walks towards Hector with determination, Hector loses his nerve and begins to flee. Zeus watches on the back wall with great interest and sadness for Hector. Hector runs full speed around Troy three times with both armies watching as Achilles pursues him. Apollo tries to protect Hector but Zeus knows Hector must die to appease Thetis so he sends a thunderbolt down as a warning not to interfere. Athena comes down and tells Achilles to stay where he is and persuades Hector to fight. Athena, who makes it look like she is going to take on Achilles with Hector, but when the battle begins she leaves Hector's side. Hector steps forward to fight. Achilles comes at Hector with a spear. Hector retaliates but his spear bounces off Achilles' mighty shield. They share blow for blow on each others' shield with their swords. Hector lunges at Achilles, and in return, Achilles stabs Hector and cuts his throat. The Greeks cheer until Achilles silences them. He helps Hector to the ground as Hector dies at Achilles' feet. Achilles takes Hectors shield and weapons and holds them over his head for a great Greek cheer and war cry. Achilles walks over to Apollo and spits on him. He then ties up Hector's legs to a rope and drags him around the stage by his legs. Before he drags the body, the Greeks came over by Hectors dead body and kick and stab it. Priam is furious at this disrespect. Paris starts down to take on Achilles. Priam slaps Paris to the ground in great sorrow and pain. He grabs Helen and throws her to the ground. Seeing Achilles drag her husband, Andromache screams in horror. She cries in horrible distress. The Greeks decide to bury their dead and leave with Achilles pulling Hector's dead body. Andromache runs down to the battlefield and screams at the Greeks. She is holding Hectors child. Priam lies down on the ground, arms reached out and begs for his son's body, but the Greeks are long gone. Zeus looks sadly at Andromache. The song and scene play out at four minutes and forty-five seconds.)

Book 23: The Funeral of Patroclus

("Riders on the Storm" by the Doors plays in the background as the body of Patroclus is on the six foot scaffolding. The Greeks stand around it as Achilles lights pyres of fire around the body. He weeps and gives many heartfelt cries out for the death of his friend. Hector's body is below the six foot scaffolding and Aphrodite is busy cleaning Hector and protecting the body from being dragged across Troy and further harm. That night, the Greeks are all sleep and Iphigenia appears to Achilles, who cannot sleep, and sits over the body of Patroclus. He is weeping. Iphigenia comes to him and she points to Briseis who is on the four foot scaffolding. She kisses Achilles on the forehead. Achilles is in shock and knows not what to say. Athena appears and touches Patroclus who awakes from his dead state. He asks Achilles to burn him so his ashes can pass through the gates of the gods. Achilles joyfully accepts and tries to hug Patroclus but he is

lying back on the ground back in his dead state. Athena and Iphigenia leave as Iphigenia blows a final kiss to Achilles. Achilles cuts a lock from Patroculus' hair and offers it to Zeus who appears on the back wall. Achilles continues to pray to Zeus as Patroclus, body is burned. Achilles climbs down the six foot scaffolding and goes to the body of Hector. He bends down over the body and starts to weep as he embraces Hector. The Greeks stand in silence and in shock. Aphrodite stokes the back of Achilles' hair and comforts him. Some of the Greeks want to attack Achilles for his love of Hector but Agamemnon stops them. Achilles rises and presents Hector's weapons to Agamemnon. The two embrace and then stand over the body of Hector wondering if the war is over. The song and scene play out at seven minutes and twelve seconds.)

Book 24: Achilles and Priam

("Another Brick in the Wall" by Pink Floyd plays in the background as the Greek army is sleeping, except for Achilles who is dragging Hector's body around by a rope. He is not in the right frame of mind and is going mad. Apollo stands on the four foot platform protecting Hectors body from any more harm from the Greek army. Thetis appears as Zeus is seen watching on the back wall. Thetis holds Achilles who breaks down. Thetis looks up at Zeus who nods. Achilles must return Hectors body to Troy. On the other four foot scaffolding, Iris appears to King Priam who is mourning with Andromache, Helen, Paris and Hecuba. She takes Priam by the hand to leads him to Achilles tent but before she does, Paris gives him a bag of gold.

Priam slaps Paris and starts beating him as the gold comes pouring out of the bag. Andromache stops Priam as he breaks down on the ground for the loss of his son. Iris takes Priam to the camp but before they go they all pray to Zeus on the back wall and offer him libations so Hector's body can come home. Zeus motions Hermes to walk with Priam and protect him from the Greek army. Priam walks into the Greek camp, led by Iris and Hermes. None of the Greeks recognize him as he is in a cloak with his face concealed. Priam enters Achilles' tent on top of the four foot platform. When he enters, Briseis is with him and she runs to Priam and hugs him. Achilles rises. He is taken back that Priam would be so bold to come to the camp. Priam gets on his knees and hugs Achilles like a child and weeps for the return of his son. Achilles becomes emotional and lifts the king to his feet and embraces him. They break the embrace and sit across from each other. Achilles gets up and starts to pace. He looks at Briseis who comes towards him. Thetis appears on the back wall and nods her head to Achilles. In an emotional state, Achilles pushes Briseis to Priam and waves them off to take Hector's body. Briseis tries to kiss Achilles but he turns his back on her. He turns to Priam and gestures and throws his weapon down to the ground. They will be at a truce until Hector is buried. Priam and Achilles shake hands. Priam leaves in the protection of Iris and Hermes. Briseis goes with Priam. She is devastated. Achilles goes to his knees and screams in agony. The war had taken over his soul. Hector's body returns to Troy with Cassandra who leads the procession of Trojans. They place it high on the six foot scaffolding as Andromache with Hector's baby kiss him and place two coins on his eyes. Finally she pours libations on his body as she weeps uncontrollably and is inconsolable. Helen, Paris, Priam, and Hecuba also mourn around the body that is lit by the pyres. Hector, hero of Troy, is finally laid to rest. Paris crosses to the edge of the six foot platform and stares across the stage at Achilles. The song and scene play out at five minutes and forty-three seconds.)

The Trojan Horse

("We Are the Champions" by Queen plays in the background as Achilles is back killing Trojans left and right, especially the new Trojan king and queen. As Achilles fights Paris from on top of the six foot scaffolding, he takes aim with his bow and arrow to Achilles' weakest spot, his heel. Apollo, in mortal form, guides the arrow. It strikes Achilles. He is mortally wounded. Achilles see's Iphigenia in the distance. He reaches for her. She will be waiting for him on the other side. Briseis comes running and tries to help Achilles. They shared one last kiss. As they do, a spear is pierced through Briseis by a laughing Cassandra. Behind Cassandra is Agamemnon who kisses Cassandra passionately and drives Paris' arrow into Achilles even further until he is dead. Giant Ajax then picks up Achilles' body and protects it from the Trojans. Priam watches from above with Paris and embraces his son. They take Achilles back to the Greek base. Giant Ajax takes Achilles' weapons and armor for himself while Odysseus fights him for it. Giant Ajax, not willing to give up the weapon and armor, threatens Odysseus who stabs Giant Ajax in the heart and kills

him and takes Achilles' weapons and armor to Achilles son, Neoptolemus. Odysseus and Diomades sneak into the Trojan army and kill Paris and kidnap Helen. She is brought to Menelaus who almost tortures her to death. They then create a wooden horse from the six foot scaffolding to honor Athena who appears on the back wall. The Greek army hides in the horse as it is rolled outside the Trojan gates. At first the Trojan are cautious until Cassandra appears and tells them it's a great omen and to accept the gift from the Greeks. The gates are open and the Trojans accept the gift with celebration and libation to the gods. As nightfall comes the Trojan celebrate with libations until they pass out. While every Trojan sleeps, a whistle blows to give the signal and the Greeks pour out of the horse led by Odysseus and Diomades. They are pitiless in their destruction of the city. They slaughter everyone. Neoptomeus slaughters Priam on the six foot scaffolding and takes Andromache as his own wife. She fights him, but he knocks her out and carries her off. Diomades, in great dramatic effect, throws Hector's one year old son, Astyanax, off the scaffolding to his death. Cassandra, who had already turned on the Trojans, passionately kisses Agamemnon. The only Trojan that escapes is Aeneas, son of Aphrodite, who she protects him with a force field and takes him far away. The Trojans are defeated. The war is over. The song and scene play out at three minutes.)

Epilogue: Going Home

("Voo Doo Child" by Jimmy Hendrix plays in the background. In a cloud of smoke from upstage center the Greeks line up on each side and Trojan bodies lie

everywhere. They drag the Trojan bodies downstage in a straight line. From center, Agamemnon, Menelaus, Odysseus and Diomades come walking downstage. They are bloody and wounded. Zeus appears on the back wall and is extremely angry that the Greeks have sacked Troy. Zeus punishes the Greeks. Agamemnon climbs the four foot scaffolding with Cassandra. Clytemnestra welcomes him home. He crosses to go into his palace and Clytemnestra and her lover, Aegisthus, stab him and Cassandra many times. After they are both dead Iphigenia appears with Artemis. Clytemnestra hugs her daughter who looks down at the dead bodies with a smile that resembles a smirk. On the other four foot platform, Odysseus is lost at sea for ten years as his scaffolding spins out of control and he collapses. On the center six foot scaffolding, Menelaus is kissing Helen passionately. When he is done kissing her she stabs him repeatedly and kills him. Helen, with a bloody knife, drops it to the ground with a smirk. Zeus appears with two glasses of libation. He joins his daughter. She gives her father a long stare. There is a long pause. They both start to laugh as they toast and drink together. They laugh for a very long time. It is a haunting laugh, one that lasts into the night. The laughter continues as the lights fade to black, and the play ends. The song and scene play out at five minutes and thirteen seconds. Suggested curtain call song is "For Those About to Rock, We Salute You" by ACDC. During curtain call, all Greeks, Trojans, and Gods come out at the same time standing on the three scaffolding for the curtain call. There should be no individual bows. Suggested post show music is "Who Are You" by The Who, "White Wedding" by Billy Idol, "Rock and Roll" by Led Zeppelin, "Bohemian Rhapsody" by Queen and "Whole Lotta Love" by Led Zeppelin.)

The Al-Mahmudiyah Incident

The Rape and Murder of Abeer Qassim Hamza al-Janabi

Characters:

Abeer Qassim Hamza al-Janabi: Young Muslim girl, 15

Soldier: Army Private Steven D. Green, 21

Time: 2008

SPECIAL NOTE ON SONGS AND RECORDINGS

For all performance songs, arrangements and recordings mentioned in this play that are protected by copyright, the permission of the copyright owners must be obtained; or other songs, arrangements and recordings in the public domain substituted.

The Al-Mahmudiyah Incident was first presented at Coffeyville Community College on May 2-4, 2007 at the Spencer/Rounds Performing Arts Theatre. The Director was Mark Frank. The production stage manager was James Hart .The cast was as follows:

Abeer Qassim Hamza al-Janabi:	Nicole Santorella
Private Steven Green:	Justin Wilson

AT RISE: *"For What It's Worth" by Buffalo Springfield plays before the play begins. On stage right is a chair in a spot of light where former U.S. Army Private. Steven Green, twenty-one, wearing a black Johnny Cash shirt and jeans sits in a chair, hand cuffed. On the other side of the stage is a prayer rug in a spot of light. Abeer Qassim Hamza al-Janabi dressed in a black sartorial hijab covering her body, face and head. She is kneeling on her prayer rug. A giant picture of the American flag is shown on the back wall. The two actors should face out to the audience during the play, and should never look at each other. The light goes faint on Abeer who continues to kneel with her head down. The lights remain on Private Steven Green who lights a cigarette.*

STEVEN GREEN: I went over there to Iraq because I wanted to kill people. Nobody takes this bony-faced twenty-one year old small town private from West Texas serious until I look right at people like yourself and start talkin about killing Iraqis without a care in the world. I could care less either way. The truth is, it wasn't all I thought it was cracked up to be. I mean, I thought killing somebody would be this life-changing experience. And then I did it, and I was like, 'All right, whatever.' *(He shrugs)* I shot a guy who wouldn't stop when we were out at a traffic checkpoint and it was like nothing. Over there, killing people is like squashing an ant. I mean, you kill somebody and it's like 'All right, let's go get some pizza.' I'd rather be there than at home where all I did was drink and get into fights with my family. Hell look at me, if a guy that drops out of the tenth grade and gets arrested for possession of alcohol can enlist in the Army, then they'll take anyone. By enlisting I was granted what the military calls, "a moral character waiver" for prior drug and alcohol related offenses that might have otherwise rejected me. They are so desperate to recruit anyone who will sign on the dotted line. Shit, I was honorably discharged from the military due to an, "antisocial personality disorder" but before the military was aware of my condition I was already training and fighting in Iraq, big mistake giving this "psychopath" a gun. *(Laughs)* Then all the shit went down in Mahmudiyah *(Laughs)* Lots of shit. *(Lights a smoke, takes a long pause)* Our unit, first Battalion, 502nd Infantry Regiment from Fort Campbell, Kentucky... we was in this town on the edge of the so called, "Triangle of Death" like for the last three years. It's labeled the "bloody center" of the Sunni-led insurgency. Its where a lot of my buddies suffered what the military calls "combat stress" because you see shit out there that will change you forever and you'll never be the same. Mahmudiyah is a place that brings about fear because it's considered by some to be on the front lines of the Iraq War. *(Pause)* The Iraq War, I thought it was over a long time ago. *(Laughs)* We go in March 2003 and shit, "Mission Accomplished" was shouted loud and proud by Bush on May 1st. So what the fuck are we still doing here four years later? I'll tell you what we're doing, killing insurgencies, dealing with guerilla warfare and a God damn civil war between the Sunni and Shiites. *(Pause, takes a long drag of his smoke)* Watch where you step now, you step on an IED, that's an improvised explosive device, and you're going home in a box. How many of our unit out of a thousand has died so far? I've lost count. Hell there's danger everywhere you turn, car bombs, mortar shells falling everyday, gunfire, rocket-propelled grenades and not enough armor or protection to fight it. Unequipped to fight, morale is shit, all of our personal shit burned, this is life in Iraq. I disagree with the war, but I support the troops, isn't that the saying of the day? I got to be there for a year and there ain't a damn thing I can do about it. I just wanted to go home alive. I don't give a damn about the whole Iraq thing. See, this war is different from all the ones that our fathers and grandfathers fought. Those wars were for something. This war is for nothing. I just got tired of people telling me what to do. Especially Americans, the Iraqis are cool. I don't give a shit if they all get waxed. We're out there getting attacked all the time and we're in trouble when somebody accidentally gets shot? Hell, we're always told if anyone looks like the enemy, shoot first, ask questions later, so fucking sue me. We're pawns for the fucking politicians, for people that don't give a shit about us and don't know anything about what it's like to be out here on the line. Maybe that's why all the shit went down in Mahmudiyah, because I stopped giving a shit. It was March 12, 2006. I remember it like it was yesterday. No sleep, no water, no nothin, but a hell of a lot of stress. *(Long drag of his smoke and a very awkward pause)* We saw her one day from the distance, a cute little teenage Iraqi girl working in the field next to her farm house. Young and hiding that beautiful virginal body under the Muslim garb they wear. A man's got needs you know when he's isolated. I mean you're in a country with thousands of US horny men with no pussy for miles around, even the women in our own brigade carry a knife with them in fear we'll rape then, so you tell me what we're supposed to do? I mean the animal kicks in and all he wants to do is fuck, you know... *(Long drag of smoke.)* I talked to another soldier over drinks discussed possibly raping the girl and he was cool with it, so we went to go visit her at her house and check it out. I had visited her many times before doing a routine check of her house and then lightly stroking my hand on her face. I think she liked it. The farm house was about two hundred yards from our traffic checkpoint twenty miles South of Baghdad, known as that "triangle of death" I told you about because of frequent attacks on soldiers there. Before going back to the farm house, we decided to drink more, get drunk, pissed drunk, and change into our black underwear, disguises or what we like to call our dark ninja suits so nobody would see us. We hit some golf balls, played some cards for awhile, grilled some chicken, and drank some Iraqi whisky mixed with energy drinks. For dessert, we popped some pills. What the hell would it hurt, we were horny, in and out, and nobody knows any better. Clockwork Orange, the old in and out. Who the hell cares, nobody really listens to the villagers' complaints anyway, even if we do it, nobody going to say a damn thing. Lots of this shit happens there you just never hear about it. So anyway, First Class Bryan Howard was left at the checkpoint to man the radio, while the four of us, Specialist James Barker, Private First Class Jessie Spielman, Sergeant Paul Cortez, and Sergeant Anthony Yribe planned the rape and headed to the farm house, armed with three M4 rifles and a shotgun, just in case we ran into trouble. With one of us guarding the door and stationed on the roof, we entered through the backyard. I covered my face with a brown t-shirt, the rest of them covered their faces with black masks. I grabbed an AK-47 rifle from the house and herded the girl's mother and father and a young girl who was I think was six or seven, in the bedroom. And then... *(Drag of smoke.)* I shot them...point blank in the head, each one of them. *(Laughs for a brief period.)* God damn did we surprise them. *(Still laughing)* You should have seen their faces. *(Pause)* While I was in the bedroom, Specialist Barker and Sergeant Cortez pushed the teenage girl to the floor, held her hands down while Sergeant Cortez lifted her dress and tore off her under garments. He raped her first, raped the shit out of her. I came out of the room as he was finishing and shouted, "I just killed them, all are dead!" Then the four of us gang raped the girl. I should say I raped her, the other three try to gang rape her but couldn't get erections because the bitch struggled so hard we couldn't get her fucking legs apart. She fought hard, struggling, screaming, sobbing... but I was hard as a rock and even though that little bitch was strong and tall, she was nice and tight just as I had hoped. When I finished, I grabbed her by the hair, lifted her head, put a pillow in front of it, and I fired two or three shots into her forehead, killing her. Practically blew her head off her shoulders. Specialist Barker got a lamp and poured kerosene on the girl. We soaked her in acrid-smelling flammable liquid and fueled the fire with blankets and left her in a pool of charred debris. We then torched the rest of the bodies to hide any evidence and got the hell out of there. We went back to our checkpoint in a hectic state, hyper, and celebrated by grilling more chicken, playing cards, drinking more whiskey, and burned our clothes with gasoline. Spielman threw his AK-47 used to kill the family in the canal. The plan worked, at least until members of our unit like Justin Watt, fucking whistle blower, began blabbing about the incident last month while they were going through stress counseling after two other soldiers of our platoon were captured at a checkpoint and beheaded by insurgents. They said it was payback for raping and killing the girl and her family. Army officials began investigating the day after hearing about the events in Mahmudiyah. I knew then, we were screwed. Now we have all been prosecuted for military crimes by our good ole U.S. government. Barker, that pussy, pleading guilty to raping that fourteen year old girl and helping to kill her family, he got life in prison with possibility of parole. He ratted us out crying like a baby on the stand to avoid the death penalty. *(Mocking Baker)* "I want the people of Iraq to know that I did not go there to do the terrible things that I did, I do not ask anyone to forgive me today." Give me a fucking break. Howard was sentenced to twenty-seven months in prison and dishonorably discharged for being an accessory to crime. Rape and murder charges were dropped due to his so called "limited role" in the crimes. According to him, he only overheard us planning the crime, but never participated. That's bullshit. *(Mocking Howard)* "If I could go back, I would not have let it happen in the first place. I definitely would have told somebody". Fucking liar testified the other soldiers weren't involved and that I was the only one crazy enough to do it. Spielman, who pleaded innocent got a hundred and ten years but he's got good lawyers who said he'd serve four years at the most and then probably get out on probation. All that idiot Yribe was charged with was making false statements about the incident and dereliction of duty. He got off easy, bastard. The rest of them are serving time in Fort Leavenworth. Yours truly, Private First Class, Steven Green, facing seventeen counts of rape and murder was spared the death penalty because the jury couldn't come to an agreement on a sentence for the so-called brutal crime. Big deal, I got life in prison with no chance of parole. I guess some jury members blamed the stress of war combat on my crime. Stress from war combat? *(Laughs)* You think? Did my family understand this? Fuck no. They didn't even show up for my trial, only my brother. No matter, I don't need them and at least I wasn't a pussy like Cortez, man, he caved, he caved bad. When they got him in front of the judge he wept like a baby and pleaded guilty to rape, conspiracy to rape, and four counts of murder as part of a plea deal to avoid the death penalty. He was sentenced to one hundred years in prison and was given a dishonorable discharge. Cortez even apologized for what we did, saying, *(mocking crying voice)* "I can't explain why I took part in such a horrible crime. I don't know why. I wish I hadn't. The lives of four innocent people were taken. I want to apologize for all of the pain and suffering I have caused the al-Janabi family." Man, fuck them. Shit, you got little Iraqi kids walking around as suicide bombers, can't be more than six, offering you a Pepsi and then blowing your ass up, got our buddies getting hung and beheaded and their bodies dragged through the streets of Baghdad and he can't explain why he took part in it? It's fucking war man, that's all it is, shit happens on the battle field and it's not pretty and it's not right but shit happens when you're stressed out in this hell called Iraq. *(Smokes his cigarette)* The Mahmudiyah Incident. *(He claps and laughs)* Now you know, bravo. *(Long pause, stares at audience)* Oh...I see you're now going to sit in judgment of me now and think of me as a sick twisted human being. *(Kicks his chair over and is angry)* where the fuck do you get off? What the hell are we doing in Iraq in the first place? Didn't the terrorists who attacked on 911 come from Saudi Arabia, you know Al Qaeda, Osama Bin Laden? Shouldn't we just stayed and hunted the Taliban in Afghanistan? Shit, they've pretty much taken over that country now. Weapons of Mass destruction? What the hell were we doing in Iraq? Where are they? So we invade a country, a president lies to the American people with false information to start a war to overthrow its dictator Saddam Hussein, and you want to put me on trial for killing an Iraqi girl? Now you tell me who the real terrorists are? What about Abu Ghraib Prison when our United States Military tortures Iraqi detainees? Soldiers went to jail for that shit but not Donald Rumsfield, son of a bitch gave the orders to torture. He's retired, sucking on marguerites in Florida now. What about the recovering soldiers who lost their arms, legs, and minds living in the shitty rat infested army hospitals at Walter Reid Army Medical Center? We can spend six hundred billion on a war and we can't even find a clean facility to put our wounded soldiers and you want to put me on trial? You're putting me on trial for murder for five Iraqis when over four thousand U.S. troops and counting, along with six hundred fifty-five thousand Iraqi citizens have been killed due to deception, manipulation, torture, retributions and cover-ups in the Iraq War by this administration of the United States of America? What I did happens everyday in Iraq and no one says a word. I guess that's war though for you. Innocent Iraqi's or terrorist Iraqi's, they all look the same and they gotta die. What's good for the goose isn't good for the gander, or some shit like that. Am I sorry for what I done to that girl? Naw, I ain't sorry, you ain't out there, you don't know what it's like and you never will. You go ahead and judge me but unless you're there seeing the shit I seen, the beheadings, the car bombs, the body parts, you got no right. You got no right. That girl that died... her family...its war man and shit happens and people die. Fuck it. (*His light goes out and up on Abeer. The American flag on the back wall is now the flag of Iraq. Arabic music plays. As she performs a ritualistic Islamic prayer on her prayer rug, the music fades out. She then speaks to the audience in broken English.*)

ABEER: When I woke from dream that morning there was still smell of burning plastic, inside our house, walls and ceilings were covered with soot at far right end of room. Under window sill, wall and part of floor were covered with thick layer of burned grease, and next to it, corner wall was stained with arc of spattered blood. I was lying there sprawled, dead in corner, my hair and pillow next to me consumed by fire, dressed pulled up to neck. In adjacent room, I see another blood-stained wall, my father was sitting there, his head slumped down. My mother was there by door, both of them swimming in blood. Their blood had spewed out of their bodies with such force that it flowed out from under door in room. And in middle of room was my five year old little sister. They all have been shot in head and there is blood everywhere. Their eyes are open; look on their faces is pure horror. I go back where my dead body lies. My uncle says that even disfigured I am still beautiful. I see my white gown was lifted to my neck when they raped me, I was turned on my face and lower part of my body was raised and my hands and feet are tied, one leg lifted and my other leg bent. Blood was still flowing from between my legs even a quarter hour after my death and in spite of the intensity of the fire in the room. My body is still smoldering from fire they put out. It burned my chest, my hair, and all flesh on my face. An American put piece of clothe over my privates and said prayer over me when they retrieved our dead bodies. These were the Americans I thought existed, I was wrong. There were a number of one inch-wide bullet holes in floor tiles. I never knew day I laid eyes on the Americans it would soon be my last days on earth. When they came by our farm house I thought they were just going to do another walk-through of our house. They did that a lot, the Americans went to many villagers' houses to look for insurgents hiding or being hidden by villagers. The Americans were dressed in all black that day and it reminded me of monsters my father would tell me stories about when I was younger. At first they approached us being really friendly and then all of sudden, they got angry with us, and they grabbed us and took my father, mother, and little sister into bedroom. I heard mother crying. My little sister was too young to know what was happening but was filled with fear. My father knew it would be last time he would look at me. He just stared at me and I could tell by his eyes this meant goodbye. It was last time I would look at his face. I never saw him cry until this moment. In room I was in, the Americans surrounded me into one of the corners of room; one soldier pushed me to floor, lifted my hijab and ripped my undergarments off me. I looked into his eyes as he raped me and he was smiling and laughing at other American soldiers in room. They were clapping and yelling. He looked me right in the eyes smiling, taking his index finger and running it down my cheek gently as he penetrated me. I could not feel pain because I was terrified. I just kept thinking of my parents and sister in other room. I wondered what was happening to them. When the second soldier took his turn with me I looked down and saw blood on him and blood between my legs and as he pulled my hair and head back. That's when I heard gun shots. I knew then my parents were dead… *(Crying, long pause)* A man came in from the bedroom and said… *(Hard to say, fighting back tears)* "I killed them, all are dead" and then he started to laugh. He pulled man off me and turned me over on my stomach. He smelled like alcohol and smoke. He…hurt me the worse, he was brutal with me. I felt him rip me open as he raped me. I felt more blood running down legs. He then struck me in head with sharp object knocking me unconscious and smothered me to death with pillow. After he finished, he lifted my head by my hair, put a pillow over my head, and shot me three times in back of head, then set my body on fire. The last thing I heard were men laughing and hollering like they were having celebration. What does America call it, life, liberty, and pursuit of happiness? Locals had not reported five-minute crime. People knew about my rape all along, but in tribes, if you can't do anything about it, better to shut your mouth. No one will say our daughter was raped because they can't do anything about it. If the Americans find out who told they might shoot villager and claim them as hostile insurgent. Honor and reputation are valued much more highly in Iraqi tribal society than property. Shame can only be wiped clean by blood and there is no worse shame for family than rape. I remember mother asking my uncle a week before incident if he could bring us to stay in his house. I told mother that Americans were harassing me as I came in and out of house. They also harassed me in field and would always touch me inappropriately. I felt so terrified and ashamed and feared for my life. Our neighbor, Omar Janabi tried to reassure my family, remove some of our fears; He told us American's would never do such thing as kill innocent civilians. He knew he was wrong when he reported, day we were killed, to hearing sound "like beating tin barrel with stick few times", and later saw four Americans leave house, one of whom carried two guns. The man who raped me could be heard saying, "That was awesome." As he left, Omar's mother claimed that she and her son went to our front door, shouting, asking if they required assistance, but received no reply. The boys, Muhammed and Ahmed, came home from school to find white smoke billowing from their house, blood and brains on the walls. In the front room, I was half nude and had been shot in the head. In the bedroom, bullet holes and red splatters peppered a corner. The right side of father's head had been blown out by a shotgun, and he lay in a thick pool of blood. The body of my mother looked broken. Little Hadeel had been killed, still clutching the stems of flowers from the garden, with a bullet through her right cheek. My two bothers stood outside the smoking building, holding hands and crying. Later they dropped out of school and "lost their futures." *(Long pause)* They labeled what happened to us "The Mahmudiyah Incident." *(Long pause)* I don't know why this happened to us. Why? America was land of free, home of brave but now my village call America land of war, home of hatred. *(Long pause)* My house is now shrine in the village of Mahmoudiyah, Southeast of Baghdad. My mother, Fakhriyah Taha Muhsin, age thirty-four, killed by five bullets in abdomen and lower abdomen; My father, Qasim Hamza Raheem, age forty-five, whose head was "smashed" by four bullets; My sister, Hadeel Qasim Hamza, age seven , shot in head and shoulders, and me, Abeer Qasim Hamza age fifteen, shot in head and burned beyond recognition. The only picture left of me is one that appeared on my Iraqi ID card, black and white passport sized photograph taken when I was maybe eight or nine, I have black hair, round face and big black eyes. (*Her photo appears on the back wall*)

They say those American men will die for what they did to me and my family. I have little faith in an American court martial. They should hand over the criminals to us, to Iraqi court, we don't trust their justice, and they should be tried in Iraq and be executed here, like Saddam. A murder can be solved in tribal council by money, but rape can only be solved by killing perpetrator. As tribe, we, Janabis, don't recognize their court. The crime will not be forgotten until criminal pays with his life. They will not stand for crime of rape which is something shameful in our tradition, thus there will be no funeral for me. The Qur'an, our holy book teaches us, "The life for the life, and the eye for the eye and the nose for the nose and the ear for the ear and the tooth for the tooth and for wounds retaliation". Those American soldiers should be turned over to my remaining family and neighbors for stoning that would be justice. For my prayers I give myself up to Allah. Our Islamic heaven is described in the Qur'an as physical pleasures, paradise as place of joy and bliss. Heaven is most often described as cool garden with running streams of unlimited food and drink. I wait here now, alone, in dark, looking for my family, my mother, father, little sister and Mohammed, God's final prophet. It is quiet. No more war, no more pain, no more breath, no more world. I wait to see eternal paradise. I wait for it, but when I die there is nothing but darkness and I have no knowledge, I'm dead, just a wandering lost voice. People will read about this crime. And they will forget about it next day. I am memory from others' voices, this burned-out corpse that used to be fifteen year old girl who never fired bullets or lobbed mortars. A memory of what I was, what became of me, and what I no longer am. I am forgotten crime. I am the Mahmudiyah Incident.

STEVEN GREEN: (*Stands up and salutes*)
I pledge allegiance to the flag
Of the Unites States of America
And to the Republic
For which it stands
One nation
Under God
With liberty
And justice for all.
(*Pause*)
Wait for it... (*There are three gun shots. He laughs.*)
ABEER: The sound of America.
STEVEN GREEN: The sound of freedom.

STEVEN GREEN/ABEER: God help us. (*"Not Ready to Make Nice" by the Dixie Chicks plays in the background as the stage lights go black. Pictures of the five tried servicemen are showed on the back wall. along with President Bush, Vice President Cheney, Donald Rumsfield, Osama Bin Laden, a picture of 911 twin towers on fire, U.S. soldiers in Iraq, and the room where Abeer was found dead. There are many pictures of Steven Green in uniform, holding an assault rifle, and trial photos. The final picture is a picture of Abeer's passport picture when she was nine. The lights fade up on both spots. The actors come center, look at each other for the first time in the play, and then leave the stage. The play ends.*)

The Rainy Trails

Based off the book, The Trails to Coffeyville

By Dr. Dusty Delso and Dr. Don Woodburn

The Rainy Trails was originally presented at Coffeyville Community College on September 18-20, 2008 at the Spencer/Rounds Performing Arts Theatre. The production stage manager was Thorr Miller and Austin Whitney. The Director was Mark Frank. The cast is as follows:

Rainy	Sarah Graham
Ah-Man	Arielle Alan
Cletis	Justin Boateng
John	Josh Kirk
Ensemble	Anthony Mount
	Jimmy Petersen
	Adrian Lopez
	Randall Pike
	Chris Auten
	Garrett Iron
	Amanda Tharp
	Caitie Almond
	Kerri Davis
	Lyndsey Cranor
	Blake Ellis
	Alyscia Harris

Cast of Characters

Ah-Man
Rainy
Cletis
John
Actor 1
Actor 2
Actor 3
Actor 4
Actor 5
Time: The Present and Past

SPECIAL NOTE ON SONGS AND RECORDINGS

For all performance songs, arrangements and recordings mentioned in this play that are protected by copyright, the permission of the copyright owners must be obtained; or other songs, arrangements and recordings in the public domain substituted.

SPECIAL NOTE ON PICTURES USED IN THE PRODUCTION

Pictures on the back wall during the production should depict pictures of Native American Life. Later in the play pictures will depict the information that is recited by different characters monologues in the play.

AT RISE:

The stage is bare except for a trash can that has a fire in it. Downstage is an extension with dirt on it. A white wall is upstage used for pictures that will be projected on the back wall during the play. NOTE: Many of the monologues will be acted out by the ensemble actors in the play. The monologues will also be accompanied by music and pictures on the back wall. The play begins with a Native American montage in pictures of the last century. The song, "Hurt" by Christina Aguilera plays in the background during the montage.

Scene 1

(Lights come up and a group of teenagers stand around the fire that is burning in the trash can. The group of teenagers are drinking beer and holding up a trophy. A young girl watches them in the distance. One boy throws more sticks into the trashcan to build the fire up. They are laughing and fighting until a loud wind is heard and the fire in the trashcan goes out and the stage goes dark. Drums are heard in the distance that builds with intensity. When lights come up again, a woman appears and comes up slowly through the dirt mound unburying herself and walks through the smoke left from the smoldering fire. Thunder is heard. She walks into a spot of light downstage and sits. A voice echoes in the background, "Who are you?" It is heard again along with wind and echoes in the distance. The young girl appears and stands behind Ah-Man.)

AH-MAN: I am Ah-Man, I am here for you, you're very special and we need you. Come sit next to me and meet my friends. *(She reaches out her hands as the wind picks up. She speaks all around her. Pictures of the animals, and tree's she speaks to appear on the back wall and they change as she addresses them. Native drums continue to be heard in the background.)* Come forward squirrel, raccoon, and wolves and breathe the smoke that surrounds you. Enjoy it as you would your finest meal. Ah badger, what may I do for you? Yes, another council and I apologize for no prior notice. Yes, we will change the responsibility of the mouse, though a rodent, he is still our friend of nature. Do not backhand the badger bear, know your place. *(A chant of "no" is heard in the background and builds as does the wind and drums. Shouting)* Come trees and grasses with your shouts of defiance grub worms, and wild onions! *(Thunder)* Yes, I am afraid wolves, as you surround me in my fear for I know not who you are. I feel you think I can do better, isn't that not so elms and bluestems? Oh cedars, am I perfect as you cry? Cedars I feel the pain of your tore branches and limbs that have been tossed into the fire. The cedars are always in the middle of it-just like their cousins, the aloe, the cannibals, and the opium. Isn't that what you always say opossum and always on your nocturnal watch? *(The chanting of "no" builds as does the wind and sound of drums.)* Silence! *(The chant stops.)* I have made my decision. *(She blows from a whistle)* Tremble trees! Leave your dropping wolves and run away. *(She blows the whistle again.)* *(Two men rise from the dirt mound (Cletis and John) and collect droppings from*

Ah-Mah as they exit.) Remove and care for the Yoe-negs and the others, do not harm or disturb them. Use plants to keep them safe. We will return shortly. The bears and horses…, collect the young people and their unfinished belongings. Eagle; leave this young girl alone, I am sure she is the one. May the creator bless our selection? *(Lighting strikes as rain is heard in a down pour. Ah-Mah opens her arms to the girl revealing a beautiful blanket.)* It's time, you must come to me now or turn and run. Never return or speak of this place and what you have seen or black snakes will stare at you in your sleep for as long as you live. *(A black snake photo appears on the back wall as a hissing sound is heard.) (The girl walks confidently to Ah-Mah and turns her back to her. Ah-Mah wraps her arms around the girl encircling her with the blanket which glows as the sound of the rain is still heard. She holds the whistle in front of the girl's mouth. The girl blows the whistle a third time and the rain and lightning stops. Ah-Mah leads the girl to the dirt mound. She leans back around Rainy and falls back into the dirt and disappear. Three men appear. Their faces are painted with white with black geometric blocks and piercing. They surround the dirt mound and hold a deer skin by three corners and stand on the dirt mound with the skin over their head. As the skin hits the ground and then removed, we see grass on the dirt mound. The men exit as the lights go to black.)*

VOICES: *(In black out)* Could I share light on this if they dig me up? They always start with big tribes and it never ends does it. Why did he put the Yoe-negs in control? If he were a she that would never happen.

(Lights come up and Ah-Mah appears with the young girl, Rainy from the dirt mound. She is lying next to her holding her in her arms as the girl sleeps. A rooster is heard it is a new day.)

AH-MAN: This was our place, it will be again, but we always have to share. *(She looks at the girl.)* You are Rainy; you are talented and will learn quickly as the chosen do. The conditions are right again. We have a chance. Let our journey begin *(Ah-Mah falls asleep holding Rainy tight as the lights fade out.)*

Scene 2

(Pictures of the underworld are shown the back wall along with the title, "The Trail to the Underground: The Teachings of Ah-Mah". Rainy and Ah-Mah awake from their sleep. The lights have changed to a red wash on stage as they are now in the underworld.)

AH-MAN: So what would you like to do first?

RAINY: I'd kind of like to know where I am and what we're doing. I know I'm here for a reason; I'm just not quite sure what it is.

AH-MAN: We took the trail to the underground. You're in the land below right now. Our people believe there are seven cardinal directions, North, South, East, West, above, at, and below. The world above is ruled by the eagle. The world at, or ground level, is ruled by the deer, and the world below the surface is ruled by the snake. *(These pictures of the animals are seen on the back wall. A large black man enters with another man with blonde hair and he looks like a surfer.)*

CLETIS: Hi ladies, I brought you something to eat, I'm Cletis, and this is our friend, John.

JOHN: Have some sweet corn cakes made from our special recipe.

AH-MAN: Cletis and John will join us on our journey. They will provide the views of our friends, the African Americans and white man when we need them. *(Ah-Mah begins to teach Rainy as they eat the corn cakes. Various pictures of the Yoe-negs appear on the back wall. The ensemble of actors acts out the butchering and slaughter of the Native American during Ah-Mans monologue. The lights turn blue. "Adagio for Strings" by Samuel Barber plays in the distance.)* Yoe-negs, our word for the white man, only believe in the four directions of the "at" world. They refuse to acknowledge the above and below worlds that are primarily spirit worlds and make no sense to them. Please remember this when dealing with the Yoe-negs. It is a most important first lesson. As with any race of people, there are good individuals, and there are bad individuals. Through your heritage, you have been given the gift to discern who is good and who is bad. That is why you are the chosen one. Native women have this gift, and you should trust your instincts when you are talking with someone. Beware your attraction to others and use your gifts wisely. You may be our last hope. *(Light rise on Rainy only.)*The bad Yoe-negs are masters at taking something they like and converting, changing, or butchering it to fit their needs and desires. *(The bad Yoe-negs (ensemble) surround Rainy as if they are ready to kill her. Pictures on the back wall depict the butchering and slaughter of the Native Americans by the white man. The monologue builds in intensity with Native-American chant.)*They have no problem slaughtering and taking advantage of the young and helpless to feed their desires and needs. *(Rainy screams)* You will learn many lessons about this as we journey through your preparation. Many of the things they tell you will be lies or misunderstandings. Other things they tell you will be true from a good heart and will help you. Listen carefully, trust your instincts given to you by the creator, and beware the foam. We'll get to the foam later, but right now you need to know where you came from and what you need to do. *(More pictures appear on the back wall as well as the title, "The Trails to North America: Native American Stories of Origin". Pictures on the back wall accompany Ah-Man's monologue as well as an ensemble of actors who act out her monologue. Music by Natalie Merchant plays in the background.)*

AH-MAN: The Yoe-negs will tell you we came to the place called America from the North. When the Bering Strait froze over, we walked across and entered North America. Our cousins, who didn't mind the cold, stayed to the North and became known as Eskimos. Those of us who didn't like the cold continued South until the weather was bearable, and we could sustain ourselves. We settled in what is now known as the lower forty-eight states and lived happily for a long time, so they say.

RAINY: That's exactly the story we learned in school. They have evidence and everything to support what they say!

AH-MAN: *(Drums. Natives dance around Ah-Man during monologue.)* I know, but our ancestors tell us that we came from many directions. You must remember, not everything you hear is true. Some things are based on ideas that are incomplete or just dead wrong. Your ancestors tell us that some of us came from the North, like the snow, some of us came from the sky, like the locust, some of us came from the ground, like the ants, and some of us came from the water, like the minnows. There are even stories that a star woman fell to earth, and children appeared from her body when she broke open. *(This is acted out)* That is why there are so many different tribes with different characteristics today. We scattered in all directions when we hit the fertile grounds of North America. Some of us followed the buffalo, some of us followed the deer, some of us stayed by the water and fished, and some of us listened to the ground and went where we were told to go. My family said we came from a land surrounded by undrinkable water. It was warm there, and our skin became darker over time to handle the effects of the sun. Our skin was exposed to the sun most of the time. *(Pictures depict Natives on back wall as actors continue to act out Ah-Man's monologue.)* Life was good in our land. There was plenty to eat, we were very good at fishing, and we even invented the gig. There were no wars, as the undrinkable water protected us from our enemies. The seven original clans lived in harmony. Each of us knew our job and contributed for the good of all. One day the earth began to shake and tremble. *(Thunder, more pictures appear on the back wall.)* Eventually it broke open and began to sink into the undrinkable water. To save our existence, we sent out seven canoes of young people from the seven clans to ensure our survival. As the canoes left the island, it sank completely into the undrinkable water. Some Yoe-negs call this the lost city of Atlantis, but it does not matter. It was brought to an end by the creator like the land of the giant turtles so many years ago. The creator had a greater job for us to complete, and he forced us to move. It was not meant for us to live in seclusion any longer. It was our destiny to search and find a different place. Our canoes encountered a new land, and we traveled North for some time until the rain turned white. We now call this snow. At that point, the ground told us to turn right and continue. We would return later to this place, but now was not the time to stay. We continued to the right, or East, and crossed the big water. It was a mighty river over a mile wide in Yoe-Neg terms. It took great effort to cross the big water, but we made it and continued our journey. After a long, long travel, we encountered some mound builders and settled with them in what is now known as the Southeastern United States. *(More pictures on the back wall with the title: "The Mounds". Music by U2 plays in the background.)* The Yoe-negs believe the mounds are sacred burial grounds used to bury chiefs, elders, and sacred artifacts. The mounds are actually just the opposite. Some of the people who lived around us were so bad, that we would not put them back in the ground. We do not bury or place things into the earth that are evil or bad. When these evil people died, we took them and their belongings, threw them in a pile, and burned them. *(A flame is brought center.)* Over time, as more and more evil people and their belongings were thrown on the pile, a mound developed. When you dig into the mounds, you release the evil and bad spirits back into the world. *(Evil spirits crawl out of the dirt mound. Native drums are heard. They try to pull Rainy into the dirt mounds but Ah-Man sends them away with a shout of, "cry".)* That is why we do not allow anyone to dig into the mounds. They are not sacred; they are evil. That is a reason why there is evil present today and your ability to discern the good from the evil is so valuable. We lived with the mound builders and others peacefully for many years. The weather was good, there was plenty to eat, and the deer made for good hunting. Things were good in this land. Then it happened, the encounters that would change our lives forever, the Yoe-negs. *(The following monologue is acted out by Rainy and other ensemble actors along with pictures on the back wall and title: "The Trails of Foam: Explorers and Contact with the White Man". Various drum music plays in the background.)* Your great-grandmother and her friend were looking out over the undrinkable water when we were in the East; she was a young girl *(Rainy)* and just entering her prime. Life was good here. The sand lined the undrinkable water; the Smokey Mountains provided plenty to eat. Everything was in harmony. Our people were happy and content. We practiced our ceremonies and dances without interruption, and everyone knew their place. We were under the White Chief who leads during times of peace. The Red

Chief leads during times of war and was getting bored. There hadn't been a dispute or battle for some time. Some foam floated on top of the undrinkable water. It moved wherever the waves rolled and had a distinct smell you couldn't miss; sweet as refined sugar, and the presence of alcohol, like whiskey. After awhile the foam landed on the beach. It lay on the sand and began to move around. The foam liked the land. It was stable and didn't move like the water. Darkness was beginning to fall on the coastline, and the foam began to take the shape of a figure. Arms and legs emerged, and the figure became a man. He walked into the brush and forest lining the coast. After awhile the girls heard loud sounds like thunder. All the birds and animals scattered from the site of the loud sound. After awhile they could see smoke from the place where he entered the forest. They crept up where they could see reflections from a fire. The man was very light skinned with light, almost golden hair. *(John enters)* He had built a fire and killed two deer and a raccoon he was skinning to eat. He had something shiny in his hand he used to take the skin from the animals. He fashioned clothes and a waterproof pouch from the deer hides, and a hat from the raccoon. After he ate, he picked up his pouch, put the shiny thing in his belt, and picked up a long stick made with the same shiny material. He disappeared into the forest leaving the fire to burn itself out and the remainder of the deer and raccoon on top of the ground. There was an eerie sense in the air as night continued and a small moon climbed in the sky. He laughed as he walked away. The scent of sugar and whiskey trailed behind him. Things would never

276

quite be the same. The girls ran back to the village and told their mother what they observed. Mother listened patiently as the girls told their story. She fed them, told them to do their chores, and get to sleep. After they were asleep, Mother looked skyward at the small moon. The day the elders spoke of was here. Things would never be the same. Where one goes, many will follow. This was the first Yoe-Neg. It wouldn't be the last.

RAINY: The first Yoe-Neg.

*(Another title on the back wall: The Trails of Money: Merchants, Traders, the Abuse of Nature and the Origin of Disease. *Most of this monologue is accompanied with various pictures on the back wall and music by U2. It is again acted out by Rainy and other actors.)*

AH-MAN: You must remember, Rainy, there are consequences to any and all of your actions, if your intentions are selfish or bad, there are negative consequences and punishment for your actions. The punishment may be delayed, even to later generations, but the punishments and storms will come. Look at the consequences of abusing the earth and nature. It caused the origin of disease and eventually contributed to the removal of our people from the East. *(Various pictures of disease culture are shown on the back wall.)* Originally, Natives, plants and animals could talk to each other. We could control the winds and weather when needed, as long as we didn't abuse our power. After we met the Yoe-Neg traders and merchants, they loved the quality of our deer skins. The Yoe-negs crossed the undrinkable water in a place called Europe wanted our deer hides. The merchants and traders would trade us for many things to get our deer hides. They also provided us with things we wanted. We began to hunt and kill more and more deer until we were killing more than we could use, other than the hides. This was a problem for the plants and animals. The plants and animals called a council to discuss the issue. The meeting was led by the grub worm. The animals complained that the humans were killing too many animals and soon there would be no more of us, like the giant lizards and turtles of the previous worlds. Something had to be done. The hardheaded bear suggested killing the humans to solve the problem. *(The following is acted out by the ensemble of actors. Pictures of these animals appear on the back wall.)* "That would throw things out of balance," said the badger. "They have their place, too." "What do you know," grunted the bear, and he swung his great paw at the badger. He hit the badger, but did not kill him. The bear's claws broke the skin of the badger and caused large white stripes in the fur on his back when the wound healed. The badger has these white stripes on his back to this day. As the bear looked to find the badger and finish the job, his eyesight became extremely fuzzy, and he could no longer see the him. He could smell the badger, but not see him, and the bear has poor eyesight to this day. The grub laughed so hard at the bear that he fell on his side and couldn't get up. The grub continues to crawl and lay on his side to this day. "Killing the humans is too severe," said the grub. "We will cause diseases and curses to inflict the humans when they leave our carcasses on top of the ground to rot without burning or burying them. They will also die slow deaths when they bring the substances of our bodies to the surface before they return to the soil and dust. The substances are very powerful and release their great energy when burned. It produces desirable things that are unclean and do not rot when returned to the earth. Their medicine men will produce these dark harmful products and become very wealthy and powerful. This will be a sign of the beginning of the end and cause the Yoe-negs to turn on each other as they become more powerful and greedy." The humans have caused us no harm and have actually helped us," said the wheat and corn. "They are great to us too," chimed in the always hungry and fickle cotton. "They even use the animal carcasses to feed us when needed. They clear places for us to grow and bring water to us when we need it. We don't want to harm them. We will make medicine to combat your disease and show them how to use it. If they begin to abuse us, we'll stop talking to them and make poison instead of medicine." You obviously know what happened after that, we can no longer talk to the plants and animals, and the oil and coal brought to the surface for energy and products are causing permanent damage to the earth. We are responsible to protect and care for the earth. As more and more people inhabit the earth, we will contaminate it more and more until it will break, just like bacteria that infest a carcass and cause it to completely disintegrate back to earth. The problem is many of the things we are making and bringing to the surface will not disintegrate, even when we put them back in the earth. Just remember, if your intentions are for your own gain, someone or something will suffer or perish. If your intentions are to help, you know it will help, and everyone comes together willfully to do the work, someone or something will flourish. Beware the Yoe-negs who make and alter things for their own gain. Look what they do to our flowing waters. This is dangerous, and the earth will give us signs from time to time that we are doing too much, just like the animals did years ago when they stopped talking to us. If they trust you, they will talk to you again. Trust your instincts when you make decisions. Your instincts will guide you and are why you were chosen. *(Various pictures are seen on the back wall and the title: "The Trails of Jesus: Pilgrims, Missionaries and a New Way of Life." Again the following monologue is acted out by the ensemble. "I went Down to the River and Prayed" from Oh Brother How Are Though plays in the background.)* Great-grandmother spoke of a meeting with some light-skinned people who lived to the North near the undrinkable water. They wore dark clothes and were very weak. Some hunters discovered them during a long hunt. A party that included great-grandmother was sent to meet with the light-skinned people. The party took skins and food to the meeting. Many in the camp had died. There was nothing to eat, and it was beginning to turn cold. The party fed and cared for the people. They were greatly appreciative of the efforts. We taught them how to hunt, farm and use a gig to catch fish. They began to recover and never forgot what we did for them. Each year during the fall harvests, we met with them and had a large meal to celebrate our coexistence together. Looking back on it, it may have been best to let them die. It changed our way of life. They sent people to live with us. They called them missionaries. They spoke of a great white man named Jesus who died for our sins and shortcomings. He was the Messiah and came to save all people, including the Indians. This was foreign to us. Our ceremonies and dances were how we celebrated our life with the creator. The smoke from the sacred fire of our ceremonies carried our prayers to the creator as we chanted and danced. Why would the creator send a white man to save the Native people? This didn't make sense, but we allowed them to stay. The missionaries taught us many things that were good, and they were caring people. Many of our people converted and adopted their life ways. We believe you are responsible for what you do and there are consequences that you must endure when you offend or hurt someone. This is your destiny. We obtained forgiveness through ceremony like the Green Corn Festival. The festival would begin with our fire keepers and medicine people. They would prepare the sacred fire with logs in all four cardinal directions. The medicine people would prepare the black drink and medicine to cleanse us on the inside. We do not share our medicine with outsiders. It is for us only. New clothes were also made before the festival and ceremonies begin. We start the ceremonies with stickball and dancing. The festival was a time of forgiveness, renewal and purification. Only those in the village who were willing to forgive others could participate in the Green Corn Festival. All the possessions, including clothes, were burned to purify the dwellings. If you continue to keep things too long, they become contaminated and harmful, just like too many bacteria in a carcass. Stickball, going to water, and scratching ceremonies purified the outside of the body. Fasting, drinking the black drink, throwing up, and asking others for forgiveness of transgressions purified the inside physical and spiritual body. *(The ceremony is acted out by the ensemble actors and Rainy.)* We did not want outsiders watching our ceremonies. We are weak and vulnerable from fasting and taking the black drink during the ceremonies. We need time to recover and come back even stronger. After four days of stickball, dancing, ceremonies, and feasting, everyone took their new clothes and fire from the ceremonial fire back to their longhouses for cooking and warmth. The missionaries taught us about marriage where a woman lived with one man and raised a family with him. This is not how we did things. We do not have words for husband and wife, only "sweetheart". It was not uncommon for women to have children with three or four different men. We believed it strengthened the bloodlines. When a woman was finished with a man, she would wrap all his belongings in a deer skin and hang it on the porch. That was his sign to leave when he returned from war or hunting. It was a matriarchal society that worked very well. The woman's brothers, the uncles, were responsible for helping raise the children. But we thought marriage was a good thing and adopted it over time. Many of us converted to Jesus and Christianity after living with the missionaries. This even caused a split in the ceremonial grounds over time. We always take and use what works as long as it doesn't damage others and is good for us. *(More pictures are seen on the back wall and the title, " The Trail of Evil: The White Rattlesnake; You Are Who You Are." The story is acted out by Rainy and Cletis. Music from the Omen, "Dies Iries" plays in the background.)* My grandmother told me this story long ago when I was a little girl, she said it was the most important story you could learn when you deal with people. Be careful, and make your decisions wisely. It is an extremely important first step to becoming a beloved woman. A young Indian boy *(Rainy)* was walking in the mountains hunting deer. It was cold and almost winter as he moved quietly through the woods. He could hear something ahead of him, but couldn't see what it was. The cloudy mist of the Smokey Mountains made it hard to see clearly through the dense vegetation. Rays of sun hit the floor of the forest, but he could still see his breath as the cool air opened his nose. He heard the sound again coming from the undergrowth surrounding a huge oak tree. It sounded like a very faint rattle. He moved back the vegetation and discovered a rattlesnake *(Cletis)* barely moving. This was no ordinary rattlesnake. He never saw a snake like this before. It was completely white with piercing blue eyes. It was as long as his arm, but very thin. The snake looked up at him and spoke to the boy.

CLETIS (SNAKE): I am going to die. Some hunters saw me even though I am white, and I had to hide from them to avoid being killed. It took so long to stay away from them, I couldn't return to my home in the underground. It began to turn cold, and I began to move slower and slower. We are required to return to the underground before the rain turns white from the cold and rest until the grass returns in the spring. It is so cold now; I can't find my way to my home. Can you help me?

AH-MAN: The boy picked up the snake and carried him back to his longhouse. The dirt-dauber wasp showed us how to build a shelter from sticks, grass, and mud, and they used this method for many years to build a home. Sometimes the houses were big enough for more than one family to live in. During the winter, the family would move to a smaller house that was easier to keep warm until spring returned. His brothers, who followed the buffalo on the Great Plains, made their shelter from poles and skins. It had a hole in the top to allow the smoke from fires built in the center of the structure to escape. The brothers who lived on the West side of the big water had to follow the buffalo herds and move often as the buffalo moved to new pasture. Not all Indians lived in moveable structures made of poles and skins like many Yoe-negs believe. The boy's family was moving to the winter house, and the boy placed the white rattlesnake in the summer house for the winter. He would bring coals from the winter house fire to keep the snake warm, and he piled skins on top of him to hold in the heat. When he hunted, he would bring back mice for the snake to eat. As he ate, the snake began to grow and get strong. Before long, the snake grew large enough to eat rabbits. He grew as big around as the boy's leg. They would wrestle and play and tell stories in the evening after the boy returned from hunting and doing his work. The snake told wonderful stories of all the things he did, places he conquered, and people he had killed, including a woman. She was smart, and he had to trick her and her husband using an apple, but they were stupid and it worked. Sometimes it takes awhile, but he could always figure out a way to get what he wanted. The boy listened to the snake in amazement. His rattle began to grow and was hypnotic when the snake would shake it as he told his stories of conquest and power. The snake continued to grow, and it began to turn warm. The woods and grasses were waking up. Young animals were out with their parents learning where to eat and play, and it was about time for the family to move back into the summer longhouse. By this time, the snake was larger than the boy and needed large animals like beaver and wolves to eat. The boy was amazed at the snake's eyes when he would eat. The snake would enter a trance state and strike his prey with lightning speed before he ate them. The snake savored the meal for hours after eating it telling the boy to bring him more after the feeling passed. If he didn't eat, he would convulse and curl up in pain. One day the boy returned with another meal, but something wasn't right. It was growing warmer as the spring season emerged, and the boy was sweating from hunting and fishing. When he entered the longhouse, the snake was curled up in the corner of the house ready to strike. His rattle sounded louder than normal, and there was something quite different in the snake's eyes as he watched the boy place the beaver in front of him. As the boy moved away from the beaver, the snake struck him on the arm. His fangs entered the boy's veins, and the venom caught fire as it moved into the bloodstream and moved slowly toward the boy's heart.

RAINY: What happened? Why would you bite me? I took care of you and helped you when you certainly would have died. I did everything you asked and made you strong. Why would you kill me?

CLETIS: Because, as his rattle played on in the background, you knew I was a rattlesnake when you picked me up. It's my nature, and just like the leopard can't change his spots, we can't change who we are. *(The story continues to be acted out by Rainy and Cletis.)*

AH-MAN: The snake coiled and prepared to strike again. With all the strength he had left, the boy raised an arrow he had in his hand toward the snake's head as he began to strike. The arrowhead passed between the snake's fangs and cut his tongue down the middle as the snake bit the boy in the neck killing him instantly. Snake's tongues are still forked to this day. The snake cursed and fought with the boy's body until he freed himself from him. He ate the boy and began to convulse violently. Arms burst from his sides, and his tail separated into two legs. He began to take on a human form with white skin. You could see the blue veins running through his arms. The snake stood up and fashioned clothes out of the skins from the floor of the longhouse. He made a hat with a wide brim to protect his fair skin from the summer sun. He could hear movement and someone calling for the boy. The snake ran from the longhouse knocking off his new hat as he passed through the door and into the woods. You could hear his rattle and laugh fade with each step as he ran farther and farther into the woods. He was sure he would return to this place someday. There were other things here that were useful to him. He would return, perhaps as a man of war or politician. The boy's uncle, (John) stepped into the longhouse and looked around. He shook his head as he saw the evidence that the boy used the place as a playhouse. He picked up the hat with the wide brim and put it on. It fit nicely and would make it much easier to see on a bright spring day. The uncle smiled to himself and returned to the others.

JOHN: Hey, how you like my new hat I made? Want to make you one?

RAINY: Tell me more of your grandmother! Tell me more!

AH-MAN: She was wonderful; she had a soft, confident voice. You always knew to listen when she talked. I've never known of her words to be false. She never gossiped about others and always found the best in someone. She told me you could always tell who someone was by their actions, not their words. It was simple, but not easy to do. *(Various pictures and another title on the back wall, "The Trails Where We Cried: Our Lands to the East and Removal." Music by Natalie Merchant plays in the background.)* We never intended to own parts of the earth. That is a foreign concept to us. We have always worked together in the spirit of Gah-Doo-Gee *(Normally spelled Ga-du-gi phonetically.)* Everyone worked together to provide what we needed. There was not a need for competition and owning land. Owning land and competition

changes the way we live. It causes people to become
selfish, and someone must lose. This is not how the
creator made us. We were destined to struggle in this
system. Grandmother talked of our time in the East
and how we arrived in Indian Territory to the West of
the big water. More and more Yoe-negs came to our
lands and settled here. They established trading with
other Yoe-negs across the undrinkable water, and our
deer skins were legendary. As they developed more
and more things to sell and trade, they moved closer
and closer to us and where we lived. The place we
inhabited to the East became more valuable, and they
needed the land to produce more and more goods
to sell and trade. Our lives were based on hunting,
fishing, and gathering only what we needed, not on
additional surplus to be sold for money and additional
things we wanted that we couldn't produce. It finally
got to the point that the Yoe-negs talked of a place to
the West of the big water where there were more deer,
fish, and trees than where we lived in the East. When
we moved there, they promised no one would bother us
again. It would be ours, and we could use it however
we wanted to use it. Some of us agreed and left our
lands for the new place. Some of us refused to leave
and were gathered into stockades. We became sick in
such a small space. Many of us died there. Others of
us fled to the mountains and hid. They never found
them, and their ancestors now live in part of the lands
to the East, but it is nothing like it originally was. They
forced the rest of us to leave, and soldiers escorted us
to the new lands. A fourth of us died before we reached
the new lands. Something was wrong, but what could

we do. *(Pictures appear on the back wall along with the title, "The Shattering Trail of Allotment: Survive, Adapt, Prosper, Excel." Bob Dylan music plays in the background, "How Does It Feel?" The monologue is acted out by actors.)* Our journey to the new lands is known as the Trail of Tears. It was a terrible time in our history, but the worst was yet to come. We made it to the new lands. It was tough, but we made it. When we arrived, it was as they said. The water was good; we could hunt, fish, gather and farm, and we set about building a new life there. We are masters at the process of survive, adapt, prosper and excel. We have shown repeatedly that we can overcome adversity and tragedy and come back better than we were. Once we established ourselves, the first buildings we built in our new home were the supreme court building and the male and female seminary buildings. The law and education are very important to us even to this day. Everyone had a home, we were literate in our language, and the white children even attended our schools. We allowed them to attend our schools as long as they didn't slow us down. One of the Yoe-Neg leaders came down to see us. His name was Senator Dawes. *(Played by John)* He told his people that we were doing fine, but we had come as far as we could go because we own our land in common. He said each of us needed to own his own land so we would strive to be better than our neighbor. The competition and free enterprise would force us to be much better than we currently were. This would help us make progress. So they cut up our lands and gave every family an equal share. They called this an allotment. Many of us sold our allotments and soon had no way to support ourselves. We did not know how to use and make money for things. When we needed something, we simply hunted, fished, gathered, farmed or asked someone for it. Using paper with faces on it to get things didn't make sense to us. Before long, most of us lost our original lands. This was a very dark day for us and changed our life ways forever. But as we always do, it was time to survive, adapt, prosper and excel. We're still doing this to this day. Some of us have adapted, a few of us have prospered and excelled, others have not and still struggle. Cletis, it's time to tell Rainy about your people. *(Ah man sits exhausted as Cletis gets up.)*

Scene 3

(African pictures on the back wall along with the title, "The Trails from the Chains: Cletis and the African Americans". "Worlds Apart" from the musical, Big River, plays in the background.)

Cletis: It's not a great mystery how we got to America. The Yoe-negs, as you call them, greatly changed our lives too, some for the better, some for the worse. Hunted us down and gathered us like cattle to work for him, gathered us up in our home of Africa, chained us in a boat, and sailed us across the undrinkable water, as you say. When we got here, they sold us to the folks in the South, and we worked their fields and plantations for them. Native Americans even bought some of us. We were no more than animals to be domesticated for their cause. Even selectively bred us for awhile and now wonder why many of us are so big, strong and fast. Its simple genetics they don't want to talk about, and now they use needles to try to keep up." *(Pictures on the back wall depicting slavery times and the title appears," The Trails from the Plantations: Life after Slavery".)* Slavery was very tough on us for a long time, till Mr. Lincoln set us free. Course the Yoe-negs killed him too while he was watching a play in Washington. Had to be that white snake you were talking about that killed the boy. After we won our freedom from slavery in the war, we had no place to go. The landowners, who took the land from the Native Americans, made life worse on us than it was before we were free through sharecropping. Many of us left the South and migrated to Texas, but we found the same chains of sharecropping there. So we packed up again and followed Paul Davis and his family North through Indian Territory and into Kansas. The word was African Americans were accepted in Kansas. We arrived in Burlington, Kansas, but we weren't accepted there. So we pushed on and were just about to drop when we found someone to help us. His name was Daniel Votaw, and he helped us settle in Montgomery County, Kansas, on the outskirts of Coffeyville." *(Pictures appear on the back wall of African American struggles and title, "The Trails to Acceptance: Our Home in Coffeyville.")* We had it good in Coffeyville. People here took us in and made us feel welcome when many other places turned us away. We set up our farms and began our new lives. The work was hard, but over time we made our way and were accepted by the people of Coffeyville. We had a great colony until the floods came, and we had to move. Many of us moved to town, and our families live there to this day. We established churches and our children went to school right alongside the white children. We had our problems with riots based on race, but we worked them out. Just like anything else, you have to keep an eye on it or it can get out of hand." *(More African American pictures appear on the back wall and title, "Our Talents and Passions: The Discovery of Our Music." James Brown's, "I Feel Good", plays in the background.)* See, they take what they like and switch it around to fit their needs. He started listening to us sing and make music when we were in the fields and in the evening time and liked what he heard. Started tapping his foot and soon, just like us, the day seemed shorter, and we'd get more done. There was rhythm to our hands and more purpose when we worked. We enjoyed what we were doing and banded together, even if it was for him. Took some years, but he figured out how to make money with it. Happened right by that big water you talk about. Let's go see it. Some of our history is on the banks of the big water, just like yours. *(Cletis takes Ah-Man and Rainy's hands, and forms a circle. He begins to dance, as everyone else moves with him. They all move faster and faster as Cletis speeds up the tempo. His feet keep perfect time as Ah-man, Rainy, and John move around the circle. Suddenly there is a great flash and thunder as the stage goes black and then lights go up again and the four of them are transported to Memphis, to a place called Sun Studios, that has a guitar on the sign. A young man is singing next to another man that's excited and tries to contain his composure. Pictures of Elvis appear on the back wall as the song, "That's All Right Mama" plays in the background.)* That's Elvis and Sam Perkins, Elvis is singing, "That's Alright Mama," his first big hit. It's based on the blues and songs he heard growing up in Tupelo, Mississippi. He picked up on our music and grew to love it. Perkins knew he needed someone white man who played our music to cross over into white America. He called the new sound rock and roll. It caught on like wildfire 'cause Elvis loved the music. He sang and performed with the same passion we did when we sang our music." *(They walked through the wall and entered Beale Street. Rainy is singing the Elvis song to herself)* Here's where it all began to cross over. We played here all night long, and the Yoenegs took notice. The beats and rhythms permeated their minds as we poured out our hearts and souls through our instruments and songs. We were making a presence, but we needed a white man who knew our music to cross over. Elvis did that. Lord knows it worked, look at his house. *(Pictures appear on the back wall of Elvis' Graceland)* Elvis's Graceland is his trophy house in the back yard. The halls and walls are filled with gold and platinum records and awards Elvis earned during his career. Elvis is a tribute to our music and our influence in the entertainment industry. He was the spark, and we eventually branched off into our own pure music which now includes soul, rap and hip-hop. You can't kill it even if you kill us. We showed that when the white rattlesnake struck one of our best right here in Memphis. *(Rap music plays. Martin Luther King pictures appear on the back wall along with music from Marvin Gaye's, "What's Going On" plays in the background and title, "Martin Luther King*

Jr. and the White Rattlesnake." The four pass back through the walls of Graceland and headed back to downtown Memphis toward the Mississippi River. They are standing in front of the Lorraine Motel Memorial to Dr. Martin Luther King, Jr. at the National Civil Rights Museum built on the site of Dr. King's assassination. The following scene is acted out by the ensemble of actors. Cletis plays Dr. King, John plays James Earl Ray, and Rainy is the black snake)

AH-MAN: A permanent wreath marks the spot where James Earl Ray shot him in the back with a high-powered rifle. Across the street from the Lorraine in a cheap apartment, the bathroom window gave a clear view of the balcony where Dr. King stood. Fumes began to emerge from the drain of the bathtub as James Earl Ray stood there with Dr. King in the scope of his rifle. The white rattlesnake emerged from the drain and entered Ray's body. Fangs began to emerge from Ray's canine teeth, and his eyes had the same crazed expression as the snake in the longhouse years ago. A strong rattle pierced the silence in the apartment. Ray pulled the trigger, and Dr. King crumpled to the cement of the balcony on the second floor. As frantic efforts to save Dr. King proved futile, a white sixty-five Ford Mustang with blood red interior, pulled away from the apartment across the street as Ray made his getaway. The damage was done; the snake struck again.

CLETIS: You can kill the man, but you can't kill the spirit, sooner or later what is just and right will always emerge. *(Dalton Gang pictures appear on the back wall and title, "The Trails to Destruction: Gangs and the Decline of Our Culture." Coffeyville Dalton Gang song plays by Rodney Lay.)* Our strength has always been our willingness to band together behind a common cause. We didn't fragment into many different tribes and clans like our friends the Native Americans. When we protested, we protested as one voice and one people. Instead of wanting to be left alone, we welcomed joining the white man and learning his game. This has always been our strength. We take our talents and apply them to the white world. Things are beginning to change. Our young people are giving up on the white man's ways and developing their own society based on lawlessness, violence and exclusion. The gang era is turning us away from our strength and turning us on ourselves. Instead of being killed and oppressed by the white man, we are killing each other over small pieces of turf in our own neighborhoods. White man won't even go in there anymore. Doesn't care that much; we're doing what he wants anyway. You'll know when it's out of hand. He'll send the soldiers in to calm it back down. Gives him something to do, and he can pay himself to do it. Our strength lies in our churches. The wise women who keep their families together against insurmountable odds are one of the keys to our society. These ladies are dedicated to preserving and teaching our children how to live in harmony instead of violence. They will revive us just like the churches did at Coffeyville when the cowboys took over. **(***Cletis sits down and eats his corn cake.***)**

Scene 4

(Pictures appear on the back wall and title," The Trails of the Yoe-negs: John, the White Man, and the Search for Gold." John rises from his spot by the fire. Music is heard by U2.)

JOHN: We've had a checkered past in Coffeyville and our relations with the Native Americans and African Americans. Like anything else, some is good, some is bad. The Native Americans originally thought some of us, like the great explorer DeSoto, were Gods. When DeSoto was looking for gold in the South, many Native Americans traveled West with him and his army in search of gold and the Promised Land. When they approached the big water you speak of, DeSoto became very sick. He died when they reached present-day Memphis. We had to sneak his body away from the party and bury him in the big water to retain his status as a God. There are special powers around the big water at Memphis. Just like the discovery of the African American music and invention of rock and roll, there are markers of the white man's relationship with the Native Americans there, too. Look at the structures around the bridge linking the East with the West. *(John lights a fire and begins to fan the flames. He holds his hat out, and an image projects onto the smoke as it rises above the flames.)* You could see the famous bridge linking Arkansas and Tennessee. It stands majestically as a tribute to the progress of industrialism. *(Egyptian pictures appear on the back wall and title, "The Pyramids." Egyptian music plays in the background.*) Look to the North of the bridge, Rainy. What do you see?

RAINY: A pyramid?

JOHN: That's right. The pyramid is a lasting symbol of another great civilization of long ago: the Egyptians. Many said the Egyptians were visited by life-forms from other worlds that showed them how to build the pyramids. They were said to possess special powers, and one of the great pyramids is said to rest in a spot where there is great power on the earth's surface. Great knowledge could be obtained from the life-forms at the site of the great pyramid. The great pyramid in Memphis, Tennessee, marks the place where Native Americans crossed the big water to their home in the East with the mound builders. It is also the site of important African American events. It symbolizes that we can work together with people of other cultures regardless of color. There is another great pyramid in America. It rests in the sands, near the big water to the West, just like the pyramids in Egypt and Tennessee. The pyramids in the new world were just completed and a sign that we are entering a new age. *(John fans the fire, and the image changes to the Luxor hotel on the strip in Las Vegas. Pictures depict Native American prosperity with casinos on the back wall. Viva Las Vegas by Elvis Presley plays in the background)* It is no coincidence that the new foundation of the Native American economy is gaming. If you follow the construction of the pyramids, they follow major eras of the Native American existence in America; the crossing of the big water to the East and back to the West during removal, and the agreements with the federal and state governments to allow Indian tribes to operate gaming facilities. The Native American tribal casinos now take in more money per day than all of Las Vegas. This is a sign that the Native Americans have accepted greed and like the other eras, it will end also. As more and more Native American casinos are opened, just like the bacteria and disease that enter an unused carcass, the gambling will become diseased and start to disintegrate. You must help your people and all people prepare for this day, Rainy. It will come sooner than we think. *(Pictures appear of historic Coffeyville on the back wall, "The Trails to Coffeyville: Trade, Cows, Oil and the Missionaries." Music by John Cougar Mellencamp, "Ain't this America" plays in the background. The ensemble actors act out monologue.)* We have a history that includes competition, greed, improvement and peace. This includes our time in Coffeyville. Coffeyville was originally established by Mr. Coffey as a trading post on the border of Indian Territory to trade with the Indians who would cross over the border into Kansas. One of the most famous Osage Chiefs, Chief Black Dog, established the Black Dog Trail and often camped in the Coffeyville area. He stood over seven feet tall and would trade with Mr. Coffey at his trading post on his way to hunt buffalo in the North. The Black Dog Trail became well traveled by the Osage, and some even settled in the area around Coffeyville. Coffeyville quickly became a rough and tumble cow town in the late 1800's. Saloons, dancehalls and other businesses quickly established themselves on, Red Hot

Street in Coffeyville, catering to reckless cowboys. Gambling became so prevalent, gamblers would hold games openly, and shootings became a nightly occurrence on Red Hot Street. The mayor tried to gain control of Coffeyville without much luck. It took the railroad, the discovery of oil, and a new majority of fearing citizens to establish law and order in Coffeyville. Coffeyville became a town of progress and even became noted for the invention of the modern cowboy boots fashioned in pairs for the right and left foot by John Cubine in his boot and shoe store. This modernization of Coffeyville happened rather quickly, and news of the change failed to reach a group who remembered Coffeyville as the wild cow town where they grew up. The Dalton Gang would make a ride into their hometown of Coffeyville to cash in on the greed they knew as outlaws. It would be their last ride. *(Pictures of the Dalton Raid appear on the back wall. Cletis, John, and Rainy become the Dalton Gang along with ensemble actors who play out the entire action of the monologue. The title on the back wall, "The Trail to Destruction: The Daltons' Last Ride.")* The infamous Dalton Gang had ties to Coffeyville before they began their assault on the Wild West. Bob, Emmett and Grant Dalton came from a large family of 15 children. Their father Lewis Dalton provided very little for his family and was generally known as a deadbeat. While most of the Dalton children held legitimate jobs of one sort or another, Bob and Grant always had a wild eye about them. They began careers as lawmen, but had no luck on the right side of the law. They became outlaws, and their little brother

Emmett followed along. He was a good boy at heart, but followed the influence of his older brothers. This is extremely important to remember. As the story of the white snake teaches, you are who you are, and you can't change the fate of your destiny. They most likely began their careers as horse thieves, but were never convicted of crimes related to stealing horses. They became quite famous as train robbers using the knowledge they acquired during training as marshals to repeatedly rob trains in Indian Territory. Their plan to amass enough money to retire in South America required one last stop in the town where they grew up, Coffeyville, Kansas. They were familiar with Coffeyville and knew just what to do to pull off one of the greatest robberies in the history of the old Wild West, two banks at once as they ran from U.S. Marshals. They camped outside of Coffeyville in October and prepared for the heist. The banks would be full from the autumn harvests. The white rattlesnake entered their bodies as they breathed the smoke from the campfire. They would hitch their horses in front of a restaurant on the street to make a clean getaway. The First National Bank and Condon Bank were across the street from each other, around the corner. They would enter both banks simultaneously, get the money, and meet back at the horses. They needed disguises since they were now famous and some townspeople would recognize them. It was a perfect plan to an early retirement. When they entered Coffeyville the next morning, something went wrong. It was not as they remembered. The street where they planned to hitch their horses for the getaway was under construction, and the hitching posts were removed. The spirit of the white rattlesnake urged them to press on. They tied their horses in an alley and walked into town heavily armed. Aleck McKenna of McKenna's Dry Goods knew something wasn't right when they walked by his store. The look of the white rattlesnake was clear in their eyes. The chink of their spurs mimicked the hypnotic signature rattle of the snake's tail, and the smell of refined sugar and whiskey lingered as they passed by. McKenna's intuition told him to follow the men as they walked through town. He recognized one of the gang as a Dalton in disguise. Three of the men entered the Condon, and two of them entered the First National. McKenna saw the Condon being robbed with rifles and yelled the alarm to the townspeople of Coffeyville. They armed themselves with rifles, pistols and shotguns from the hardware stores and waited for the robbers to emerge from the banks. When the robbers appeared, they opened fire. After exchanging fire for fifteen minutes, the battle ended in what is now known as Death Alley. Four citizens and four gang members were dead or dying. Dick Broadwell was the only gang member to make it out of town on his horse. He was found dead a half mile outside of Coffeyville. Emmett Dalton was shot twenty-three times and did not die. He was basically good at his core; his association with his evil brothers distorted his view of the world. Remember, you can't change your destiny. He survived and after a long prison sentence, changed his ways until his death forty-five years later. Bob and Grant Dalton are buried in those baskets right over there in the cemetery with their accomplice Bill

Powers. They are face down as a final sign of their eternal evil. White foam that smelled of refined sugar and whiskey oozed from the burial basket coffins. Do not touch the foam. It will forever distort your views of good and evil. The Dalton Defenders and the Coffeyville citizens are a lasting symbol that good will ultimately overcome evil. If the citizens had not changed Coffeyville from a rough and tumble cow town based on gambling and entertaining cowboys to an upstanding community founded on legitimate businesses and a lasting belief in God, the Daltons may have pulled off one of the most aggressive bank heists in history and escaped to South America. *(New Orleans devastating flood pictures appear on the back wall and title, " The Signs Along the Trails: What Mother Earth is Telling Us If We will Listen." Natalie Merchant, "I Don't Want to Beg" music plays in the background.)* The Native Americans are keepers of the earth and responsible to care for it. When you artificially redirect the waters, strip the land, and bring the ooze to the surface, the earth will break. Look at the disasters involving the water. They are signs of things to come when you artificially use nature. It will balance itself out over time. Sometimes this requires an aggressive action or disaster to regain balance. It is why moderation and living a balanced life are so critical and a hallmark of your people. It is why you were chosen to keep the earth. But, you are straying from your strength, New Orleans was a sign. The storms that broke the barriers show that it is dangerous to change and abuse nature. The only thing worse than the disaster of Hurricane Katrina, was the portrayal of the African Americans after the flood by some of the mass media. It shows racism is still alive and well in America. The New Orleans disaster just confirmed it. Floods in Coffeyville destroyed the original African American colony during the 1800's and half of Coffeyville in 2007, spreading the ooze of the refinery across the earth's surface. The floods and natural disasters will return again. It is just a matter of time. Las Vegas will experience this too, just like the lands of Memphis and Egypt. Flooding is necessary to cleanse the earth just like the green corn festival ceremonies. The big water and abusing the natural balance of moderation links our cultures together. Coffeyville sits at an epicenter to address racism, just like the great pyramids of Egypt sit at an epicenter of communication. Coffeyville is neutral turf with all the conditions and elements necessary to fix our prejudices. The tolerance, acceptance, settling of African Americans, flooding, dependence on ooze, the reclamation of a wild gambling cow town on the border of Indian Territory to trade with the Indians by the merchants and the churches make Coffeyville the ideal place to address racism. If we don't act soon, the worst is yet to come. What we have witnessed is only birthing pains of what will come if we continue. It is up to you, Rainy. *(John stands up and put out the fire. The images dissolved into the smoke as it climbed into the sky. John sits down and becomes distant as he stares into the dark of the underworld.)*

Scene 5

(Picture of Coffeyville Community College appears on the back wall with the title, "The Trail to the Future:

Where Do We Go From Here?") U2's song, "Beautiful Day" plays in the background.)

RAINY: So, where do we go from here? I know where we came from and where we're at, what's next? *(The underworld begins to cloud up and darken. The storm clouds began to boil, and the wind picked up. Thunder and lightning surrounded the group as they sit around the site of Ah-Mah's grave. A tornado is heard coming down from the cloud scattering debris everywhere, but leaving the group untouched. The storm cloud split, and a ray of sunlight falls directly beside the group. The storm holds angrily around the ray of sun, rolling and boiling as the sunlight touches the ground illuminating the area. The ensemble actors bring out and cradle a crystal clear globe turning slowly on its axis. The globe hovers just above the ground. Pictures of three children descend from the light are shown on the back wall sitting around the globe, a Native American girl, an African American boy, and a Caucasian boy. A spring emerges from the ground and forms a pond beside the globe and the children. Three spirits descend from the storm cloud, a Native American, (Rainy) an African American, (Cletis) and a Caucasian, (John) They reach the ground, and the storm clouds settles into an uncomfortable quiet. The three are holding paint cans and brushes and begin dancing counterclockwise around the globe flinging paint on the globe as they move. The Native American use red paint, the African American use black, and the Caucasian use white. It was a competitive contest to see who could get the most paint on the globe. The red, white and black paint stain the globe causing it to crack and ooze substances from within. They began to push and fight as they bump into each other and put each others paint on each others face . The Caucasian knocks the Native American and African American down, kicks their paint cans from them, and stands on their chests as they lay on the ground. Ah-Mah, Cletis, and John each take the globe and lower it into the pond formed by the spring. Each time the globe emerges unchanged. The paint seemed permanent, and the substance oozing to the surface of the globe seems to continually weaken the integrity of the sphere. The globe shakes uncontrollably from time to time. The spirits continued to struggle on the ground as Ah-Mah replaces the globe suspended above the ground in its original spot. A deep voice comes down from the clouds and the sunlight.)*

AH-MAN: Rainy, you and your people are responsible for the earth, it's up to you!

AH-MAN/CLETIS/JOHN: We have failed, it's up to you! *(Rainy stands and looks at the stained globe, the spirits and the water for what seemed like an eternity. She thinks carefully before responding as the weight of the responsibility she inherited weighs heavy on her shoulders. "Chasing Cars" plays in the background by Sno Patrol plays in the background as Rainy turns to the back wall and see's all the American pain through out the century that has affected Natives, African American, Caucasian, and every culture in America through pictures as they stream quickly before her eyes. When they finish her eyes widened as she looks at Ah-Mah and smiles.)*

AH-MAN: You can do it. *(Intense Native drum music and thunder and lighting accompany this scene. Rainy collects reeds that emerged from the pond and weave a perfect reverse weave basket. She checks it by lowering it into the spring. It is water tight. She empties the basket and returned to the "at" world. She goes into the grass and forest surrounding the cemetery. She holds the basket just above the ground, and puts the plants into the basket. As she enters the forest, she puts additional plants the basket. The animals begin to applaud as she returned to the below world. She places the basket down and gathers mud from the bottom of the pond formed by the spring. She fashions a bowl from the mud and etched the words Gah-Doo-Gee in Cherokee syllabary on the side of the bowl. *In the Cherokee language, Gah-Doo-Gee means to come together willingly to do meaningful work. She makes a fire from cedar and began heating the bowl. She adds water from the pond and ground the plants from the basket, adding the mixture to the water as it began to boil. After it simmers, she removes it from the fire. After it cools, she passes the bowl next to the spirits (John, Cletis, Ah-Man) sitting around the globe. The children now depicted by Cletis, John, Ah-Man, each drink from the bowl as Rainy offers it to them. The drink is clearly pleasing and wonderful as they drink. Rainy takes the children by the hand and they lower the globe into the water. The globe emerges from the pond unchanged, still stained and damaged. Rainy is puzzled and upset.)* You can't skip to the future; you must address the past and present to make the change. That's why it's difficult and hasn't been done. It requires discipline, confrontation, negotiation, cooperation and compassion. These are rarely found in a common place between different adults of different race. *(Looking at Ah-Mah and her confidence, Rainy knows what she must do.)* You can do it, you are the last hope. *(Rainy stares solemnly into the rays from the clouds. There is no reply as she contemplates what to do. Ah-Mah, Cletis, and John stare patiently as Rainy gathers her strength for another attempt. Her eyes fills with rage as she knows what has to be done. A rattle and laughing can be heard in the distance. Thunder is heard. Rainy takes the bowl and returns it to the fire. She approaches the men who are still struggling around the globe and holds out her hand. The men are immediately paralyzed as Rainy approaches them. Taking a cedar stick, she scrapes the sweat from each of the children into the bowl and adds the substance that is oozing from the globe to the bowl as she stirs it carefully. It immediately turns black, and steam begins to emerge from the bowl. But instead of ascending to the clouds, it rolls counterclockwise around the bowl and sizzles as it enters the cedar fire burning under the bowl. The fire stains the bowl as the steam enters the cedar flames. Grabbing each child by the hair of the head, Rainy holds the bowl in front of them as she sits them up. She does not force them to drink, but looks sternly into their eyes as she holds the bowl in front of them. Each child drinks from the bowl with the look you only get when genuine hate is present within the chest. After the last child drinks from the bowl, they all begin to throw up uncontrollably. The blood vessels burst in the whites of their eyes from the strain of their convulsions. Rainy holds the bowl out to them again.)*

RAINY: You know what to do, It's up to you; no one can do it for you this time.

(The children look at Rainy, and their eyes well up with tears.)

AH-MAN/CLETIS/JOHN: We ask your forgiveness, we can make this work.

(The drink was bitter, but this time they held it down. They walk to the circle with a humble, grateful attitude. Rainy signals to the children to try again. The group enters the pond and lowers the globe. It emerges from the water in pristine condition. The stains are gone, and the oozing cracks are healed into their original condition. They hand the globe to Ah-Mah, Cletis and John as they come out of the pond. Ah-Mah, Cletis and John raise the globe above their heads and walk to the place where the globe originally descended from the actors. As soon as they reached the spot where the globe would remain suspended, a huge bolt of lightning erupted from the storm clouds striking the globe. The repercussion and force of the thunder knock Rainy to the ground. She regains her bearings and stumbles to her feet. Smoke surrounds the spot where Ah-Mah, Cletis and John are holding the globe. The smoke begins to clear, and she can see the outline of Ah-Mah, Cletis and John still holding the globe above their heads. A sand-like coating covers their bodies and the globe. The children are still sitting undisturbed looking up at the sand-covered figure. Sunlight cuts through the

storm clouds as the dawn of a new day arrives in the below world. The Earth begins to shake again, and the sandy coating covering the figure begins to crack and fall to the ground as the sunlight strikes the trio holding the globe. The coating immediately returns to sand as it hits the ground around the pond. It swallows the foam that oozed from the graves of the Dalton Gang. The smell of sugar and whiskey are replaced with the smell of fresh water only experienced after a cleansing rain. A crystal clear figure of Ah-Mah, Cletis and John holding the globe above their heads remains in the middle. There are no colors in the figure, just the unmistakable impressions each one has etched into the crystal as they hold the globe. The actors appear again and cradled the figure. Rainy joined hands with Ah-Man, Cletis, and John as the actors ask the audience to stand and all join hands in a show of peace and unity. The song, "Chasing Cars" plays throughout this scene. Pictures appear of the back wall of racism at first but by the end of the song show pictures f peace and harmony between all cultures of the Earth.)

RAINY: Let us not forget what we learned here today, and the sacrifices Ah-Mah, Cletis and John made for us, the wisdom we have gained will serve us well as we continue our journey into our own community. We must always remember our intentions have consequences. Our instincts will always guide us in the right direction if we avoid selfishness. We have work to do here; we better get started. *(Rainy, Cletis, and John begin to dance clockwise around the figure. Sunlight pours through the glass doors and passes through the globe producing a prism of colors.)*

AH-MAN: The colors of peace. The trail of our journey, "The Rainy Trail" as it shall now be known will be the trial and tribulation of all men and women and it continues...*(Wind blows, "A Beautiful Day" by U2 play in the background as a picture montage of African American, Native American, and White American struggles through the ages are seen again. The last image is Rainy walking upstage in a spot of light with the globe over her head. The last picture on the wall is a child holding a cross in their hand. It fades out. Rainy is now the only thing seen on stage holding the globe. The lights fade and the play ends.)*

HUMPTY DUMPTY: THE MUSICAL?

Characters:

Humpty Dumpty

Director

Stage Manager

Lighting Guy

All The Kings Horses and All the Kings Men

Humpty Dumpty: the Musical? was first presented by *Coffeyville Community College on September 17-19, 2009 at the Spencer/Rounds Performing Arts Theatre. It was directed by Mark Frank. The production stage managers were Melissa Delfft and Lauren Bell. The cast was as follows:*

Humpty Dumpty	Randall Pike
Director	Brandon Jackson
Stage Manager: Sheila	Brianna Cordova
Lighting guy	Clifford Lee
Kings Horses/King's Men	Phillip Morris
	Randy Skidmore
	Mead McMurphy
	Jimmy Petersen
	Zach Bartz

AT RISE: (*The play begins with many stage hands putting up Humpty Dumpty's Wall. The actor playing Humpty Dumpty has an English accent, (Think Christian Bale) and is in a huge Humpty Dumpty costume smoking a cigarette and going over his lines on one side of the stage. He is a brutal method actor and very on edge. On the other side of the stage are six actors that portray three horses and three Kings Men. They are in full costume. All the men are dressed in black and have toy riding horses for the horses and fake armor and helmet costume for The King's Men, they wear black underneath their armor. They are all stretching doing Yoga exercises. The stage manager is running around calling places. The Director enters; his character is modeled after Charles Nelson Reilly. He approaches Humpty Dumpty.*)

DIRECTOR: Jim, we need to talk.

HUMPTY: God Damn it! Look how many times do I have to tell you to call me Humpty Dumpty. How do you expect me to get into character in this costume if you keep calling me Jim, for fuck sake!

DIRECTOR: Okay method acting, that's right. I'm sorry, look we got get this musical on its feet. We are three weeks behind schedule, we open in two weeks, and I can't even begin to tell you how much we are over budget. We need to find the right style for this thing to really sell the shit out of our tickets; we have a lot of backers who risk losing millions of dollars on this, plus think of my career.

HUMPTY: Is that my fucking fault, talk to the flaming idiots you cast for the King's horses and King's men, I mean look at them, they fucking suck man! *(The King's Horses and King's Men take exception to this and yell obscenities back to Humpty.)*

DIRECTOR: I'm working with them, believe me Jimmy, I'm doing the best I can.

HUMPTY: FOR FUCK SAKE! CALL ME HUMPTY FOR THE LAST FUCKING TIME YOU PRICK!

DIRECTOR: Humpty! Humpty, I'm very sorry!! You are wonderful in this, just wanted to say…

HUMPTY: Get the fuck away from me!

DIRECTOR: Okay people places. Let's try to find this musicals voice!

HORSE: Um, excuse me um…I have a fucking run in my tight.

HUMPTY: For fuck sake can we just get started!

DIRECTOR/STAGE MANAGER (SHEILA): Places!!!

DIRECTOR: Okay going country first….action!

SHEILA: *(Going out to the house to watch.)* Going country!

KING'S HORSES/KING'S MEN: *(They sing the song in a country style. Humpty Dumpty is sitting on the wall. He looks pissed until the director yells action and he totally becomes a happy, wholesome*

Humpty Dumpty that kids would gush over. During the performance a lighting person crosses behind the set with a light. *Note: Anytime the Humpty Dumpty song is sung it can be repeated or be choreographed into the given style or length per the discretion of the director.)

"Humpty Dumpty sat a wall
Humpty Dumpty had a great fall
All the Kings Horses and all the Kings Men
Couldn't put Humpty together again!"

HUMPTY: Stop for a fucking second. Bring that lighting person over here.

LIGHTING GUY: Yeah? (*Wearing a ripped up shirt and jeans*)

HUMPTY: Am I going to walk around and rip your fucking lights down in the middle of a scene? Then why the fuck are you walking right through? Ah-da-da-dah like this in the background. What the fuck is it with you? What don't you fucking understand? You got any fucking idea about, hey; it's fucking distracting having somebody walking up behind me in the middle of the fucking scene? Give me a fucking answer! Fuck it! Let's do it again. Stay off the fucking set.

LIGHTING GUY: Ok, sorry man.

DIRECTOR: Next up classic rock. Action!

SHEILA: (*Going back out to the house to watch*) Going classic rock!

KING'S HORSES/KING'S MEN: *(The lighting guy comes on stage during the performance and looks at a gel he holds up to the lights right in front of the performers.)*

"Humpty Dumpty sat a wall
Humpty Dumpty had a great fall
All the Kings Horses and all the Kings Men
Couldn't put Humpty together again!

HUMPTY: Stop! Stop! What the fuck! What don't you get about it man?

LIGHTING GUY: I was looking at the lights.

HUMPTY: Ohhhhh, goooood for you. And how was it? I hope it was fucking good, because that run.... its useless now, isn't it?

LIGHTING GUY: Ok.

HUMPTY: Fuck sake man, you're amateur. Mr. fucking director, you got fucking something to say to this prick?

DIRECTOR: I didn't see it happen.

HUMPTY: Well, somebody should be fucking watching and keeping an eye on him. *(Sheila and Humpty get into it.)*

DIRECTOR: Okay, okay, fair enough!

HUMPTY: It's the second time that he doesn't give a shit about what is going on stage, all right? I'm trying to fucking do a scene here, and I am going "Why the fuck is lighting guy walking on the set? What is he doing there?" Do you understand my mind is not in the scene if you're doing that?

LIGHTING GUY: I absolutely apologize. I'm sorry; I did not mean anything by it.

HUMPTY: Stay off the fucking set man. For fuck sake, Alright, let's go again.

DIRECTOR: Let's just take a minute.

HUMPTY: Let's not take a fucking minute, let's go again.

DIRECTOR: Let's move on to techno....and action!

SHEILA: (*Goes out into the house*) Going techno!

KING'S HORSES/KING'S MEN: (*The light guy starts to eat a long meatball sub sandwich during the song smacking his lips while he eats. Marinara sauce is all over his mouth and t-shirt.*)

"Humpty Dumpty sat a wall
Humpty Dumpty had a great fall
All the Kings Horses and all the Kings Men
Couldn't put Humpty together again!"

HUMPTY: For fuck sake! Stop! Stop! I'm going to fucking kick your fucking ass if you don't shut up for a second, all right?

KING'S HORSES/KING'S MEN: Humpty, Humpty, its cool.

HUMPTY: I'm going to go... do you want me to fucking go trash your lights? Do you want me to fucking trash 'em? Then why are you trashing my scene? Standing there eating a fucking meatball sub, smacking your fucking lips! *(Mocks him eating it)*

LIGHTING GUY: I'm not trying to trash your scene. *(Still eating the meatball sub)*

HUMPTY: You are trashing my scene! *(He throws the meatball sub upstage. The director goes and retrieves the sub off the floor.*

LIGHTING GUY: Humpty, I was only...

HUMPTY: No...No...No...! You do it one more fucking time and I ain't walking on this set if you're still hired. I'm fucking serious. You're a nice guy, but that don't fucking cut it when you're fucking around like this on set. Let's do it again!

DIRECTOR: Let's move onto opera! And action!! *(Eating the meatball sub.)*

SHEILA: *(Going back into the house to watch)* Going opera!

KING'S HORSES/KING'S MEN: *(During the performance the lighting guy blows his nose)*

"Humpty Dumpty sat a wall
Humpty Dumpty had a great fall
All the Kings Horses and all the Kings Men
Couldn't put Humpty together again!"

HUMPTY: You fucking asshole, I'm going to kick your ass! (*Humpty Dumpty jumps off the wall and chases the lighting guy around the set. All the Kings Horses and All the Kings Men try to stop Humpty Dumpty. Humpty tackles the light guy into the set of the wall and knocks it over. Humpty is just laying into the Light Guy with rights and lefts. The Kings Horses and Kings Men pull Humpty off the Lighting Guy.*)

HUMPTY:No!No!Noooooooooooooooooooooooooooo! (*Black out*)

VOICE OVER: And now ladies and gentlemen. Straight from Broadway, Humpty Dumpty, The Musical! (*The musical begins and the music sounds like something right out of Disney's Little Mermaid, "Under The Sea."*)

King's Horses and King's Men:
"Humpty Dumpty sat a wall
Humpty Dumpty had a great fall
All the Kings Horses and all the Kings Men Couldn't put Humpty together again!"

(*The lights go black the performance is over. The lights come back up and Humpty Dumpty is taking his curtain call with all of his King horses and all of his Kings Men. The Lighting Guy runs on stage and yells, "Union!" and tackles Humpty Dumpty the fight is on with everyone involved. Black out.*)

Epilogue

(*The lights come back up and all the Kings Horses and All the Kings Men are back on stage.*)

HORSE: According Wikipedia, Humpty Dumpty is a character in a nursery rhyme typically portrayed as an egg. Most English-speaking children are familiar with the rhyme. The rhyme does not actually state that Humpty Dumpty is an egg. In its first printed form in 1810, the rhyme is posed as a riddle and exploits for misdirection the fact that "Humpty Dumpty" was also 18th-Century reduplicative slang for a short and clumsy person; the riddle being that whereas a clumsy person falling off a wall would not be irreparably damaged, an egg would be. The rhyme is no longer posed as a riddle, since the answer is now so well known.

ALL: We just thought you should know that...okay? Goodnight everyone! Toodles!

HUMPTY: *(Walks back on the set.)* Go fuck yourselves!*(The lights go black as the play ends.)*

TROUBLE'S REVENGE

Characters

Trouble, A 21 year old cat

Tiger, Trouble's brother who is dead.

Han Solo, A Japanese fighting fish.

Jasper Jax, A crossed Siamese eyed cat.

Jilly, A dense Shiatsu.

Time: Present

Place: Mommy's House

For JD and Honkey

Who we love and miss everyday!

**SPECIAL NOTE ON SONGS AND
RECORDINGS USED IN THIS PRODUCTION**

For performance songs and recordings mentioned in this play are protected by copyright, the permission of the copyright owner(s) must be obtained; or songs, arrangements and recordings in the public domain substituted.

Trouble's Revenge was first performed at Coffeyville Community College on September 17-19, 2009 in the Spencer/Rounds Performing Arts Theatre. It was directed by Mark Frank. The production stage managers were Melissa Delfft and Lauren Bell. The cast was as follows:

Trouble	Zach Bartz
Tiger	Clifford Lee
Han Solo	Brianna Cordova
Jasper Jax	Phillip Morris
Jilly	Lauren Curley

AT RISE: *Lights come up on Trouble, a twenty one year old cat, just waking up from a nap. The play takes place ten years after A PURRFECT LIFE. The other cat, Tiger, has passed away and appears in the play as a ghost. NOTE: The actors playing the two cats should capture the essence of a cat and not be a cat. The performance should be honest without being too cartoon like. The costumes can be simply pants or a turtleneck of the same or different colors with cat ears and a tail. The word "mommy" should sound like a "meow" and the word "perfect" should be purring.*

TROUBLE: *(Moving very slowly, looking rough and unkempt, he throws up.)* God Damn I'm old!

TIGER: *(Enters from upstage looking magnificent)* Let's go then!

TROUBLE: Not yet...not yet...still holding on.

TIGER: Holding on, to what? I mean look at you, your furs all matted, you have no teeth!

TROUBLE: So...I can gum my food to death.

TIGER: You're so fat, old, have arthritis in your back legs really bad and you can't even clean yourself anymore.

TROUBLE: Hey give me a break that's a hard to reach spot, I seem to remember you had trouble cleaning back there also tubby.

TIGER: Every spot on you is a hard to reach spot, you stopped grooming yourself a long time ago, and you have so much brown crap in your ears, I mean, what gives?

TROUBLE: Look I'm tired; I mean what's the point anyway Mommy *(Sounds like "meommy")* doesn't care about me anymore.

TIGER: Yes she does! What are you talking about?

TROUBLE: No she doesn't, not since *"that"* came into the house.

TIGER: What's *"that"*?

TROUBLE: You know, *"that"* *(He points to a picture on the table which is of a little girl. He mocks her, acting like a little girl)*

TIGER: You mean the little girl she adopted?

TROUBLE: Yep that would be *"that"*! Ever since she came into the house I no longer exist.

TIGER: Come on your over reacting.

TROUBLE: Over reacting? Over reacting? I don't even exist in this house anymore. She kicked me off the bed! I mean I can't even sleep by her head anymore because *"that"* is always in my spot.

TIGER: Well it also may be because you puke almost daily and she's tired of washing the bedding.

TROUBLE: I'm twenty one years old for Pete sakes what is that like hundred and twenty in cat years, I'm going to puke once in awhile, I can't digest like I used to.

TIGER: Still pass the gas with ease I bet.

TROUBLE: She never picks me up anymore because *"that"* is always on her lap.

TIGER: You can't even jump up on her lap even if you wanted to. You're old!!!!

TROUBLE: If I skid mark on the carpet or even have a slight bought of arthritis in my back legs she takes me to the crazy fat lady who sticks things in me and up me.

TIGER: See now there you go, if she didn't care she wouldn't take you to the fat lady to get checked out, and you wouldn't have lasted this long. I mean hell, I died ten years ago.

TROUBLE: Well you were disgustingly fat; you never knew how to eat. You ate all the time and all the wrong things, after you left us it was the Science Diet every day, dry and moist!

TIGER: Taken out of this world by the dreaded Diabetes.

TROUBLE: That damn vet mis-diagnosed you or you'd still be with me.

TIGER: Yeah, Mommy tried to give me insulin shots but it was too late, I withered away to nothing.

TROUBLE: Hell you lost ten pounds like in a week. That was the best you looked.

TIGER: Ah, yeah right, I pissed myself and could no longer walk. Mommy took me to the fat lady and I got the dreaded death shot right in the back of the head, didn't know what hit me. Gone like that!

TROUBLE: That was the saddest day I ever lived.

TIGER: Saying goodbye to mommy was hard, I gave her one last, "meow". *(He meows)*

TROUBLE: I didn't even get to say goodbye to you, I woke up one day and you were gone, I remember spending days looking for you everywhere.

TIGER: But I was gone.

TROUBLE: Only clumps of your fur around the house remained. I knew when mommy came home you were gone, I could tell by how sad she was. I slept with you clump of fur for months carried it in my mouth hoping you'd come back.

TIGER: She was the best mommy.

TROUBLE: After you died I got lots of attention, I was living the purrfect life until she adopted *"that"* little girl. *(Puts picture face down on table.)*

TIGER: Hey, come on, that little girl loves you.

TROUBLE: Are you kidding me? She tortures me. She picks me up wrong, carries me awkward, and pulls my tail. When Mommy's not around, I hiss at her *(Laughing)*

TIGER *(Laughing)* you….hiss! Hilarity….hila-ri-ty!

TROUBLE: What do you mean hilarity? What the hell does that mean?

TIGER: You hiss? Come on, you couldn't scare anything at your age.

TROUBLE: I have a bad ass hiss.

TIGER: Oh...okay...whatever you say, let's see this bad ass hiss.

TROUBLE: I have no reason to hiss right now so I'd rather not show you.

TIGER: Here, hiss at the new Japanese fighting fish they got up in this see through glass bowl up there. *(He taps on the glass.)* Tink, tink, tink,. *(The fish is looking at them sitting on the table reading a magazine. Tiger winks at the audience since there is no prop for a fish bowl)* Look, he's looking at you.

TROUBLE: You mean Han Solo?

TIGER: Han Solo?

TROUBLE: Yeah that's what they named the fish, pretty moronic if you ask me.

TIGER: What a pathetic name, Han Solo. *(Laughs)* Go ahead, let me hear this mean, terrifying hiss you possess.

TROUBLE: Alright smarty but stand back I don't want to scare you. This can be pretty terrifying.

TIGER: Just do it.

TROUBLE: Hey, Han Solo! *(He hisses which comes out and sounds pretty pathetic. He tries to more times very unsuccessful.)*

HAN SOLO: *(Laughing. The actor playing Han Solo is dressed like a fish. He speaks in broken English being Japanese.)* Fuck off old cat!

TIGER: *(Laughing)* He said fuck off old cat...wow, how terrifying you were.

TROUBLE: Alright, alright you made your point.

TIGER: Look, it's time to let go. I really miss you, let's leave this world and come with me?

TROUBLE: Where? Where are you? What happens when you die?

TIGER: Well...some would say when I died I went up to the beautiful clouded sky, found myself in front of a pearly golden gate, it opened, I walked in and heard beautiful music from a harp. Then all of a sudden, a kind gentle man with a bright light behind him with long hair and a beard picked me up and petted me. I had no pain and heavenly bliss! I was in Kitty Heaven!

TROUBLE: *(Excited)* REALLY!!!

TIGER: No, I was kidding about all that basically when you die there's nothing, just blackness, hell you don't even know your dead.

TROUBLE: But how are you here...aren't you from Heaven? Aren't you my angel?

TIGER: No, I'm just a figment of your imagination trying to convince you to die.

TROUBLE: So dying is no big deal?

TIGER: Not really, its sucks for the people who are left on earth that miss you like mommy, who feels lots of pain, but you don't feel a thing. It's a big cat nap you just never wake up from and best of all there's no weird dreams! There's nothing, absolutely one hundred percent nothing after this.

TROUBLE: No shit?

TIGER: That's right my good fiend so if you want to go do a giant skid mark on the carpet right now, or puke up your moist, and stain the carpet so bad that no carpet cleaner on earth can remove the stain, go ahead. There is no remorse, and there is no forgiveness, you simply are born, live and die like everything else on this earth.

TROUBLE: So this is it. This is all we got?

TIGER: This is all we got.

HAN SOLO: This is all we got? You mean I'm flushed and that's it?

TIGER: That's all there is so fuck off fish! (*Han Solo mumbles in Japanese to himself*)

TROUBLE: But I still love Mommy, I'd miss her.

TIGER: You're never dead as long as you're remembered.

TROUBLE: You remember when Mommy first got us a long time ago. We were only three weeks old.

TIGER: Yeah, we both sucked on her hair because we thought she was our real mommy and we wanted to still nurse.

TROUBLE: You remember getting up in the middle of the night and chasing each other.

TIGER: Hanging off the curtains getting our claws stuck in the furniture?

TROUBLE: Jumping off of high places, running like a bat out of hell after dropping a great shit!

TIGER: Faster than a speeding bullet!

TROUBLE: Able to leap tall counters in a single bound!

TIGER: It's a bird!

TROUBLE: It's a fish!

TIGER/TROUBLE: It's Tiger and Trouble!

TIGER: Those were the days.

TROUBLE: They are long gone. Time goes by so quickly.

(Long pause)

HAN SOLO: You guys remember when you used to watch me swim back and forth and you would get dizzy and fall backwards and then I would just flop

334

over and laugh. Good times. (*They both stare at the fish in disgust and then look at each other.*)

TIGER: You weren't even around when I was alive so shut the fuck up fish before we eat you.

HAN SOLO: Shutting fuck up.

TROUBLE: Seemed so easy back then.

TIGER: Then we get old and die. Not much time for us like humans.

TROUBLE: It sucks.

TIGER: It sucks.

TROUBLE: You know my bladder is failing. I haven't peed for two days.

TIGER: It's time.

TROUBLE: Lost so much weight.

TIGER: It's time.

TROUBLE: I'm dragging my back legs.

TIGER: It's time.

TROUBLE: I can't hear or see very well.

TIGER: Let's go.

TROUBLE: I can't leave Mommy no matter how bad she treats me.

TIGER: She'll get over you, she has someone new in her life that she needs to care for, a new kitten but this one is of her own kind, and she's human. There's more of a connection.

TROUBLE: I love her.

TIGER: I loved her too and always will.

TROUBLE: It's so hard to say goodbye knowing you'll never see her smiling kind face again.

TIGER: I know.

TROUBLE: And her kisses, I'll miss her kisses, the baby talk, her pettings and scratches.

TIGER: Petting's and scratches, hell yes, she knew where to scratch.

TROUBLE: She did. She'll cry when I'm gone, she cried for weeks when you left us.

TIGER: And you and I will cry right with her.

TROUBLE: You think she'll forget about us?

TIGER: Never.

TROUBLE: How do you know, you're not even real, just a figment of my imagination?

TIGER: You know deep in your heart she'll remember you.

TROUBLE: Will she bury me like she did with you with a cool grave marker and all?

TIGER: Well it's not like she's going to cremate you and leave you on her mantle in a urn, I mean come on what do you think?

TROUBLE: Okay you convinced me, I'm ready. She'll come home and find me very sick and then take me to the fat lady and...

TIGER: Yes....yes I'm afraid... the dreaded death shot in the back of the head, you won't feel a thing, just get really tired and go to sleep.

TROUBLE: Will she stay with me during the shot.

TIGER: Probably not, you know in case you go all bug eyed after the shot, some of us react poorly to it. You know drool, or make a weird death face, not pretty, not pretty at all. (*He makes the cat death face.*)

TROUBLE: I thought the cat death face looks like this? (*He makes a more disgusting death face.*)

HAN SOLO: No cat death face look like this. (*She makes a weird face.*)

TIGER: No, the cat death face is this (*Make an even uglier face.*)

HAN SOLO: Being flushed is so much easier, it's over in seconds. The fish death face looks like this. (*Makes a disgusting face.*)

TROUBLE: I thought the dead fish face looked like this? (*Makes an even uglier face*)

TIGER: No, dead fish face looks like this (*Makes an even worse face*)

HAN SOLO: I don't think so.

TIGER: I should know I've died. Have either have you died? No, I have so I should know what the death face looks like and it looks like this. (*Makes a disgusting face*)

TIGER/TROUBLE: So shut up!

TROUBLE: I'm going, but can I go my own way?

TIGER: It's your life my friend, you can leave it as you choose!

TROUBLE: It was a purrfect life wasn't it?

TIGER: The best any cat can live. Now come join me.

TROUBLE: I will but first, this… *(The lights change to a spotlight and Tiger puts a stool and a microphone onstage. Trouble sits on the stage like a lounge singer. A wall behind him flashes a power point of pictures of the real life Tiger and Trouble cats from young kittens to elderly cats.)* This song goes out to my mommy who I love and will miss very much, and to Tiger, my playmate, that I've missed for many years and convinced me it's time to go. *(Trouble sings the song, "My Way by Frank Sinatra" as the power point of pictures flashes behind him. Han Solo and Tiger are the back up dancers behind him. When the song finishes he puts the microphone down.)*

TROUBLE: Let's go to sleep Tiger.

TIGER: Let's go to sleep Trouble. *(They walk arm and arm into the darkness. As the play ends the lights fade down only to be interrupted by Warner Brothers, "Looney Tunes" music as another cat, a male Siamese that is crossed eyed, and a dog, a female shiatsu not so bright, runs on stage. The dog is chasing the cat.)*

JASPER: Hey, hold those lights.

TROUBLE: Who the hell are you two?

JASPER: We are the replacements that mommy got for you two old scoundrels. *(He gives a playful punch to the chin to Trouble. They eyeball each other.)*

JILLY: What's going on? *(Starts to laugh and looks confused)* Ooh my tail! *(She starts to chase her own tail)*

TIGER/TROUBLE/JASPER: *(All look at each other.)* Dogs!

TIGER: *(To Trouble)* That cat is crossed eyed and spastic!

TROUBLE: And the dog is dumber that a door knob.

JASPER: We'd like to stay and talk old chaps but we gotta get moved in.

TROUBLE: Yeah…yeah good luck with all that.

TIGER: Yeah...take care.

(Jilly and Jasper leave chasing each other off accompanied by "Looney Tune" music.)

TROUBLE: That little girl is going make their lives so interesting....

TIGER: That dog's probably not even house trained... look a piss puddle.

TROUBLE: What a little piss bag. I hate dogs.

TIGER: Not our worry. Where were we? *(Put arms around each other.)*

TROUBLE/TIGER: Black out. *(Lights black out and the play ends.)*

A Christmas Play

Characters:

Glory, An Angel

Holly, Mother of Noelle who is in a coma from a car crash.

Noelle, age eight.

Uncle Nick, Noelle's Uncle.

Doctor Michaels

Santa Claus

Rudolf The Red-Nose Reindeer

Jack Frost

Frosty the Snowman

Christmas Tree

Gingerbread Man

Christmas Elves

Jesus

Ebenezer Scrooge

SPECIAL NOTE ON SONGS AND RECORDINGS USED IN THIS PRODUCTION

For performance songs and recordings mentioned in this play, (Mariah Carey Christmas music) that are protected by copyright, the permission of the copyright owner(s) must be obtained; or songs, arrangements and recordings in the public domain substituted.

A Christmas Play was first presented by Coffeyville Community College on November 20th, 2009 in the Spencer/Rounds Performing Arts Theatre. It was directed by Mark Frank. The production stage manager was Amber Long. The cast was as follows:

Glory The Angel	Sarah Rush
Holly	Bethanie Frank
Noelle, Holly's daughter	Atlantis Frank
Uncle Nick	Chris Cameron
Doctor Michaels	Nick Rush
Santa Claus	Caleb Coffman
Rudolph Red-Nose Reindeer	Zach Bartz
Jack Frost	Jimmy Petersen
Frosty the Snowman	Brandon Jackson
Christmas Tree	Melissa Delfft
Gingerbread Man	Anthony Mount
Jesus	Clifford Lee
Elves	Mariah Lovett
	Kerri Davis
	Reyna Ponce de Leon
	Sarah Hagebusch
	Lauren Curley
	Brianna Cordova

AT RISE: *The play begins with Glory, the Angel singing, "Christmas, Baby Please Come Home" by Mariah Carey center stage with a choir of Angels behind her as the lights come up. As the song ends and the lights fade down and up to a hospital room stage left with a lady in bed unconscious with a little girl seated at her bedside. A doctor and an old man are looking at a chart.)*

DR. MICHAELS: I think we might want to talk in another room in private.

NOELLE: I want to hear. Please no secrets. She's my mother I deserve to know what going on.

UNCLE NICK: Noelle please…

NOELLE: Uncle Nick, it's Christmas, please let me stay and hear how she doing.

UNCLE NICK: Okay.

DR.MICHAELS: Are you sure? It's not very good news.

UNCLE NICK: Noelle's a strong girl, she's been through a lot already-I think she prepared for the worse if it can get as bad as it already has.

DR MICHAELS: Well the news is not good. Holly status has not changed and she is still in a coma that she's been in for the last two weeks with no change. We thought the bruising of her brain from the car accident may have brought her out of her coma but still no change.

UNCLE NICK: Give her more time; she'll come out of it.

DR. MICHAELS: I'm afraid there's more. Her brain activity is in a state of decline. She could be brain dead in a matter of days if her condition worsens and then we need to discuss some serious decisions your family has to make.

UNCLE NICK: Well it's just me and the kiddo. Her father was killed many years ago while away at war and my wife passed many years ago.

DR. MICHAELS: I'll know more by tomorrow but it doesn't look good. You may want to call a priest in tomorrow.

UNCLE NICK: Thank you doctor. Can we stay with her tonight? I know its past visiting hours but its Christmas and Noelle really want to be with her tonight.

DOCTOR MICHAELS: It's against policy...

NOELLE: Please?

DR. MICHAELS: ....but policies are meant to be broken during certain special circumstances. You two have a Merry Christmas and I will see you tomorrow.

UNCLE NICK: Thank you doctor. *(Doctor Michaels exits as Glory the Angel enters and sings "Miss You Most At Christmas Time" by Mariah Carey. Uncle Nick just stares as Noelle in anguish. When the song ends, Glory leaves. She cannot be seen by Uncle Nick.)* You're going to be okay kiddo that was some pretty heavy news about your mother. *(She does not answer and only stares at her mother.)* You know there have been many people in worse shape then your mom that woke up from a coma after many years. I once read about a man who woke up thirty years later. Of course everyone he knew was dead and gone but he still woke up.

NOELLE: You're not helping.

UNCLE NICK: You just need to pray to the good Lord and maybe she'll come back to us.

NOELLE: *(Whips around in her chair angry.)* There is no God, no Jesus, no Lord! What God would take both my parents from me? *(She breaks down crying)*

UNCLE NICK: It's not for us to understand. Sometimes God has his reasons and we find out these reasons after we die. You must continue to have faith in him no matter what happens in your life.

NOELLE: Okay. I'm sorry.

UNCLE NICK: Look I'm going to leave you here so you can have private time with your mom. I will be right outside that door if you need me. Talk to your mom, she may be able to hear your voice. Tell her how much you love her. She'd like that.

NOELLE: What if the doctors right about her condition.

UNCLE NICK: Let's not talk about that right now. Let's just focus on good thoughts. Okay? How about a kiss for your old uncle?

NOELLE: *(She kisses and hugs him)* You smell like Beef Jerky!

UNCLE NICK: Had some down the hall in the vending machine, now I got it stuck in my teeth. I need to find a toothpick. *(He exits, and then comes back in.)* Noelle...

NOELLE: Yes?

UNCLE NICK: Don't forget about prayer, it's a powerful healing thing.

NOELLE: I love you Uncle Nick.

UNCLE NICK: I love you too kiddo. *(He exits. She sits next to her mom on the chair. She gets up, kneels downstage, looks up, and puts her hands together. Glory appears behind her singing "Holy Night" by Mariah Carey. Her choir of children dressed in white is behind her.)*

NOELLE: Are you an angel?

GLORY: *(Put finger to her lips and nods, "yes")*

NOELLE: Are you here to help my mother get better?

GLORY: You first must believe in him, the Holy Spirit. Come sing with me and believe in his holy power. He is the true meaning of Christmas. *(Glory and Noelle sings, "Jesus Born on This Day", and "Jesus Oh What*

349

a Wonderful Child" by Mariah Carey with the her choir of children.)

NOELLE: I didn't think he was real because he took my dad away and now my mother…but I do believe in him after seeing you and know you must be her guardian angel.

GLORY: I am Glory and I'm here to teach you there are many wonderful things you should believe in that simple people do not.

NOELLE: Like what?

GLORY: Santa Claus.

NOELLE: He's not real, none of the Christmas characters are. They are just make believe to make us enjoy the holiday more. My friends told me Santa is really just your parents.

GLORY: Well they would be wrong now wouldn't they?

NOELLE: What do you mean?

GLORY: Listen, hear that lullaby, he's almost here. Go open that closet door

NOELLE: This one?

GLORY: That's the one!

(Christmas characters come dancing out of the closet including Rudolph, Jack Frost, Frosty the Snowman, the Gingerbread Man, A dancing Christmas Tree, Elves, and Santa Claus and his wife. They dance all around

the room dancing with Noelle singing, "Santa Claus Is Coming To Town" by Mariah Carey. They go into the audience with the elves and Christmas characters and pass out presents to all the children.)

NOELLE: Wow, they are real and a lot of fun.

GLORY: If you believe in your heart anything is possible to come true, even miracles. *(She looks over at Noelle's mother.)* Hey you guys back in the closet! *(The Christmas characters go back in the closet except Jack Frost.)* You too Jack!

JACK: Fine but it's going to be a long, cold winter. (*He goes into the closet.)*

NOELLE: Can you make her wake up?

GLORY: No, but you can. You just need to share with Jesus in a prayer from your heart and he will do the rest.

NOELLE: *(She runs to the bed)* Did you hear that mother? You're going to wake up! You're going to wake up!

(Uncle Nick comes running in armed with an umbrella.)

UNCLE NICK: What in the world is all that yelling? *(The room is now empty; Glory and the characters of Christmas are gone.)*

NOELLE: Glory? *(She runs to the closet, its empty.)* Glory!

Mark Frank

UNCLE NICK: Are you okay?

NOELLE: I just had the strangest dream, but it was so real. It was right here. At least I think it was a dream.

UNCLE NICK: Well look I'm going to get a cup of coffee and then let's just sit you down and you can rest your eyes while I spend time with your mom okay? I'll be right back. Hope I got enough change, stupid vending machines. *(He exits)*

NOELLE: Glory? Are you there? *(There is only silence. Noelle resumes her position downstage center in a kneeling praying position. She then stands up.)* Believe! Will you all stand and join hands with the person next to you and sing Silent Night with me and believe with me the power of the Lord. *(Glory sings "Silent Night" by Mariah Carey with everyone as the Christmas characters come back out of the closet and join in the song. Glory holds Noelle's hand.)* Nothing happened

GLORY: Now tell Jesus with your heart why you want her back. I'll sing your thoughts. Go on-tell him. *(Glory and her children's choir go stage left and sing, "All I Want for Christmas is You." by Mariah Carey The Christmas Characters return to the closet. Noelle kneels to pray again. During the song Holly, Noelle's mother wakes up and stands directly behind Noelle. As the song ends Noelle see's her mother and breaks down and gives her a hug. They all dance as the Christmas characters come out of the closet again and dance with the choir children, Glory and Noelle. Uncle Nick enters in shock.)*

UNCLE NICK: I got jipped only a half a cup of coffee. *(He see's Holly awake along with Glory and The Christmas characters.)* By the love of Pete! *(He spills his coffee all over himself.)* Hot! How? *(Glory appears and sing, "Hark the Angel Sings" by Mariah Carey with the children's choir.)* It's a miracle! I have to go find Doctor Michaels. Doctor Michaels!!*(He runs off.)*

NOELLE: Welcome back mom, we missed you!

HOLLY: I missed you my beautiful daughter and I will never leave you again.

(Uncle Nick storms back into the room pulling Doctor Michaels in by the arm.)

UNCLE NICK: *(Talking a mile a minute)* It's a miracle! Look Holly's awake! It was amazing, I came in drinking my coffee and this angel appeared with these other people in robes and started to sing and I spilled coffee on myself and let me tell you that was hot coffee...

DOCTOR MICHAEL: Slow down! Your rambling and I cannot understand a word your saying. Holly, how do you feel?

HOLLY: Like I just woke up from a long nap.

DOCTOR MICHAEL: Well you sort of did. *(They all laugh. He examines her.)*

UNCLE NICK: It's a miracle I tell you. Where's that angel lady? Angel lady come on out here and bring your Christmas friends.

DOCTOR MICHAELS: I think your Uncle Nick is so overjoyed with jubilation he's losing his mind. We have a good psyche ward if you'd like to keep him overnight for observation.

UNCLE NICK: What's a psych ward. They got coffee there? Beef jerky?

NOELLE: How is she doctor?

DR. MICHAELS: Perfect, healthy. It's a miracle.

NOELLE: Thanks to Glory, my Christmas friends and Jesus, right mom?

HOLLY: Right daughter but just to make sure, let's ask Glory herself. *(Glory comes out and sings, "Joy to the World" by Mariah Carey with everyone. She hugs Noelle.)*

UNCLE NICK: Told you! Told you! See, she's right there. There's your psych ward!

DR. MICHAELS: I wouldn't believe it unless I saw it and I'm seeing it.

NOELLE: Merry Christmas mother!

HOLLY: Merry Christmas Noelle! *(They hug and during the pickup of the song, the Christmas characters come out of the closet and dance with Holly, The Doctor, Noelle and Uncle Nick who is being chased by the Christmas Tree. The cast sings as the elves get the audience to stand and sing with them. Jesus appears and comes downstage and hugs Noelle as the play ends.)*

Iphigenia Rising

Characters:

Iphigenia

Orestes

Electra

Aegisthus

A messenger

SPECIAL NOTE ON SONGS AND RECORDINGS USED IN THIS PRODUCTION

For performance songs and recordings mentioned in this play that is protected by copyright, the permission of the copyright owner(s) must be obtained; or songs, arrangements and recordings in the public domain substituted.

Iphigenia Rising was first presented by Coffeyville Community College on September 17-19th, 2009 at the Spencer/Rounds Performing Arts Theatre. The production stage managers were Melissa Delfft and Lauren Bell. The cast is as follows:

Iphigenia	Lauren Curley
Electra	Brianna Cordova
Orestes	Zach Bartz
Aegistius	Brandon Jackson
Messenger	Jimmy Petersen

AT RISE: *(The Palace of Argos in Athens, Greece. Orestes and Electra are ransacking the palace looking for valuables.)*

Scene 1

MESSENGER: Princess Iphigenia! *(Iphigenia enters into the palace room. Aegisthus sits at the throne lost inside his soul. A large pool of blood is present downstage where Clytemnestra died.)*

IPHIGENIA: *(Looking down at the blood stain, where her mother's lifeless body was, talking to Aegisthus.)* What happened here? I said what happened here? *(Calls over a messenger)* You, clean this up.

ORESTES: Don't ask him, he's afflicted by the drink and out of it. If you ask me he killed her.

IPHIGENIA: How?

ORESTES: He didn't stop her. Let her drink herself to death. There's blood leading to the next room which means Mother crawled in here and died. She bled to death. *(Iphigenia is silent, looking at the pool of blood.)* Here, I drew a picture of what she looked like dead before they took her away. She looks like a skeleton, probably hasn't eaten in months and we can thank this son of bitch for that *(He kicks Aegisthus who is sitting in a corner wrapped in a knitted blanket. He has a blank look on his face.)*

IPHIGENIA: Stop it! Leave him alone! She was afflicted by the drink for years, he couldn't stop her.

ORESTES: Could not stop her? You want to see what Electra and I found in the palace. Here…look… *(He empties out a dozen bottles, small and large that contained alcohol)*…hidden all over the palace, under the couch, behind things, under things. I mean how could he let her go on like this? How could he buy it for her when he knew it was killing her?

(Aegisthus sits and cries.)

ELECTRA: Where are her Greek lamps? They are mine, she promised them before she died, and they are worth a fortune. *(Grabs a messenger)* Just don't stand there, find them!

ORESTES: Keep looking, I took her rings and jewelry. *(Crosses to Aegisthus)* He's not getting anything even if he is king, and I don't give a shit because as I see it, we are done with you, you're not our father. Never was.

IPHIGENIA: Stop it, he's *my* father.

ORESTES: He killed Mother.

IPHIGENIA: She killed herself; he didn't lift the bottle to her lips. She would have figured a way to drink even if he tried to stop her.

ELECTRA: Can you two please stop arguing for two seconds and help me find her lamps!

IPHIGENIA: What happen to the palace, what happen to Aulis since we left?

ORESTES: You like it? This place is infested with bugs crawling all over the place, dishes and old food scattered everywhere, sheets over the windows stained from the smoke.

ELECTRA: I think what you should do is help me find the lamps.

MESSENGER: Here! *(He brings the lamps to Electra.)*

ELECTRA: Where did you find them?

MESSENGER: They were in the cellar.

ELECTRA: Put them down here. Go! *(Messenger leaves)*

ORESTES: Wow that chest is filled with bugs. There is so much dust on them.

ELECTRA: Who cares, you know how much each of these are worth... fortune. I'm taking them, any objections? *(Looks over at Iphigenia who looks away)* Any objections? *(Dead silence)* I'm surprised she didn't sell them, she sold the antique chest she had them in and everything else worth anything in the palace.

ORESTES: I got her jewelry and rings, I got what I wanted.

IHIGENIA: May I take these two items?

ELECTRA: What are they? *(Cleaning the lamps, not even paying attention)*

IPHIGENIA: It's a blanket she was crocheting, looks like its half done. I'd like to take it with this little hourglass.

ORESTES: Why do you want that old hourglass? It's cracked.

IPHIGENIA: We would play together with it when I was a child.

ORESTES: Whatever.

IPHIGENIA: I'll just take these two things. What will happen to the rest of these items? What will happen to Father?

ORESTES: You mean our father, The king or Aegisthus here?

IPHIGENIA: Aegisthus, our father.

ORESTES: Our father is King Agamemnon!

IPHIGENIA: What will happen to Aegisthus and the palace?

ELECTRA: We will burn anything left behind including the palace and Aegisthus will be banished. Never to be seen again.

IPHIGENIA: Where?

ELECTRA: Far away from me. I do not ever want to see his face again.

IPHIGENIA: Whether you two like it or not he's our father.

ELECTRA: He is *not* our father. *My* father is King Agamemnon. This man cheated with our mother when Father was away fighting a war. Took her away and ruined her life.

IPHIGENIA: Agamemnon was a drunkard like mother, he abused her.

ORESTES: So did Aegisthus!

IPHIGENIA: Agamemnon gave us up when he came back from war. Don't you two remember? He came back with a mistress. He spread lies about Mother killing him, but in truth he ran off with Cassandra and had three more children. Those are his children now, not us. He gave up all claim to us, gave up all royal blood to us. This man Aegisthus raised us, fed us, and took care of us, especially when mother was not in the right frame of mind. How can you banish him now when he needs us the most?

(Electra slaps Iphigenia)

ELECTRA: What planet Sister have you been living on? Do you not remember that this man had us work when we were children like slaves? This is the man who beat us when we were small within an inch of our souls because we were not of his blood? We never celebrated holidays? This is the man who made Aulis and his reign as king a laughing stock by robbing the people of this city. This is the man who beat mother when he was afflicted by the drink to a bloody pulp. Am I forgetting anything or don't you remember?

IPHIGENIA: I also remember Agamemnon beating Mother when we were small when he was afflicted by the drink as well.

ELECTRA: Aulis was great after our father, Agamemnon came home victorious after a long war. He was a hero to our country. Aegisthus ruined all that and now Aulis is a joke everyone laughs at.

IPHIGENIA: Agamemnon was a drunkard who abused people.

ELECTRA: I remember him buying you and us everything we wanted when we were younger, you seemed to love him then.

IPHIGENIA: You can't buy love. I'm older and wiser now and saw past his tricks. I guess you forgot when we were little how he dropped the three of us off in the early morning in the nursery of the palace and didn't come pick us up until late night when he reeked of wine and could barely walk.

ORESTES: Mother couldn't walk! Do you here this? She couldn't walk for the last year and that son of a bitch right there did nothing! He would watch her crawl into another bottle and die!

IPHIGENIA: I talked to her recently and she never mentioned it to me.

ELECTRA: *(Clapping)* Never mentioned it to me! Go to hell!

IPHIGENIA: It's been ten years since I've seen you and you still hate me. Why?

ELECTRA: I don't even know you to hate you or even care to so drop it.

IPHIGENIA: You resent I went off to school and you couldn't because you were with child.

ELECTRA: Drop it!

ORESTES: Come on you two, stop it! You talked to her recently? When? How recent?

IPHIGENIA: I wrote her every month since I left ten years ago. I saw her last at your wedding. Why?

ORESTES: I hadn't talked to her for half a year.

ELECTRA: I got you beat by twelve years, she hated me.

ORESTES: I stopped stopping by the palace because they always would ask for pieces of gold?

IPHIGENIA: Asked for gold?

ORESTES: They were broke, spent all their money on luxuries of the drink and gambling. I gave when I could to buy food, but they bought wine instead.

IPHIGENIA: But they are king and queen of Aulis. They used to be so wealthy, they had anything they wanted.

ORESTES: Were king and queen of Aulis? You see anyone here? Aulis has been abandoned for years give or take a couple loyal messengers who stayed with them out of pity. Embezzlement of a kingdom and those that supported them left them with their riches. The gold they did have was spent on wine alone, hidden away in this room for years.

ELECTRA: I'm leaving. I got what I came for.

IPHIGENIA: What about Mother?

ELECTRA: Talk to her, fill her in.

ORESTES: Need any help?

ELECTRA: No. I got this chest. *(Calls over to messenger)* How many more chests full of lamps are there in the cellar? Hey! How many more chests are in the cellar?

MESSENGER: Another two or three, shall I retrieve them for you?

ELECTRA: I'll come back for them later. Just clean them up and have them ready for me.

ORESTES: I'm heading out too. Make sure everything in here is burned to the ground after the burial tomorrow. This here is for you two; thank you for your duty to my parents *(Gives the messenger gold pieces.)*

MESSENGER Thank you prince. What about the king?

IPHIGENIA: I'll take care of him. You may go.

(The messenger leaves)

ELECTRA: You will never understand Sister, maybe one day you will when he's used your life up like he did with Mothers. Someone should clean that up, after all it is *your* mother's blood. (*She leaves*)

ORESTES: We will bury Mother tomorrow. I'll see you then?

IPHIGENIA: See you then.

ORESTES: I miss you. I think about our childhood all the time and wonder what if things were different and you had not gone away to school, we may have been closer, maybe even saved Mother. I love you

IPHIGENIA: I love you too. (*Orestes exits and the lights dim as Iphigenia stares at Aegisthus who stares back at her with tears in his eyes. Iphigenia starts scrubbing the blood of the floor as Aegisthus is still seated in his throne is drinking. The room is dark and quiet. She never looks at her father during the following scene. A messenger enters.*)

MESSENGER: Princess, you do not need to do that, we will be burning the palace tomorrow after the queens burial.

IPHIGENIA: I'm fine thank you, you may go.

(*Long pause*)

AEGISTIUS: I fell asleep and when I woke up I found her laying there in all that blood. Her eyes were open, her skin was blue, and I knew she was dead. I was so scared. I didn't know what to do, I needed you. *(He breaks down.)*

IPHIGENIA: It's alright, I'm here now. *(Continues to scrub the blood off the floor)*

AEGISTIUS: Your brother and sister hate me. They've always been selfish, always worried about themselves and no one else. You were the only one.

IPHIGENIA: I didn't know my father, they did. All I knew was you. You raised me.

AEGISTIUS: They left home right away but you stayed with us for a time before you left for school and took care of your mother and me. You knew what we were and still did not abandon us.

IPHIGENIA: You can't abandon family no matter how bad it gets. You may hate it, but it's who you are, where you came from, and you love that unconditionally.

(Long pause)

AEGISTIUS: I was a horrible father to you three.

IPHIGENIA: No you were not.

AEGISTIUS: I beat you. Your sister was right about that.

IPHIGENIA: We probably deserved it.

AEGISTIUS: Not as bad as I beat you.

IPHIGENIA: You probably need to stop drinking now, you look terrible.

368

AEGISTIUS: I am fine.

IPHIGENIA: Your skin is a shade of gray, you have almost died three times, and you are not in good health. You are going to die like mother if you don't...

AEGISTIUS: Don't do that...I know. *(Iphigenia keeps scrubbing the blood up off the floor as there is an awkward pause between the two.)* Why did you stick by my side all these years when the other two did not. Why?

IPHIGENIA: You loved me and Mother did not. She loved Orestes. Agamemnon loved Electra. That's just the way it was. You each had your own child to lean on.

AEGISTIUS: Your mother loved you.

IPHIGENIA: She loved Orestes. He could do no wrong in her eyes and I could never do anything right. She always made me feel stupid when I made a mistake, comparing me to Orestes and how he was perfect, humorous, and her only son.

AEGISTIUS: She was so proud you went to school.

IPHIGENIA: I know but so were you.

AEGISTIUS: Hardest day in my life when you went away. We were pals weren't we, we did everything together. It was hard to say goodbye. I cried for days after you left. I missed you.

IPHIGENIA: I grew up with you. You were my father.

AEGISTIUS: You took care of me, put aside my faults, and accepted me as your father, the other two didn't.

IPHIGENIA: I think Orestes accepted you until you would come to him for gold so many times. He sold some of his prize possessions to aide you in your many troubles when you had gambling debts or lost riches for using your gold unwisely.

AEGISTIUS: He was always concerned about *his* riches.

IPHIGENIA: Electra was not.

AEGISTIUS: I don't want to talk about her, she never saw me as her father, only Agamemnon. I cannot help that.

IPHIGENIA: What happened between her and mother after she moved away? She never talked to her again. Something happened but she never would tell Orestes or me about it.

AEGISTIUS: I don't know. All I know is she hated me, has never talked to me since. All she cared about was finding those lamps, forget about her dead mother lying on the floor, those lamps were more important.

IPHIGENIA: She looked for those things like her life depended on it.

AEGISTIUS: That's because your mother never wanted her to have them. She wanted you to have them.

IPHIGENIA: I know, she told me in her last letter she wanted me to have them. I do not care, Electra can have them. I got the two items I wanted.

AEGISTIUS: If you loved me, or your mother do not let her take anymore of those lamps. Promise me you'll take them and hide them away so she never finds them. Your mother would return from Hades if she knew Electra got them.

IPHIGENIA: That's going to cause some serious problems between her and me if I take those lamps.

AEGISTIUS: Tell her I took them, she hates me already. Please do not let her have those lamps. Promise me. Promise!

IPHIGENIA: I promise. *(There is a long silence and Aegisthus falls asleep with the drink in his hand. Iphigenia removes his drink and covers him up with her mother's knitted blanket. She kisses him on the forehead.)* Goodnight Father. *(Lights fade out)*

Scene 2

(Iphigenia, Electra and Orestes enter with a messenger. They are returning from their mother's burial.)

IPHIGENIA: Not many people came to the funeral.

ORESTES: Not many people cared she died.

IPHIGENIA: She's Queen of Aulis

ELECTRA: She was Queen of Aulis, not anymore. Aulis is gone forever, at least the Aulis I once knew.

ORESTES: The people who came gave gifts to show their sympathy to the queen. There's quite a bit of gold here, probably enough to get her a pretty decent burial marker.

IPHIGENIA: Are you alright?

ORESTES: *(Breaking down)* I should have been there for her. I should have saved her. She loved me and I didn't even get to talk to her before she died. I stopped going to see her because I was sick of giving them my riches and I knew they were just drinking it away.

IPHIGENIA: Orestes it's not your fault. Pull yourself together

ORESTES: It is my fault! I took care of her when you left. I took her to get medical assistant when she couldn't walk and I left her alone with Aegisthus thinking he would take care of her but instead he killed her!

ELECTRA: I'm glad he left before I told him off. I hope he goes off and dies somewhere.

IPHIGENIA: For what? She drank for years even before she met Aegisthus. To say that he killed her or could have stopped her is ridiculous. She was a drunkard. She always was, growing up we would hide the wine from her and she would still find it, fill it up with water to trick us into thinking she was not drinking it.

ELECTRA: Aegisthus was abusive. She served him like she was a slave. He never did anything for her. We've been through this same argument before, he stole from the citizens of Aulis, gambled away all their money, and lay with other women whenever he deemed necessary and you call that a king? You call that your father?

IPHIGENIA: No different than Agamemnon who gave us up after he left our mother. He did not want to deal with the responsibility of providing for us, he couldn't afford it because he was too afflicted by the drink to understand. He went off with Cassandra and had three more children, three more sisters we never met and don't even know.

ELECTRA: He was nothing like Agamemnon. Agamemnon was military, he *never* hit us, ever, but Aegisthus did.

ORESTES: He beat us pretty bad.

ELECTRA: So bad as a matter of fact that we couldn't show our faces in public. He beat us with everything you could imagine or don't you remember because he favored you, you never got it as bad as Orestes and me because you bought into all his lies!

(The following dialogue is said on top of each other)

IPHIGENIA: You mean beat us as bad as Agamemnon beat her when he would drink from the bottle?

ELECTRA: He never beat her as bad as Aegisthus beat us.

ORESTES: He never beat us as bad as Aegisthus!

IPHIGENIA: They were all drunkards! Alright, so let us stop this!

ELECTRA: Well at least Agamemnon loved me enough not to rape me in my mother's palace.

IPHIGENIA: Come again?

ORESTES: Aegisthus raped her?

IPHIGENIA: You knew?

ORESTES: Mother told me.

IPHIGENIA: What the hell's going on here?

ORESTES: Nothing.

ELECTRA: It was hardly nothing.

IPHIGENIA: What else do I not know that you two told each other? Huh? Did Orestes tell you about us?

ELECTRA: About what?

IPHIGENIA: We laid together when we were children? Experimenting? Did he tell you that? *(Long silent pause as Iphigenia glares at Orestes who cannot look at her.)*

ELECTRA: What?

ORESTES: We were young we didn't know what we were doing.

ELECTRA: That's sick.

IPHIGENIA: Yes we did.

ORESTES: That was a long time ago. It's was no big deal.

IPHIGENIA: But not forgotten.

ELECTRA: At least you two decided, I had no choice.

IPHIGENIA: He raped you. Aegisthus our father, raped you?

ELECTRA: Yes, *your* father raped me, not my father.

IPHIGENIA: It's why you hate him.

ELECTRA: Yes.

IPHIGENIA: And mother?

ORESTES: Did not believe it happened?

IPHIGENIA: Did not believe you?

ELECTRA: Thought I was lying because I did not like him growing up beating us. I didn't appreciate him spanking me bare bottom in front of his subjects at thirteen years of age.

ORESTES: She never believed it happened.

IPHIGENIA: Did it?

ELECTRA: Yes it happened. What the hell is wrong with you? It happened!

ORESTES: It's why she left.

IHIGENIA: She left because she laid with a messenger and was with child....

ELECTRA: ...and what?

IPHIGENIA: It killed you and Mother.

ELECTRA: No, the rape killed me and Mother, she made her choice. I wasn't it.

IPHIGENIA: Are you sure that is the truth?

ELECTRA: Yes?

ORESTES: Is it?

IPHIGENIA: ARE YOU SURE THAT'S THE TRUTH?

ELECTRA: Yes!

IPHIGENIA: You knew and you didn't confront mother about it? She loved you the most. Why didn't you convince her it happened?

ORESTES: I could not afford to lose her love by taking sides.

ELECTRA: He did not want to take sides. (*Laughs mockingly*)

IPHIGENIA: Did not want to get involved. Why didn't you tell me?

ELECTRA: Are you kidding? Tell you? You loved him the most, you would have never believed it or believed me, I can tell you do not right now.

IPHIGENIA: He is the only father I knew. It's why you both were pulled back to Agamemnon. You forgave everything he did and went back to him. You, Electra, was his favorite, always was.

ORESTES: Aegisthus raped Electra, killed mother and took every piece of gold I had to satisfy his hunger to gamble and drink, do you blame us for running to blood. Aegisthus is not part of us. He's no relationship to us at all. Agamemnon is blood; he's our father, our rightful family.

IPHIGENIA: You cannot escape one thing they all had in common. They were all drunkards and they all lived for the moment and never for the future and never, ever for us.

ELECTRA: Fine, are we done here because I have to get back to my family and I'm tired of rehashing the same nonsense over and over.

ORESTES: Yes, I need to be leaving as well.

ELECTRA: I need to come by the palace and get those other chests of lamps. I thought I would send you both one if you want.

ORESTES: Sure.

IPHIGENIA: No thank you. I got what I came for.

ELECTRA: Fine. Goodbye. *(She starts to leave and summons the messenger.)* Let's go. *(He doesn't move, he just stares sadly at Iphigenia)* I SAID LET'S GO! *(He starts to leave but before he does he gives Iphigenia her mother's blanket and the hour glass. Iphigenia touches his face and smiles as he exits followed by Electra.)*

IPHIGENIA: Then it is done, I guess.

ORESTES: I will talk to her, smooth things over.

IPHIGENIA: You were always the peacemaker.

ORESTES: And you the favorite daughter. Give me a hug!

IPHIGENIA: I'm sorry I brought up...

ORESTES: Shhh... Let us not revisit the past; it was a long time ago.

IPHIGENIA: Take care.

ORESTES: You'll see me, I promise. We will keep in touch. Yes?

IPHIGENIA: Yes.

ORESTES: Love you.

IPHIGENIA: Love you. *(Orestes exits as Iphigenia looks down at where her mother's blood spot was. Black out)*

Scene 3

(Lights come back up with Orestes in a spot of light. It is ten years later.. Iphigenia is reading his letter center stage.)

ORESTES: Iphigenia. Will you be coming to Agamemnon burial? It's been ten years since I saw you last at mother's funeral. It would be great to catch up, with love, Orestes. *(Lights fade on Orestes and up on Iphigenia on center stage. She crumbles the letter and then throws it down. Lights fade out on Iphigenia and up on Orestes)* I wish you would have told us all along you had no intentions of coming to the funeral. It would have saved some time...as our three sisters wanted to wait.... Agamemnon died with a lot of regrets in life.... this meeting wasn't even really even about *him*...more about family....don't lead these girls on, they are your half sisters and really wanted to meet you....they have dealt with enough pain in their lives...and all turned out fine...*Your* biggest regret in life will be not showing up....I'm busy too, Electra had all the lamps packed up ready to give you whatever you wanted.... if you wanted it.... just to make peace because I convinced her you would show. Iphigenia, if this is the real you.... tell me...because I made every excuse possible as why you were the only one that could not show up, without trying to make you look selfish. I love you Iphigenia, but it's been ten years, ten years to long...I have family that I love....wish it were mine...as I get older I really love bonding with people that look like me and share my blood.....*family!* Let me know if I am off base or if you are in a part of your life where you don't want to look into the past. Because I will defend you forever... because I love you ....you're my sister...I just wonder if you let others escape your mind? If you have... I'll give up and leave you alone, with love, Orestes. *(Lights up on Iphigenia. Electra now joins Orestes in the stage right spot as they read the letter together from Iphigenia.)*

IPHIGENIA: So Electra was going to give me the some lamps to mend fences? What does that mean? I will never believe anything she has to say because

I know in the end; she is only looking out for herself. Anyway, I really wanted to meet my three half sisters of Agamemnon but I also remember you writing me telling me that the three of them were fighting over his military gold and burial plans recently with Electra. I simply told you I didn't care what she did with his riches. I didn't want any of it because I never knew the man. I got cold feet coming because I didn't want my relationship with Aegisthus thrown in my face by you and Electra. I haven't talked to his family since he died, I'm too ashamed to. I should have been there the day he died. He was my father…I have tried writing Electra over the years and she ignores me. Why the hell would I want to see someone who doesn't even like me? I love you Orestes. I have no hard feelings I hold against you but so much time has passed all we have to talk about is growing up together and nothing else. I would have felt like a hypocrite going to a memorial for a man I hardly knew, and pretty much didn't know enough to love. I understand I haven't been the best aunt to your children or Electra. If you two have any anger towards me it should be for that. It seems the only time we connect is when tragedy strikes. That's not a family. I didn't want to get into with Electra in front of three sisters I never knew. The right five children went to Agamemnon's memorial. I had no right to be there. I'm not part of that royal family and never will be. He wasn't perfect, and you're right, he was emotionless with us. Both of our fathers had their faults, but both made their peace before they died. It's too bad mother never got the chance. Don't take me not coming as a slap in the face or an insult. I will always love you and cherish our childhood together. Three parents who each chose a different child to love and ripped us apart in the process. There is no place for all of that at a memorial of a man you five loved, wanted to remember, and called father. I hope this helps you understand why I wasn't there. Take care, with love Iphigenia. *(Orestes leaves the stage as Electra is now in a spot of light downstage left. Iphigenia stays lit center as she reads the letter from her sister.)*

ELECTRA: Iphigenia, I'm sorry I haven't contacted you since Agamemnon's death. The last thing you wrote me was, "thanks, got it." I guess I just assumed you really didn't want to talk to me. I don't really think you hate me. For the most part I think you feel the way I do, we don't really know each other anymore. Iphigenia, there are so many things you don't know or understand about me. For the most part it doesn't matter. I asked Orestes why you didn't come and he tried to explain. I think I understand. He told me that he had mentioned to you that I wanted to give you the lamps to fix things between us. I need to clarify that. That is not my purpose at all. The last time I talked to mother, I asked her if we could set up a deal so that there was something of hers to pass down to her granddaughters. I told her that her lamps were what was important to her and would be perfect. We shared a bottle of wine and had probably our only and last mother daughter moment, but after as time passed, she used those lamps to hurt me. Saying things like I would never have them or I didn't have enough gold to buy them from her. I really don't want them for myself. I never have. The one chest I took the day she died

Mark Frank

has been in my cellar for years. I guess Aegisthus took the rest of them because when I came for the rest of the chest of lamps, the messenger told me they were weren't there and he didn't know what happened to them. Probably for the best because I really didn't know what to do with them because Orestes didn't want them and I am afraid our other relatives would sell the lamps. But now you have a daughter I hear. And I know you cared about Mother. I just think it would be justified if you had them to give to your daughter. To say, these were your grandmother's, and some day she could give them to her daughter. Anyway, I don't care about the lamps, and I don't think our differences have anything to do with chests of lamps...I think you are much more mature than that. Iphigenia, I just want to be your sister. I don't ever expect that we will be good friends. You have a great life and are blessed with a happy family, and I have mine. I guess I just want us to be able to be happy for each other with no hard feelings. I hope you are enjoying your life and your daughter. Time is way too short to get caught up in the past. No matter what you believe, I do love you, Electra. *(Lights fade out on Electra. Iphigenia crumbles up her letter. The song, " Show Me What I'm Looking For" By Carolina Liar plays in the background.)*

IPHIGENIA: Electra, I am sending you the chest of lamps Aegisthus took after Mother died. I appreciate your offer of giving them to my daughter, but I do not want them, I want you to have them. They should be with you, Iphigenia. *(Iphigenia opens up a chest next to her and takes out a lamp. She looks at it for a long time. She places the lamp carefully back in the chest.*

382

She takes a sword and shatters the lamps inside the chest. She slams the lid of the chest shut.) And with that, I'm done writing. *(She throws down the sword and exits off. The lights fade except for the chest that is in a pool of light. The stage goes to black slowly as the play ends. The song plays out.)*